TR Laszlo, Andrew
850
.L38 Every frame a
2000 Rembrandt

778.5 Laz

EVERY FRAME A REMBRANDT

ART AND PRACTICE OF CINEMATOGRAPHY

D0209313

Watkins College
of Art & Design

EVERY FRAME A REMBRANDT

ART AND PRACTICE OF CINEMATOGRAPHY

Andrew Laszlo, A.S.C.
with additional material by
Andrew Quicke

Focal Press
Boston Oxford Auckland Johannesburg Melbourne New Delhi

Watkins College
of Art & Design

Focal Press is an imprint of Butterworth–Heinemann.

Copyright © 2000 Butterworth–Heinemann

A member of the Reed Elsevier group

All rights reserved.

All trademarks found herein are property of their respective owners.

No part of this publication may be reproduced, stored in a retrieval system, or transmitted in any form or by any means, electronic, mechanical, photocopying, recording, or otherwise, without the prior written permission of the publisher.

Recognizing the importance of preserving what has been written, Butterworth–Heinemann prints its books on acid-free paper whenever possible.

Butterworth–Heinemann supports the efforts of American Forests and the Global ReLeaf program in its campaign for the betterment of trees, forests, and our environment.

Library of Congress Cataloging-in-Publication Data

Laszlo, Andrew, 1926-
Every frame a Rembrandt : art and practice of cinematography / Andrew Laszlo, with Andrew Quicke.
p. cm.
ISBN 0-240-80399-X (pbk. : alk. paper)
1. Cinematography. I. Quicke, Andrew. II. Title.
TR850.L38 2000
778.5—dc21

99-058083

British Library Cataloguing-in-Publication Data
A catalogue record for this book is available from the British Library.

The publisher offers special discounts on bulk orders of this book.
For information, please contact:
Manager of Special Sales
Butterworth–Heinemann
225 Wildwood Avenue
Woburn, MA 01801-2041
Tel: 781-904-2500
Fax: 781-904-2620

For information on all Focal Press publications available, contact our World Wide Web home page at: http://www.focalpress.com

10 9 8 7 6 5 4 3 2 1

Printed in the United States of America

CONTENTS

CONTENTS

ABOUT THE AUTHOR

Andrew Laszlo's career in film and television spans nearly fifty years, from the original *Phil Silvers Show* ("Sergeant Bilko") (1954–1958) to Walt Disney Pictures' *Newsies* (1992). Mr. Laszlo came to the United States in 1947 as an emigrant from Hungary, where he started his motion picture career as an apprentice at the Motion Picture Studios of Budapest.

He served in the U.S. Army Signal Corps as a cameraman from 1950 to 1952, and after being honorably discharged from the Service, worked in many jobs allied with photography and the entertainment industry. In connection with his professional activities, he has traveled extensively throughout the world. He is a member of The International Cinematographers Guild, The Directors Guild of America, The American Society of Cinematographers, and The Motion Picture Academy, and has served two terms as Governor of The National Academy of Television Arts and Sciences. He received Emmy nominations for *The Man without a Country* in 1973 and *Shogun* in 1980.

In addition to his activities in motion pictures, Mr. Laszlo lectures extensively at such institutions as Dartmouth College, New York University, The American Film Institute, and is an Adjunct Professor at Montana State University, Bozeman. In addition to his lecturing in the United States, he has given seminars for industry professionals as well as future filmmakers around the world.

Mr. Laszlo's hobbies include, quite naturally, photography, writing, flying, wood- and metal-working, and above all, fly-fishing. He lives with his wife on Long Island, New York.

FOREWORD

It gives me great pleasure to write this foreword to Andy Laszlo's book on the art, craft, and experience of cinematography. It will take only a few turns through the pages of this wonderful book to impress readers with Andy's abundant talents as a creator of moving images designed for theatrical presentation and television and with his skill as a problem solver and teacher. I remember my first contact with Andy on the set of *Poltergeist II: The Other Side* (1986) on the historic MGM lot in the mid-eighties. I was beginning my career as a sales rep for Kodak in Hollywood with responsibilities to call on feature film directors of photography. I asked Andy about setting exposures, and he pulled out of his ditty bag an exposure calculator he had customized that elegantly and accurately displayed the variables of exposure, which included film stock speed, T-stop calibrations, shutter speed, and so on. He then proceeded to give me a tutorial on how this ingenious system worked. He was always inventing new ways and tools to improve things or to solve problems on the set, and he never tired of sharing his insights and experiences with others.

Every Frame a Rembrandt is a splendid distillation of Andy's more than fifty years as a cinematographer and of his work with Kodak for the past decade. In the early nineties Kodak launched a worldwide program for film school students called, appropriately enough, the Kodak Worldwide Student Program. One of the key components of this effort was a seminar called Visiting Artists, which featured Andy talking about the art of image creation and illustrating this concept from his rich inventory of experiences in feature films, television, commercial production, and documentary. Andy's work on numerous high-profile feature films is well known; not as well known but just as significant is his work in other fields. Andy traveled with Ed Sullivan to film one of the first (if not the first) interviews with Fidel Castro after Batista was ousted in Cuba. Andy was on the field at Shea Stadium as director of photography when The Beatles took America by storm at the legendary concert there in the early sixties. In 1963 he filmed one of the early truly independent films, *One Potato, Two Potato,* a film about race relations that was well ahead of its time. His experiences have all added immeasurable richness to Kodak's Visiting Artists Program, which has been presented to hundreds of film school students at dozens of colleges and universities around the world.

Andy Laszlo "the man" is even more impressive than his achievements. His story represents many of the qualities and virtues we as a nation most admire and would want others to model. Andy came to this country from Hungary by way of Germany right after World War II, arriving in New York in January 1947. He taught himself photography in Hungary, but the motion picture situation in Budapest after the war was practically bankrupt, so he came to America to start a new life and career. He was penniless, and he didn't have much more going for himself beyond his desire and dreams. In 1950 he was the first draftee from New York taken for the Korean War, and he essentially learned photography while in Army service during that conflict. By the mid-fifties he was shooting television films in New York—and the rest is history.

The story of Andy Laszlo is the story of a person who fought hard for what he believed in and gave everything to succeed. He mastered his craft and, throughout a most distinguished career, was able to make worthwhile contributions to the art of moving images. He is loyal and generous, and *Every Frame a Rembrandt* and the Visiting Artists Program both represent his characteristic way of giving something in return for a life and industry nobly served.

John Mason
Manager
Kodak Student and Emerging Programs,
United States and Canada

PREFACE

The first movie I helped to direct took place on the island of Cyprus in 1960. I was lucky enough to be working for Peter Montagnon, who later made the famed documentary series *Civilisation* (1968) and *The Heart of the Dragon* (1985). He was making a 16mm documentary film about working in the Royal Air Force. That summer we found that freelance cameramen were hard to find, and we ended up hiring a wonderful director of photography who had been prominent in silent cinema in the twenties. I was naturally nervous when I directed my first sequence, but he was very helpful. We had dinner together every night and talked about movie-making. Listening to him was an education; I learned a great deal from his stories and the way he set about making a movie. I never found a textbook that matched his ability to convey what making movies was really like.

Thirty years later, after I had directed film in thirty-three different countries, I retired from the industry to teach motion picture production at the university level. In 1995 I was lucky enough to meet a very distinguished director of photography at the Kodak Visiting Artists seminar at Regent University Graduate School of Cinema-Television. Andrew Laszlo had more than knowledge, he had a brilliant way of imparting it. Though a book can never be the same as a live seminar, I felt sure that some of his wisdom could be transferred to the printed page, so I went to Long Island to try and persuade him that a book was possible. He showed album upon album of photographs, and I became convinced that somewhere there was a publisher who might see the wisdom of publishing what is not a textbook, but an account of how a talented cinematographer brought movies to life on the screen. And what movies they were, many of them very innovative for the time.

I saw my role was that of a catalyst, helping Andrew Laszlo to convert his lifetime of experience as a cinematographer into a permanent document for a new generation. Our book consists of five chapters, each describing one particular film that posed interesting challenges. All are available on videocassette for further study, and some are on laser disc or DVD as well. My students were asked to read the first draft of the book, and the questions at the end are a distillation of their questions on the five chapters. They are there to help the student reader, to round out the chapters, and to give additional insight into the world of filmmaking.

Some people work to live; those who love motion pictures and television live to work. If this book conveys some of Andrew Laszlo's passion for excellence, then we will have achieved our purpose.

Andrew Quicke
Professor of Cinema-Television
Regent University
Virginia Beach, Virginia,
U.S.A.

INTRODUCTION

"Every frame a Rembrandt" is an expression heard on the sound stages of motion picture studios all over the world. It refers to the images that flash before our eyes, twenty- four individual pictures (or frames) per second, as we watch a movie in theaters or on television. For the past half a century while I have been a cinematographer, this expression, "Every frame a Rembrandt," became as much a fixture on the set as lights, cameras, cast, and crew. Although in most cases the expression is used lightly, and not infrequently with a certain amount of sarcasm, its true meaning speaks highly of most cinematographers' commitment to produce the best, most interesting, unusual, and memorable images for the screen.

"Good morning! I am Andrew Laszlo. For the past half a century I have been knocking around in the motion picture industry in one capacity or another, but mainly in the area of cinematography."

This, more or less, is how I introduce a two-day seminar presentation about cinematography, which I conduct a number of times a year at universities around the country and the world where the best film courses are taught. These seminars are sponsored by the Eastman Kodak Company. When I take the spotlight, after the seminar organizers have briefly introduced the movie industry, I usually open by saying: "Now that you know all about the industry, I'd like to add that none of what you've just heard would amount to beans, if it weren't for people like me who create the images for the films that people pay to see. And that's what I'm here to talk about." I follow with an outline of the seminar, and for the purposes of this book, I would like to outline what the following pages will contain and why.

My seminar, which is the basis for this book, evolved over a number of years of visiting with filmmakers already in the profession, young people aspiring to enter the profession, and film students at various institutions around the country and abroad. Teaching this course continues to reinforce my belief that most film students, although they get an increasingly good foundation in filmmaking at school, hardly ever get a chance to hear about filmmaking at the industry level from an industry professional. On many occasions, as my seminar presentation wraps up, students tell me that they have learned more about cinematography and filmmaking in general in two days than during an entire semester. I sincerely hope that this book will have similar success in passing on such information to the readers. Information, after all, is what our business is about. I am a strong proponent of the precept that our art and craft can be most successfully learned by practice, by the observation of others in the field, and by the analysis and exchange of ideas and information. One does accumulate a lot of experience and knowledge in the course of a half a century. It is time to pass some of it on!

Consider this book your private seminar. It will describe and discuss cinematography as it deals with five of my films, ranging from the seemingly simple to the most complicated. All of these discussions will contain information on such varied subjects as the day-to-day activity of a cinematographer before, during, and after filming a project; the equipment, film stock, testing, and labs necessary to make a film; the unions and agents cinematographers need to work with; and so on.

I will be talking about "good" photography, "bad" photography, "good/bad" photography, and "bad/good" photography. These general judgements may sound confusing at the moment, but before you get very far into the first chapter they will take on meaning and begin to comprise the most central subject of this book—the creation of the image and the art and practice of cinematography.

It is not the intention of this text to teach the "nuts and bolts" of basic or advanced cinematography. I do not intend to include a photograph of a light meter and spend a chapter teaching the use of the light meter. I do not intend to give lighting diagrams. I believe that each and every situation that requires lighting demands its own particular plan and approach. I do not intend to use the following five films as examples of photography to follow or imitate. I intend to use them to illustrate individual aspects of the cinematographer's experience, which, as illustrated by these five examples, will add up to understanding what goes into the creation of the image, technically and artistically. Photography is too much of an individual art to impose one's own technique on others. The examples will serve simply to illustrate how I approached and executed the photography of these five films, and to talk about the problems I encountered as well as my solutions to those problems.

Throughout this book, my main concern will be the creation of the image. The five films I have chosen from my repertoire of some forty feature films, perhaps a couple of hundred television shows, and commercials too numerous to even guess their number, are *Southern Comfort*, *The Warriors*, *First Blood*, *Streets of Fire*, and *Innerspace*. As a supplement to this book, I would recommend viewing these films, presently available on videotape or laser disks, prior to, and perhaps again after, reading the chapters that follow.

A large portion of each chapter will be devoted to "war stories." These are incidents that happened on and off the sets of these and other films. Some of these war stories are technical in nature, others are political, some are funny, and some are sad. But all will have elements of interest, as they include reflections on half a century of cinematography and filmmaking.

And now, onto the first film.

1
SOUTHERN COMFORT

During one of my visits with film students, I was asked to describe the secret of photography. Frankly, the question threw me. I knew that some students who are film aficionados have an almost religious zeal when it comes to film, nevertheless I didn't expect the question, didn't know exactly what the questioner meant, and wasn't prepared to give a satisfactory answer. Until then it had never occurred to me to think that indeed there might be a secret to photography. Perhaps because I have a tendency to be a bit caustic at times, I answered by saying that the secret of photography was having a camera with a lens, film, and the determination to point it and shoot.

And that brings me to the most basic type of photography, which I call Point and Shoot. As the term implies, Point and Shoot simply means pointing the camera in the direction of the subject matter and pushing the button. This type of photography is practiced daily worldwide by millions of people taking pictures with their still cameras. In the professional film industry, it is generally practiced on an outdoor location, usually during the day without lighting or the use of sets. On a "Western" location, for example, where the panorama is the important element, riders might be seen in the distance in a picturesque valley surrounded by mountains. Artificial lighting is not required, and, indeed, it would be of no use. Simply set up a camera, point it at the subject, and shoot. Simple! Or is it?

As I said in the Introduction, we cinematographers are constantly striving to create an image that is interesting, unusual, and memorable. Does Point and Shoot photography meet those requirements? Clearly not! Point and Shoot photography will record an image, but it will not make it any more interesting, unusual, or memorable. In fact, in many instances—due to the shortcomings of even the best state-of-the-art equipment, film stock, and laboratory techniques—the image comes up short of emphasizing or bringing additional values to the subject matter. Yet there can be hidden values, even in an image that photographically is not quite as good as the original subject matter. Certain shortcomings can take on artistic virtue, as I will discuss throughout this book.

Let's start with Point and Shoot photography. In my own repertoire of films, there is one very good example of Point and Shoot, a theatrical feature called *Southern Comfort* (1979–1981). When the script came in from my good friend director Walter Hill, certain aspects of the movie became obvious even on my first reading. All of the film and the entire story were to take place in exterior locations. Most of the film was going to be exterior day photography and, with the exception of one sequence, called for no sets. None of the film was to be shot in the studio or on the back lot.

The story depicts a couple of days in the life of a squad of National Guardsmen on weekend maneuvers in the swamps of Louisiana. Early in the story, some men in the squad shoot blanks at the local Cajun trappers and poachers who live on the swamp—and they shoot back with live ammunition. From this point on the film deals with the Cajuns, an unseen enemy, killing off the Guardsmen one at a time in the most ingenious ways. Only two escape in the end.

The photography of the film was scheduled to begin in late summer. Even before the preproduction period, Walter, producer David Giler, first assistant director Pat Kehoe, and I would meet

Figure 1.1 Location scouting in an airboat

on weekends to scout potential locations for the film. As I was shooting another film at the time in South Carolina, the three of them would pick me up in a small jet on weekends, and we would go from swamp to swamp in South Carolina, Florida, Georgia, Mississippi, Louisiana, Alabama, and Texas (see Figure 1.1).

Until this time I'd never been in a swamp. My idea of a swamp was lots of mud, brackish water, rotting timber, snakes, alligators, and flies—none of which was high on my list of priorities of places to visit. But filmmaking, which can take filmmakers all over the world to the most interesting places, is not restricted to the beautiful spots on earth alone. Swamps, caves with millions of bats, tunnels deep under New York City, the frozen regions of the Arctic, garbage dumps, and blood-splattered emergency wards, to name a few, are all potential sites for filmmaking. A location is whatever place the script describes as where the action is to take place. Expecting the worst, I wasn't prepared for the beauty of the first swamp we visited in northern Florida (see Color Plate I).

The sky was the most vibrant blue, with huge billowing white clouds. The water, a faultless, endless putting green, was covered with a lush green carpet of duckweed. The immense old oaks were richly decorated with Spanish moss swaying gently in the breeze, and brilliant white egrets completed the panorama. There was beauty all around me—and all of it, I knew instinctively and immediately, was totally wrong for the story of the film. The actions and situations of the story would have clashed head-on with the beauty of the scenery.

We found this beautiful scenery in swamp after swamp, but, as magnificent as the scenery was, it was disheartening to know that for our purposes this kind of beauty was all wrong. Walter and I were very concerned with the "look" of the film. Neither one of us wanted a glossy, pretty look. We wanted to emphasize and underline the harsh aspects of the story, add to the discomfort of the audience, and manipulate their emotional response by the style, the "look," of the film.

After reading the script for the first time, I dug out one of my favorite photo books, *This Is War*, by the famed photographer and photojournalist David Douglas Duncan. Duncan covered the Korean War for *Life* magazine. On one of the opening pages of this book there is a full-page photograph of a Marine sitting on a rock, wearing a wet poncho and a steel helmet. Having just taken part in a two-day withdrawal, without rest, food, or sleep, the Marine's face reflected the hardships and perhaps the horrors of his experience. The photograph was in black and white; it was grainy and dark, and some of its details were obscured by the mist and late afternoon twilight. The Marine's eyes, for example, were almost totally swallowed up in the shadow of his steel helmet. I thought this photograph was an outstanding example of the old adage, "a picture is worth a thousand words." It told the Marine's story eloquently, and I sensed it would be our guide in determining the "look" for our movie. Walter agreed.

But how was this look to be achieved? Duncan, having spotted the Marine, seized the opportunity, pointed his camera, and shot. A moment masterfully captured, but how were we going to do that throughout an hour-and-a-half-long feature film? And if we wanted to get close to that wonderful look Duncan had captured, how was that to be achieved technically, and how was it going to mesh with the endless beauty of the swamp? At least one part of the answer was obvious. Whatever I was going to do with the photography, the story would not fit into the beauty of any of the swamps we had visited.

We thus had a major problem before the film had even started. But, as so often happens, the solution came from an unexpected source. In the course of scouting swamps in northwest Louisiana, we were introduced to a former college professor, Greg Guirard, who had chucked the academic world for the beauty of the swamp, where he had moved with his family. He supported himself by building very interesting and unusual furniture from wormwood that he harvested from the swamp, and by the results of his other hobby, photography. He had several photographic books published, all dealing with the same subject matter: the swamp. One of these books, *Seasons of Light*, was full of the most beautiful and interesting photographs taken in the swamp, mostly during the winter. Looking through the pictures was a revelation. The swamp looked grey, monochromatic, almost totally devoid of the vivid colors we saw during our scouting trips. His photographs brought us closer to that "hostile" atmosphere we thought would be right for the film. There were some colors, of course, but the colors were subtle and very subdued. The monochromatic quality of the swamp was shrouded in a mysterious semidarkness under the tall canopy of the trees. Unlike the swamps we visited at the height of their summer glory, these pictures portrayed another kind of beauty, one which, in my opinion, could not have been better for the background against which our story was to be told. There was no question that the photography of the film had to be rescheduled for the winter.

As portions of the film I was working on in South Carolina also took place in a swamp, I had opportunities to shoot a few tests and send them off to the lab for processing. The purpose of these tests was to see if I could come close to the "look" David Duncan captured with his still camera, but on motion picture film. His image lacked detail. It allowed—I should say demanded—that the viewer fill in the detail. I knew that if I underexposed the film it would deteriorate the quality of the negative by not allowing portions of the detail to register. It would also result in a grainy image, without deep harsh contrast. In other words, I felt I had to go against the rules of the textbooks, of Kodak's specs, of past and current practices, of everything I considered "good" photography, in order to get the "look" I wanted, the "style" I hoped to create for the movie.

I wanted a bad image. Or perhaps "bad" is not a good description. I wanted a "bad/good" image. At this time in preproduction I knew more about what I didn't want than what I did want. What I didn't want was a "good" image, a pretty image, with well-exposed, sharp, vivid colors, and everything in focus to infinity. The film had a rough story, so I wanted to present it in an equally rough manner. I wanted the audience to be disturbed by the look of the film, just as the characters in the film were disturbed by their environment and circumstances.

When my tests came back to South Carolina, I was delighted to see that certain aspects of what I was looking for were achievable by the underexposure. Even though I did not have the actors dressed as soldiers, the underexposed results clearly showed that, indeed, I was getting one step closer to that "bad/good" image I sought. But, photographed in September with lots of sunshine, the footage still had a lot of color and contrast. Further tests photographed with reduced exposure and the addition of heavy neutral density filters allowed me to shoot almost wide open, defeating the depth of field to the point that background objects melted into one another, losing their contrast and definition. I liked the effect of some of the details disappearing into shadows. Little by little I was getting closer to the "look" I was hoping for, which would not have been possible with good, "normal" exposure.

It has always been my practice to "bracket" the exposure over a wide range whenever I shoot these kinds of tests. Though underexposing two stops made the image bad, I actually loved it. It was scary at first to go against my years of training and experience. It was scary to know that I was purposely deteriorating the negative stock Kodak had developed and perfected, probably at the cost of millions of dollars, beyond acceptable limits. But I knew I was on the right track. I also counted on, and hoped for, Mother Nature's help: providing me with the winter look of the swamp with very little—or better yet, no—sunshine at all, and allowing the undesirable elements in my test footage (color and contrast) to be minimized or disappear altogether. I was discovering "bad/good" photography. The question now was, what other elements could I bring to the image to make it more interesting, memorable, and effective enough to exert an influence over the emotions of the audience, so that they would feel the discomfort, fear, and paranoia of the characters in the story?

When my film in South Carolina wrapped, I could turn my full attention to *Southern Comfort*. The rescheduled start date of the film was drawing closer. I continued my testing and research for anything I thought would further enhance our footage. Every time I discussed what I wanted to achieve with colleagues, lab people, and supply houses, everyone had advice and suggestions, but no definite solution to my dilemma. My assistant suggested that I try "black dot filters." Frankly, until that time I'd never heard of them. We located a set, but looking at them and through them, I was dubious. They looked like rectangular pieces of glass splattered with muddy water. There were varying numbers and sizes of irregularly shaped dots and blotches of different density imbedded in the glass in a random pattern. The filters came in gradations from one to five, one being the lightest and five the darkest. As the start date of photography was closing in on me, I decided to try them, though I had strong misgivings.

In the first place, I knew that anything with a pattern placed in front of wide-angle lenses would register, particularly at small T-stops used in daylight photography. But I was also aware of an old practice of putting a small, solid object directly in front of a long focal length lens for portraiture, which disturbs the optical characteristics of a long focal length lens to produce a very pleasant, soft effect. I couldn't help wondering if black dot filters would somehow produce similar results. They did. My tests not only showed a definite improvement in further knocking down contrast, but also showed that the black dot filters had slightly softened the image, and even imposed a soft veil over the subdued colors of the winter swamp. When I used them in connection with neutral density filters, shooting at close to wide-open apertures, the results were as close to the desired "style" as I had hoped for and thought I could get. It was a great relief.

If these filters had not worked, the next process I was going to experiment with was "fogging." I abhorred the idea. I have never been a proponent of fogging of any kind. In my opinion "fogging" was, and still is, a less than precise technique. Pre-fogging the film by the lab, rightly or wrongly, I would not trust. Fogging the film during photography with the devices available then was, in my opinion, inconsistent and required a great deal of lab work after the film was edited to balance the inconsistencies of fog densities from cut to cut. I considered pre- or post-development fogging equally undesirable. I even rejected print fogging, though this method held the least danger, as it didn't impose a quality on the negative that couldn't be removed. My experience with any techniques of "fogging," before *Southern Comfort*, and since, was less than satisfactory. Yet, as a last resort, prior to my discovery of "black dot" filters, I was considering it.

While scouting one particular location in the northeast Texas swamps, we came across a crew shooting a film for Disney, I believe. The director of photography was complaining bitterly about the deep contrast, even on lightly overcast days. He was skeptical about the black dot filters, and I didn't think they would help either when shooting in the bright summer sunlight. I knew that the winter look of the swamp, coupled with the black dot filters, was going to eliminate the aggravation of dealing with contrast. The black dots turned out to be a godsend that freed me from having to resort to fogging.

As my tests proved the validity of these filters to achieve the "look" of the film, the photographic "style" based mainly on their use was locked in. But I discovered, to my dismay, that only one set of these filters was available. There wasn't much demand for them and rental houses did not stock them. Most cinematographers shied away from black dot filters, and for good reason. They *did* deteriorate the image. Most motion pictures didn't require this effect; on the contrary, most cinematographers wanted to improve the image, maintaining better focus, better depth of field, better color definition, and so on. But for *Southern Comfort* I wanted the opposite of all that. Yet, to leave for location to start shooting the film with only one set of these filters on hand would have been playing Russian Roulette. By this time I knew that one or another gradation of the black dot filters would be in front of the lens for just about every shot. I also knew that most of the time I would be shooting with two cameras and in some instances three. I had to have matching sets of these filters for all cameras.

We frantically called every rental house in Hollywood, New York, London, Rome, and Hong Kong, but it seemed there was only one set of these filters around—and I had them. Fortunately, their manufacturer agreed to make several additional sets for me. I didn't know if they would have the same qualities as the ones I had tested, but they turned out to be identical. For some reason, all of our black dot filters, unlike any other we carried, were very susceptible to temperature variations. If the temperature dropped abruptly, which happened frequently at night in the winter swamp, the filters would separate, or shatter in their cases while stored in the camera truck. Time and again I managed to have new ones made and fortunately they also turned out to be identical to the original set. With these filters on hand, the photography of the film started on schedule, producing results we all wanted and were pleased with.

I believed that the "look" all of us wanted, which was now locked in, would add an unusual element to the film. The "look" of *Southern Comfort* was now as close to David Duncan's Marine as I could get it on motion picture film. The grainy monochromatic images, in which certain details were hard to see or disappeared altogether, was right for the story and was an important part of the film, supporting the story, the actors, the situations, and the locations.

When I examined this technique of underexposure coupled with the use of black dot filters, interesting contradictions surfaced. The negative emulsion, Kodak 5247, was a fine-grain negative stock, with excellent ability to render color, and with a good range of exposure for most conditions. As I mentioned earlier, the Eastman Kodak Company probably spent millions of dollars developing this emulsion, and perhaps an equal amount to perfect it over the years. Their guidelines regarding exposure, use of filters, processing, printing, and so forth were designed to achieve the best results this negative stock was capable of producing. Knowing and understanding the "rules" for how to get the "best results," I decided to go against them, chuck almost everything I knew, and opt for "bad" exposure, "bad" processing, and deteriorating the good qualities of the film. In other words, I decided that in the case of *Southern Comfort* it would be more appropriate not to use "good" photographic techniques in favor of what I and most others considered "bad" techniques and procedures. I was convinced that "good" photography for *Southern Comfort* would have made the film ordinary. In my opinion, from an artistic viewpoint, "good" images—properly exposed, properly processed, sharp, and colorful—would have been wrong and unacceptable for the film. "Good" photography was consciously rejected, to be replaced by what, on all technical bases, was known to be "bad" photography. But in our case, "bad" photography turned out to be the desirable way to go. "Bad" photography was good for the film and I decided to refer to it as "bad/good" photography.

I have been using that term since *Southern Comfort*, and I find that every time one deviates from the norm or the proper techniques of cinematography for artistic considerations, the terms bad/good or good/bad photography take on special meaning. This concept will crop up throughout this book in connection with the other films I'll be talking about as well. At this point, let me just cap this off by saying that by "discovering," and using, bad/good photography, I had created an image that was unusual, interesting, and memorable—and which, I hoped, would help make *Southern Comfort* an interesting film.

I had found what the "look" of the film should be and formulated the techniques to achieve it. My problems were solved, but sometimes, solving a problem creates new problems. For example, the underexposed quality of the "look" just about negated the need for any sort of lighting. Had we deliberately gone into the dark portions of the swamp for its obvious look, and then lit it and the actors to studio quality, not only would we have defeated our purpose, but we would have come up with an unnatural, untrue, and contradictory look. I deliberately further deteriorated the "look" of our film by not lighting.

Some time ago, during one of my visits with film students at a leading northeastern college, a young fellow expressed resentment at the fact that I, as a professional cinematographer, had at my disposal everything one could possibly need to make a movie, while he, a film student, had to make do with minimal equipment. He felt that as a young filmmaker, his abilities were curtailed by not having, as he put it, "truckloads of lights and equipment," to make his films. His plight, self-imposed and imaginary as it was, represented certain misconceptions about cinematography.

This young man and his idea of what a cinematographer needs to shoot movies gave me an opportunity to talk about lighting and the equipment a cinematographer uses to execute the photography of a motion picture. I talked about the process, starting with reading the script for the first time, making notes, meeting with the director, gaffer, art director, and others, and slowly arriving at a list that would represent the equipment necessary to film the movie. I pointed out that the only piece of equipment that I, and all cinematographers, absolutely must have is a camera.

There could be no motion picture without this one, vital piece of equipment. Everything else is subject to availability, budget, size of production, crew, and other limitations. I also pointed out that the cameras I use in the course of filming a movie, though bigger and more expensive and sophisticated, with more accessories, lenses, tripods, and so on, nevertheless are the same cameras that any student would be using for student films. All motion picture cameras have a film transport mechanism, at least one lens, and they all use film. Yet no matter what I said, this young man's envy and animosity remained obvious. Oddly enough, there were others in the same group who seemed to agree with him.

Rather than continue a "no-win" type of academic argument, I showed a segment from *Southern Comfort*. This film, I thought, would be a good representation of my side of the discussion. When the lights came on, I talked about how this motion picture was lit. I pointed out that the entire film was shot on location in the swamps of northern Louisiana and Texas. We did arrive on location with truckloads of lights and every other possible piece of equipment we thought might be needed. I pointed out that, contrary to all my training, I came to the realization that I didn't have to light every scene, and that, indeed, how wrong it would be to light the scenes. Though it wasn't an easy or secure decision, I ended up not using the lights in our "truckloads" of equipment. We even devised ways of withholding existing daylight from the image to be photographed with overhead silks, tarps, and smoke. Withholding the light was the decisive step that created the film's "unlit," "hostile," and "natural" look, and a sense of pall that the story so strongly demanded.

It is difficult at times *not* to use the equipment one has at one's disposal. One feels obligated to use the equipment just because it's there, or because it was ordered and approved for the production by the production department at the cinematographer's request. It is also very difficult to deny the opportunity to one's crew to do their best for the film. In the end, however, only the demands of the film, as interpreted by one's convictions, must be considered.

By the time I would arrive on the set in the morning, my electrical crew, a wonderful bunch of people, had already been at work for a couple of hours. Their smiling faces were a testimonial to their pride in accomplishing the seemingly impossible task of running cable deep into the swamp and carrying heavy lights and stands to our locations. But every time I turned on a light and the eyes of the actors sparkled and their dark, muddy faces lit up in the warm glow of our lights, it convinced me that conventional lighting was all wrong for this movie.

This was hard for my crew to accept. At first I tried to resort to diplomatic means. When a light, such as a large HMI was turned on, I would immediately ask for two double nets. They appeared in the light before I even finished my request. Then, scrutinizing the image further, I would ask for a silk in the light, and then another about three feet in front of the light. Additional cutters, flags, and more nets prevented just about all the light of the HMI from reaching the actors. My gaffer, today a cinematographer himself, exchanged meaningful looks with his crew, leaving no doubt that they were not fooled for a minute. It would have been unfair (and, I might add, foolish) to go on with this charade, so after the first couple of days of shooting, my gaffer and I had a meeting. He assured me that he knew what was going on and why, and he told me that he agreed with me. Most of our lighting complement was shipped back to Hollywood the following day, leaving only some "security"—or perhaps I should call them "insecurity"—lights, a few small units that I knew I would use towards the end of our schedule.

Sunlight was not as easily controlled. Even though we were fortunate to have mostly overcast days in the winter swamp, the sun broke through the clouds at times, creating contrast and in some cases a pretty, cheerful atmosphere that we didn't want. By varying the degree of neutral density and black dot filters, and by pushing the underexposure to the absolute limit, I could deal with the contrast to some extent, but I had no "filters" that could magically eliminate sunlight from our footage. Other methods had to be resorted to.

One of these, a time-honored and much-used method, was stretching silk panels overhead. In the past this worked well for me on relatively small shots, but putting silk panels above the tall trees in the swamp was not always possible. One of the scenes in the film, which depicts our squad being attacked and mauled by hunting dogs, was photographed during a sunny day. In comparison to the rest of the film, the sunlight brought, along with other unwanted aspects such as contrast, an element of cheer to the scene. It just didn't fit. The scene was rescheduled to be shot again at the end of our schedule, which was to be in March, the beginning of summer in the Texas/Louisiana swamps. All of us knew that by March there would be more and more sunny days. I had to prepare for not shooting the scene in sunlight again. I selected a portion of the swamp where the trees were topped at a certain height. I also had a wire grid constructed to support a double-silk panel, about a hundred by hundred and fifty feet, with side walls made of silk curtains. This way we were reasonably certain that we would be shooting the scenes in subdued light, similar to the qualities the rest of the film was shot under. The tent was also going to be utilized for picking up other shots to complete or add to already photographed sequences, which were being edited as the shooting was going on (see Figure 1.2).

There was one additional method by which, on a few occasions, we were able to control sunshine. As many as four large fog machines would be located a couple of hundred yards on the up-wind side of the shooting location. These fog machines would shoot a dense curtain of smoke straight up until a cloud formed over the shooting location, blocking the sun (see Figure 1.3). This method worked, but it was a very limited and tedious solution. When the cloud of smoke was dense enough, the noisy fog machines had to be turned off for sound takes. Usually, by the end of the first take, the cloud would dissipate, and the procedure had to be started again. On breezy or windy days, particularly when the wind kept changing direction, the fog machines had to be located around the perimeter of the shooting area, and in high winds this method didn't work at all. Those were the

Figure 1.2 Shooting the dog fight under the tent

Figure 1.3 Fog machine in action

days when shots that could be shot in limited sunlight, or backlight, would be selected for photography.

One of these shots was of Corporal Casper, played by Les Lannom, charging the unseen enemy. After he fixes his bayonet and orders his buddy, "Get out of here!" he runs away from and towards the camera. We shot his charge in sunlight. As the swamp looks the same in all directions, we turned the shot 180 degrees, setting up both of the angles in backlight. Not only did this make the shots acceptable, but it also enhanced them. I selected a 300mm focal length lens for the shots and decided to run the camera at 128 fps.

The combination of the long focal length lens and the slow motion coupled with backlight picked up the splashing water, which added an element of beauty to the shot, underlining the futility of the corporal's charge. His unlit face, the shaded camera side of the trees, and other objects in the shot were dark, so the visual continuity of the film was only minimally interrupted. When he is shot and killed in subdued light, the change from the almost poetic beauty of the backlit shot contrasts with the underlit, bleak, grainy qualities of the rest of the film and seems to underscore the tragedy of his death. None of us, and no one with whom I ever discussed this sequence, ever objected to this inconsistency in visual continuity. A shot photographed in accordance with our "bad," standard grainy "look," followed by the backlit shot, then returning to the drab "look" of the film seemed inconsistent. But this sort of inconsistency is at times forgivable and may even be desirable from an artistic point of view.

Now let me deviate for a moment and talk a bit about relationships with one's crew and other members of the company during the making of a film. I already touched on this subject in regard to informing my gaffer about the reduced lighting requirement of the film. It was a difficult situation. It is not hard to understand how awkward it is to tell one's close associates, friends, or colleagues that they should not do their job to the full extent of their ability and desire. I certainly would resent it if someone asked me to do my job badly (it happens occasionally), or not as well as I could, or not as I would want to. During my fifty years in the film business, I recall only a handful of people on the crews I worked with who did not want to do their best for the picture. This can happen for a myriad of reasons—that one takes shortcuts at times or performs one's job below one's best—but never against one's strongest convictions, and never deliberately against the best interest of a project. In fact, the entire photography of *Southern Comfort* was below industry standards, but by design. And this brings up one of the war stories I promised in my introduction to this book.

This story touches on the close collaboration—or hostile relationship—that at times exist with one or a number of service organizations that surround the production of a film. In this case, it was the lab. I have already written about the lengthy testing that I did during the preproduction period of *Southern Comfort*. I shot tests, trying to arrive at a safe but effective underexposure to create the "look" of our film. All the tests had to go through the lab as the final proof that our "look" was not only possible, but also would stand up to the laboratory procedures all the way to the release print of the film. Once the tests were determined to be conclusive, the procedures were "locked in" and followed precisely on a daily—or I should say minute-to-minute—basis with almost religious fervor.

You can imagine my astonishment one morning as I got out of my car at our location and a note was handed to me from the production office. The note simply said, "Call the lab." There may be no other message received by a director of photography during the photography of a movie that can create such a sinking feeling. I have received a few of these messages during my years in the business. When a message starting with "Call the lab" is delivered first thing in the day, one knows instinctively that the message spells disaster. In this instance, I didn't even have to wait to call lab to find out how bad the news was: the rest of the note spelled it out: "80 percent of yesterday's close-ups are unusable."

Though mistakes occasionally happen in connection with almost every picture, no cinematographer is ever hired to make mistakes. When 80 percent of one day's close-ups are unusable, that is not a mistake, it is an unforgivable disaster of major proportions. But I wondered how the close-up coverage could be unusable without the rest of the footage being affected. I soon had the answer. Let me tell you the sequence of events as they happened.

As *Southern Comfort* was shot long before the advent of cellular telephones, and we were in the middle of a large swamp, I had to get into a boat and motor to one of the summer homes closest to our location to make a phone call. I was fortunate to find people in a house, who, in spite of being awakened sometimes between 6:30 and 7:00 in the morning, were gracious enough to let me use their phone. When I called the lab in Los Angeles, I was connected to someone I didn't know instead of my usual contact. My contact, the man who had followed my testing and handled our footage from the first day of photography, I was told, was not available. This new man told me that he was going to look into the case and was going to call me back. Obviously, this would not be possible, and I asked him to look into my problem while I was holding. I held for what seemed a very long time. My stomach was churning, and questions were racing through my mind as I tried to find a reason that could have explained my problem. I knew that the entire company and I were facing a terrible dilemma.

As it happened, we were scheduled to blow up the "Trapper Shack" that very day. The Trapper Shack was a small wooden building that we had built in the swamp as the home of one of the Cajun poachers who were believed to be killing the National Guardsmen. Blowing up this building was the continuation of the scene we had photographed the day before, which, as I was now told, had 80 percent of its coverage unusable. That being the case, I knew we couldn't blow up the building. If we did, we would have to rebuild it in order to rephotograph the unusable portions of the scene preceding the blowing up of the shack. As I was thinking about the consequences of this delay—not just the loss of a day's work, but rescheduling the rest of the film, and possibly keeping cast members beyond their contractual terms on penalty pay—I was, figuratively speaking, beginning to contemplate suicide.

When the man at the lab came back on the phone he told me that the production office had misunderstood the original message. It wasn't 80 percent of the *close-up* coverage of my footage that was unusable, it was 80 percent of *all* the footage photographed the day before that was unusable. He explained that the negative, was too thin, beyond his control, for effective printing. Not wanting to make the same mistake again, I asked him for his description and recommendation to correct the problem. He said he would have to run densitometry tests on the negative, but had no recommendation as the negative was "too far gone." He suggested that I call him in about an hour.

That, of course, was out of the question for many reasons. The people whose house we had invaded at that early hour possibly would have let me use their phone again, but I didn't want to hold up production while I was motor-boating between the telephone and our location. Besides, the whole thing didn't make sense to me. I had to get to the bottom of this and by this time I also knew that I wasn't going to get any help from the lab. As long as the lab told me the footage was a write-off, I knew that shooting for the day would have to be suspended. I told the man at the lab I wasn't going to call back. In spite of his objections, I instructed him to reprint our entire footage from the day before, effecting the best correction possible, and I asked him to messenger the film as soon as the prints were ready by the quickest way possible to our headquarters at the Hilton Hotel in Shreveport, Louisiana.

On the way back to our location, my head was spinning trying the find the least painful way to tell Walter Hill (the director), David Giler (the producer), and everyone else concerned that we had a disaster on our hands. We could not blow up the shack since 80 percent of all the footage photographed in front of the shack the day before would have to be reshot. I couldn't even guess about the financial loss to the company. I have heard of cases where the cameraman was replaced for much smaller problems. Frankly, I expected to be fired, but I guessed everybody wanted to see the reprinted footage first. I should also mention that if we had been in a studio environment, we normally would have gone to another scene while awaiting the new prints from the lab, but in the swamp, being two hours from our hotel, we had no "cover sets." We did not have the entire cast made up and in costumes with us, and we were not prepared to swing to other scenes. Obviously, shooting was suspended for the rest of the day.

Whenever a problem such as this surfaces, the first place to look for explanations is at one's own level. By the time I got back to our location, Dick Meinardus, my first assistant, had all the camera reports out and had checked all the magazines and the shutter (it might have closed accidentally or suffered mechanical failure). He checked the lenses to see if the T-stop rings might be loose and could have set the iris incorrectly. My crew and I checked everything we could think of. But everything came up negative. Nothing at camera level could have caused or accounted for the problem. That left only one thing—the lab.

Something must have gone wrong at the lab. Far-fetched as it was, one possibility entered my mind. The lab mistakenly underdeveloped our footage. Perhaps it had been swapped somehow with footage that was to be "pulled," or underdeveloped. If that were true, underdevelopment, added to the deliberate underexposure of my negative, would have rendered it unusable. But I knew it would have been futile to call the lab again and ask if this was the case or even a remote possibility. Very few labs during my fifty years in the business have ever admitted mistakes. It would have been as useless to call them for an explanation as asking the hospital why the surgeon had removed the good kidney. We had no choice but to stand down. No one spoke during the two-hour trip back to our hotel. Sitting in the backseat of the limo, I felt that I was at the focal point of our problem.

It was past 11:00 at night when the phone rang in my room. Our reprints had arrived. I hopped out of bed and into a pair of pants, and ran barefoot and shirtless down to our editing suite. As I entered the darkened room, the footage was already running on a flatbed editing machine. Walter, David, most of the editing staff, our production manager, and others were already looking at the footage. It looked—great! The only thing I could think of was that somehow the lab was able to correct the problem and my ass was saved. "This is great," I exclaimed. "They were able to correct the problem!" David Giler looked at me. "This is the uncorrected footage," he said, very quietly. It was as if lightning had struck. High-speed images of the day's events, as though projected by a runaway projector, replayed in my mind. In a flash the explanation became clear. There was nothing wrong with the footage!

I couldn't talk with my contact at the lab because he wasn't there. I was told "he was not available." He could have been sick, his car could have broken down, his mother-in-law might have died. For whatever reason, I knew he didn't show up at the lab that morning to time and shepherd my footage, as he had from day one of our testing and photography. Somebody totally unfamiliar with the special, highly nonstandard considerations of my footage and photography had covered for him. When he saw our purposely underexposed thin negative—after the strong, fully exposed, sharp, saturated qualities of a television series he might have been servicing—and wasn't prepared for the thin negative that was shot that way on purpose, he just simply classified it as 80 percent unusable.

Had he simply told me that the footage was "underexposed," I could have told him it was underexposed intentionally. I could have told him to compare our printing lights to the previous day's lights. I could have told him to run densitometry tests on our dailies and compare them to any of our previous footage. Had he told me my contact was not at the lab but at home sick, I could have told him to call my contact at home, or I could have called him myself and asked him to call the lab for me. All these thoughts were swirling around in my head, and I asked myself:

Should I have known that there was nothing wrong with the footage? Should I have had more courage and conviction to say, "There is nothing wrong, let's go on with our scheduled shoot, let's blow the shack"? Was I justified in canceling an entire day of our scheduled work? Even today these questions haunt me, but as more time goes by, the more convinced I am that indeed I was justified. I had no other choice! In the face of the message received from the lab, there was no other choice. As much as the loss of that day cost the company, the alternatives would have been far worse if the lab report turned out to be true. What price to pay for good photography! Even if it's *bad/good* photography.

Why did I relate this war story? Because hardly a day goes by on a film in production without something unexpected happening, and because it illustrates how "bad/good" photography can create its own problems, and most importantly because dealing with the unexpected is so much a part of the cinematographer's life.

And now that I'm telling war stories, how about another one. It also has a great deal to do with the cinematographer's life and, in particular, with the collaboration that should exist between the cinematographer and the director. Many creative people contribute their talents to the making of a motion picture. The individuals who write the story as a screenplay, put the production together, pick the locations—the list is too long to name all who leave their mark on a film. But it is my conviction that as the film goes into photography, although many people still contribute, only two figures on the set are responsible for the final creation and execution of the image. They are the director and the director of photography. The collaboration between these two people must be as close to perfect as possible (see Figure 1.4).

Collaboration does not mean surrendering one's ideas and convictions. In fact, at times, collaboration is strengthened by a point of view that's different from one's own particular perspective, but one that's always offered in the best interest of the film. Disagreements between creative people are often labeled as "creative differences." That expression usually suggests an irreconcil-

Figure 1.4 Discussing a shot with Walter

able difference that is decided by the stronger of two wills—and very seldom ends up in the best interest of the project. In some cases these creative differences end in a parting of the ways between two people who just cannot work side by side with one another. But to me, "creative" or "artistic" differences mean something entirely different. To me they mean that there is a difference in the thinking of two creative people, each of whom is convinced that his or her idea is right, but each of whom should be willing to consider the other's idea, and then go with what he or she believes is best for the film.

Walter and I found ourselves having just such a creative difference concerning a shot while filming *Southern Comfort*. The scene was the burial scene of five members of the squad killed by the Cajuns. The remaining members of the squad line up at the head of five fresh graves, as one of the Guardsmen, the Coach, is about to conduct the service. Each grave is marked by a rifle stuck

Figure 1.5 Burial scene

into the ground at the head of each mound of earth, with the steel helmet of the dead soldier on the rifle butt. It was a very powerful, graphic shot. Even on my first reading of the script, I scribbled a note that we should shoot this scene from the foot of the graves, looking up into the stricken faces of the squad, with a wide-angle lens on a low camera. I also felt that the wide-angle lens would exaggerate the perspective of the shot, making the graves appear to point at the Coach, as he is reading the service, about to go mad (see Figure 1.5).

But Walter had also made notes in his script. And his notes must have preceded my notes by a good several months, as he was one of the authors of the script. I'm convinced that even as he wrote the scene, he must have thought about how to visualize it. His notes called for a high-angle shot, slightly from the side and behind the squad, looking down on and over the soldiers' shoulders at the graves. Having mentally seen the scene hundreds of times, long before the photography began, his mind was set, locked into the high-angle shot for the burial scene. Our two opposing ideas did not clash until the day we were ready to shoot this shot. As he described his idea, I told him that I also had an idea and that I felt mine was better for the scene. I described my shot, and I think Walter liked it. Having lived with his visualization for so long, however, it must have been impossible for him to abandon his long-time thinking and adopt something entirely new and opposite to his vision. But he also must have seen some merit in my description of the shot, for he agreed to shoot the scene twice: his way and mine. As we discussed our "artistic differences," we even considered that both of the shots, or parts of each, might wind up in the finished film.

This incident is a clear example of what true creative differences can be. It also speaks highly of a director whose integrity and commitment is for a better product rather than for any false ego. Months after the shot was photographed, in the editing room, without any consideration for egos or politics being allowed to play part and in the best interest of the film, Walter chose my shot.

This kind of collaboration might be considered unusual. But during my fifty years in the business, I have been very fortunate to work with directors and other creative people whose self-esteem permitted such collaboration. Of course, there were also some whose egos—in some cases as big as the Universal back lot—did not permit them such unselfish decisions. Such egos (and the industry is full of them) have at times spelled the difference between the success or failure of many films.

But not everything works out all the time to the liking, design, or satisfaction of the cinematographer. Like it or not, there are conditions, "givens," attached to just about every project, which a cinematographer has to live with. One such a situation came up during the shooting of *Southern Comfort*. The scene was not part of the original script and came about as the film was being photographed. As "rough assemblies" of the sequences emerged, it was decided that the film needed a scene explaining the special predicament the last three Guardsmen were in and the personal relationship (which wasn't exactly what it should have been) between two of our heroes, portrayed by Powers Boothe and Keith Carradine. A scene was needed to round out the action through the spoken word. We added a scene in which the three remaining soldiers prepare to bed down for the night.

Photographing a night scene was "all in a day's work" for me, but a predictable request from the studio politely inquired about the intended lighting for this scene. It pointed out the shortcomings of night scenes for television reproduction, which at that time, the studios felt, was unable to reproduce underlit, low-key, photography. Although I was aware of the shortcomings of television, I did not fully subscribe to the studio's ideas of what television could or could not reproduce. I had my own ideas of what night photography should be. First, the style had to be in keeping with the day portions of the film regarding the visual qualities of the scene, before the restrictions and shortcomings of television could be considered. The creation of an image is not a precise or exact science. It is an art, and art doesn't recognize specific boundaries defined by, or restricted to, day or night. The image one creates starts with the primary purpose of telling the story. Day or night is a condition set by the story. The image must be effective in its portrayal of the story, regardless of the time of day or night.

The first gentle prodding of the studio is hard to ignore. A cinematographer knows that the studio's concern, unfounded as it may be, deals with the release of the film on television after the film has had its run in the theaters. The studio wants to make certain that the photography is not going to hurt, or possibly eliminate, the film from being rereleased on television at the loss of considerable revenue. But trying to convince the studio, as represented by an executive without adequate photographic background, that your photography will be wonderful for television, or arguing that the primary purpose of the film is a big-screen release and compromising the photography for the sake of a second release will hurt the picture's chances in the theaters, is very seldom successful. I learned a long time ago that by far the best way to handle such a situation is to acknowledge the studio's concern and assure them that you will do everything possible to comply with the studio's request for the type of photography that will stand up to the limitations of television without compromising the quality of the film in the theaters. In other words, the studio will have the best of both worlds. It is hard for the studio, or any executive, to argue with that kind of response, and the issue is generally put to bed. But the concern that I and all cinematographers face is that we do not want to sell out our own ideas, shortchange our artistry, or compromise what we believe is in the best interest of the picture.

And that brings me back to the creation of the image and "good/bad" and "bad/good" photography. Regardless of any requests or directives, the task at hand was to photograph the scene of the three soldiers bedding down for the night. Even without the studio's concern about television release, I knew I had to introduce light into the shots. This is not hard to explain or understand. Go into the woods at night; if you can't see in the darkness, you can't photograph effectively to tell the story. This is where Point and Shoot photography must give way to creating an image, as opposed to recording an image. The audience will accept the scene as taking place during the night, if an artistic illusion of darkness is created. Without this illusion of darkness, the audience would be looking at a totally black screen, only hearing the dialogue. At times that can be an effective way of presenting a scene, but in our case such an effect was not called for. The cast and their facial expressions had to be seen. Only after this "illusion of darkness" is created, can we worry about how to accommodate the shortcomings of television. By using techniques of backlighting, side-lighting, and in some cases not lighting the faces of the actors, the story line of the film was well served—and permitted a future television and videotape release.

And now we come to the real purpose of telling this war story: to illustrate how at times solutions come out of the unexpected corners of film production.

I learned very early in my years in cinematography that one must always expect and, as much as possible, be prepared for the unexpected. Because there were many times I was not prepared and could not photograph something that was unexpected, I decided a long time ago to always have a loaded camera within reach, just in case the unexpected did happen. I missed many beautiful sunrises and sunsets, because by the time a camera could be set up the sun dipped below the horizon or was high in the sky. Just such an occasion of an unusually beautiful sunset happened as I was on my way back to our hotel in Shreveport after one of our days' work in the swamp. Fortunately, this time I did have a small, hand-held camera next to me on the seat. It was loaded with film, ready to point and shoot. As I saw the sunset, I asked the driver to pull over and stop the car. Resting the camera on the car's roof, I shot several 15 to 45 second takes of the sunset, bracketing the exposure. I knew I had a very nice shot of an extraordinary sunset. (See Color Plate II.) I also knew that the script did not call for a sunset shot. Why shoot it then? First, because it was beautiful. Second, the studio's film library would have another sunset shot to add to the hundreds already in the library. But by far the best reason was, what if the film could use a sunset shot, photographed in the actual location of the story, even though it wasn't scripted? Many times during the editing process, long after the photography of a film is finished, an unforeseen story point could demand such a shot, or use a sunset, or any other pretty or unusual shot, for no other reason than it is nice to look at. If it fits into the story, it will bring an extra bit of what we like to call "production value" to the film.

Such was the case with my unscripted sunset shot. The script didn't call for it, but during the editing it turned out to be the perfect bridge between the daytime portion of the story and the scene of our heroes bedding down for the night. Not only did it tell us that night was coming, but it also left the exact time of the evening up to the audience. Was it late at night? Was it just getting dark in the evening? In either case, the lighting of the scene, the creation of the darkness, was now justified. How dark is dark? I can't define it, and most of the time, if the story is good and the imagery is appropriate, the audience doesn't care! Besides, the audience doesn't know which shot was scripted and which was not.

With that principle in mind, I would forego lunch on a number of occasions, grab a small, hand-held camera, and foray into the swamp looking for interesting, beautiful images to photograph—what I call "Targets of Opportunity," or whatever presented itself. Whether it was a colorful fallen leaf floating on the surface of the water, the reflected image of a heron fishing, or just the dark silhouettes of the huge, magnificent tree trunks reaching skyward from the still waters of the swamp, being surrounded by such beauty made me quickly learn how believable our soldiers' predicament was. Going from shot to shot one day I realized that I had wandered too far from our base camp. It was no longer in sight and the swamp looked the same in all directions. I had no idea where I was, or in which direction I should go to find the base camp. Then I heard a truck start up in the distance and headed toward the sound.

Let me talk about lighting the interiors of one of our sets, the Cajun Village. The last remaining two soldiers are picked up by an ominous looking truck, driven by an equally ominous looking Cajun couple (who, incidentally, are played by the local resident photographer Greg Guirard and, I believe, his wife). The two are driven to the Cajun Village where a *boucherie* (a party) is in progress with lots of people, food, drink, and music. The buildings are weathered board construction, built along the shore of a lake. Inside one of the buildings a Cajun band is playing, and people are dancing and eating. Our two soldiers are ushered into this building and urged to eat, drink, and have a good time. Under the circumstances, with the paranoia caused by the events of the past few days, having a good time is difficult, particularly for one of the soldiers played by Powers Booth.

As I was getting the scene ready, listening to the Cajun musicians rehearse, I realized that just like the beautiful swamps we had scouted, this room was also a contradiction to the story. The music was lively, unusual, and interesting, making me want to tap my feet. The enormous spread of Cajun food was inviting, and the smiling, happy faces of the dancers created a festive atmosphere. But unlike the case of the beautiful summer swamps, I was not unhappy with this circumstance. The festive mood and atmosphere in the large room was to serve as an ominous, threatening contrast. Having read the script, I knew that the soldiers' troubles were not over. Likewise, I knew that by this time, the audience watching the movie would also be somewhat paranoid, expecting further trouble to emerge from the merriment and happy surroundings of the village. Because of this feeling, I instinctively knew that the main theme of my photography should not change. It was to be the common denominator that continued unchanged beneath the story line, maintaining the suspense and the sense of threat.

At times a cinematographer must rely on instinct. No analysis or falling back on formulas can provide solutions as good as instinct can. This was particularly true in the case of our Cajun Village. The village was not a studio set, it was "real." Built on location, as opposed to in the studio or on the back lot, the room in which we were to photograph was real. The lake, the swamp visible through the windows, and the environment that we had left just a short time ago and that had been the background to the soldiers' story throughout the movie, these were all real. "Why should I light this scene?" I asked myself. I hadn't lit the rest of the movie and that became the strength of the film's style. Why not continue with that approach? Everywhere I looked in the room, the images were interesting, graphic, real. It could have been a real Cajun Village; it could have been a real *boucherie*. These sorts of parties, I was told, were characteristic of that part of the country and the Cajun people who lived there. The word *boucherie*, a word derived from the French, simply meant a festive get-together with lots of food, music, and good times. But my light meter told me that, as much as I wanted to photograph the reality of the situation as it existed without lighting, the film stock and the slow lenses, would not have allowed me to come up with satisfactory results.

Had I shot without lighting, even with the lenses wide open, I knew I would have been hopelessly underexposed.

To add insult to injury, the exterior light conditions were the lowest of our entire shooting schedule. Heavily overcast skies dropped the exposure to the absolute bottom of the scale, though the look of the swamp and the lake was exactly what I had always hoped for. But we were going to photograph them from inside the large room. Exposing for the exteriors, as seen through the windows, would have left the interior of the room much too dark for any kind of exposure that could effectively tell the story. This was a classic instance in which a cinematographer has to strike a compromise or, better yet, come up with a solution that turns an obvious disadvantage into an advantage.

There were two natural sources of light inside the building: daylight, which came into the room through the windows, and the bare electric bulbs in the rafters. The ratio, or the relationship and scale between the exterior light and the electric bulb-lit interior of the room, had to be established in key positions. The rest of the photography in the large room could be done using "artistic license." A bit cynical you might ask? Of course, but it is true. After all how real must "real" be? As long as the key elements tell us that we are in a real environment and that the story is continuing, uninterrupted, in a new environment, the cinematographer can do whatever he or she feels is right for the scene. Make the image serve, help, and enlarge the story, and underline and enhance the situations by making the image interesting and memorable. Of course, this has limitations beyond which a cinematographer should not go. However good or interesting an image might be, if it is not tied to the story in some way, it will be counterproductive.

With this reasoning in mind, the actual task of lighting the set was relatively easy to accomplish. I pumped some HMI lights through the window from the outside, just enough to supplement the existing light a bit and being very careful to maintain the characteristic diffused qualities of the actual overcast daylight (see Figure 1.6). The reality of the atmosphere was preserved. I then

Figure 1.6 HMIs pumping light through windows in *boucherie* scene

changed all the light bulbs in the rafters. Now that more "daylight" came through the windows, I installed 100- and 150-watt bulbs, instead of the 40- and 60-watt one, in the rafters. Above each of these bulbs, just out of the camera's view, I added a small 1000-watt to 2000-watt unit. I had to deal with two considerations that were created by this type of lighting. I knew the large bare bulbs would flare in the shot. Although I like flares under certain conditions, I didn't think that flares would be attractive or add anything to the shot in this case. The solution to this problem was simple. I used what I call "liquid dimmer," which is really hairspray that is sold in drugstores in many different colors. My favorite colors are black and brown. Varying amounts of this spray on the camera side of the bulbs will effectively mask or reduce the glare of the filament to the point that it becomes acceptable, or at least not objectionable. Even if this sprayed spot becomes visible in the shot, it is OK, as it makes the bulbs look old (a bulb that has turned black with age or has had dirt settle and cake on it). As only the camera sides of the bulbs were sprayed, none of the light output from any other portion of the bulbs was affected. The bulbs continued to look real and very much in keeping with the other appointments of the interior. Most importantly, they did the job and were completely acceptable visually. In fact, they helped maintain the character and the reality of the setting.

The 1000-watt and 2000-watt units, installed above each of these light bulbs, however, did create a problem in that they lit up the rafters. This light spill is visible in some of the shots on videotape in the standard video frame. I will come back to this problem a bit later in the chapter.

This type of lighting was completely in keeping with the rest of the "natural look" and the unlit quality of the film. In a few instances, as the happy tones of the interior scene slowly change back to horror, I did allow a few liberties with the lighting. The Point and Shoot aspect of the film gave way at times to "created" imagery as the last two soldiers are being attacked in the sheds surrounding the dance hall. Though the sheds were real, the images were lit in a way that helped underline the horror of the scene, without deviating too far from all that had preceded these shots in the movie. We still showed bare bulbs and simulated daylight even in places where no windows existed. The only difference was that the lighting, and the framing of the shots, was allowed to become more graphic and low key, thus underlining certain elements of the shots and lending emphasis to the situation. The low-angle shot of one of the Cajun killers, towering over one of the solders as a threatening, dark silhouette against the glaring daylight of the exterior, was created by lighting an artificial exterior of a brightly backlit silk panel. The empty shell casing that drops to the floor after the soldier is shot is softly spotlighted.

Let me deviate a bit at this point, I feel that I must discuss some other aspects of motion picture photography. Unlike a painter who can set up an easel with a blank canvas anywhere, assemble paints and brushes, and paint whatever he or she might have in mind—a portrait of a person, a still life, the landscape, or even an abstract image—a cinematographer is strongly guided by many factors. The first and most important guideline is the story as depicted in the screenplay. Then there also are the visions of others on the creative team; budgetary limitations; scheduling requirements; availability (or unavailability) of equipment; sensitivity of film emulsions; laboratory techniques—all of which are factors that affect, limit, or enhance the creation of imagery for a film.

I have already mentioned my approach to a script, but let me discuss it in a bit more detail. When a screenplay first comes to me, it has not always been decided that I will do the movie. But I have to read the script to decide if it is a project for me and to be able to discuss it with the director and others, who will decide if I'm the one for this screenplay. Once I'm attached to the project, I read the script again. In both instances, I like to read the script uninterrupted from beginning to end. I usually retreat to my den, turn off the phones, and lock out the outside world as much as possible. Reading a script from beginning to end gives me an overall picture of the story, close to what one would experience watching the movie from beginning to end. Even after the first reading, details and images begin to form in my mind. By the time I read the script for the second time, I'm already looking forward to some scenes that stand out in my memory as unusual opportunities to do interesting photography.

As I read, notes begin to appear on the blank left pages of the script. These notes deal with execution, with questions seeking clarification, with comments—all of which will affect the photography. Even before photography begins, the script will undergo changes: shots might be dropped or rewritten and new ones added. Shots that are too outlandish, expensive, or complicated may be simplified. Other shots will be photographed with standard or nonstandard approaches. In some cases, because of some unusual demands of a shot, new equipment has to be found or designed. These are just some of the considerations that will affect the photography of a feature film. Other considerations are financial and some are technical, but regardless of how simple or complicated the shots may be, all must be approached with the intention of doing them in the best, most interesting, unusual, memorable, and artistic manner possible. The dictates of the story are paramount.

Additional factors enter into the planning of how the image is to be created. For example, what will the format be? Years ago, when I first started in the business, the cinematographer had no such concern. There was only one format. It was known as the Academy Aperture. The Academy Aperture, which refers to the shape of the image, was an almost square, horizontal rectangle. This shape evolved from Edison's format, as it was thought to be more pleasing to look at than square images, and also, I suspect, because it more readily accommodated the four perf per frame film format. With the addition of sound, space had to be allocated for the optical sound strip, which had to be carved out of the picture area on the side of the image, making the frame almost square again. In order to continue the horizontal, rectangular presentation that the audiences had gotten accustomed to, the top and bottom of the frame was shaved a bit to create the same aspect ratio as in silent films, now known as the Academy Aperture.

In the ensuing years, as television began taking over as the number one form of entertainment, the movie industry desperately searched for new twists in hopes of bringing audiences back into the theaters. One-strip color photography, as opposed to the three strip, black and white negative, technicolor process, or some inferior color processes, was one obvious difference between theatrical and television presentation, but perhaps the major format difference was the wide screen presentations, going back to the early fifties. There were many of these formats. Most required the design and manufacture of new equipment for photography, film stock, print stock, processing, editing, and, finally, projection. Vista-Vision, a Paramount Pictures wide screen process, was a completely new approach, requiring all the changes listed above. Though the cameras used standard 35mm film, the film ran through the camera horizontally using a film area of eight perforations, effectively doubling the size of the negative area used and presenting the images in a wide horizontal format. Some of the other formats minimized the new requirements. The anamorphic format, even as it is used today, uses standard 35mm film stock, a standard camera, and a projection apparatus equipped with special lenses. Other than the special lenses, all other phases of filmmaking in the anamorphic format, such as editing, printing, and mixing, are accomplished with standard equipment.

Over the years, as it became clear that theaters all over the world could not afford to purchase and maintain all the various projectors necessary to accommodate all the different formats, anamorphic photography became the standard wide screen process. The requirements for equipment and techniques for anamorphic photography have changed little since its birth in the fifties. The new wide screen formats, as primitive as some of them were in the beginning, became very popular with audiences. Perhaps the most striking of these wide screen presentations was an early process called Cinerama. In spite of tremendous technical problems, visible even to the uninitiated, audiences loved this spectacular process. Three side-by-side cameras shot three equal-sized sections of the image, which made the side-by-side images vibrate along the frame lines in projection. Unmatched colors in all three frames were readily overlooked as other new innovations such as surround sound and the "wrap-around" images gave this process an almost three-dimensional quality. Because of insurmountable technical imperfections, Cinerama fell by the wayside and was replaced by better processes, such as Todd-AO, Vista-Vision, Cinemascope, and others.

The demand for films shot in the wide screen formats grew quickly. Because equipment was scarce as these new formats were developing, and because some aspects of production became substantially more expensive, a less expensive, less complicated wide screen process was sought. Some of the early wide screen formats used four times the normal amount of light, therefore increasing the amount of lighting equipment needed, the size of crews, and the time necessary to light sets. The solution the industry came up with was affectionately referred to as the "poor man's wide screen process," the 1.85:1 aspect ratio photography. The only difference between the 1.85:1 aspect ratio photography and Academy Aperture photography is that a narrow, horizontal area at the top and bottom portion of the picture area was eliminated, therefore projecting an elongated image that on the wide screen appears to be comparable to a film photographed with the anamorphic format. There are many advantages to this format: cost, ready availability of equipment, and no special or expensive production requirements to accommodate the process. Nor is distribution impaired as the films shot in this format are projected on standard projection equipment. Production companies love the 1.85:1 aspect ratio. With practically no adjustment at all, a film shot in that aspect ratio can be shown on television or transferred to videotape. With the current standards of television, no other wide screen format can make that claim.

But there are also some major problems built into this process. One of these is the unreliability of projection. Though the 1.85:1 aspect ratio uses standard projection equipment, projectionists, whether inadvertently or due to carelessness, can and do project portions of the frame that were photographed but not intended for projection. This is also true in the case of television reproduction where, due to the different shape of the screen, unintended portions of the image are seen. In some cases these areas of the negative contain lights, microphones, crew members, and so forth, none of which, of course, was intended to be part of the image. Adding to the problem, the top of the frame, as marked in the viewfinder, may not necessarily be the true top of the frame as the image is captured on film. It is difficult at times to determine how to frame a shot, knowing that it may not be projected as the truly intended composition for the shot. The same is also true for the bottom portion of the frame, where an image is photographed but also isn't supposed to be seen. Because of these and some other problems associated with this format, the industry came up with the "hard gate." The Academy Aperture aspect-ratio film gate, the part of the camera that determines the size and shape of the frame, is replaced with one that is the exact size and shape of the 1.85:1 ratio. This eliminates all the problems and fears of photographing unwanted elements, misframing in projection, and showing images that are not part of the original composition. As the top and bottom portions of the standard frame are no longer recorded on the negative, no mistakes can be made in projection.

But the studios dislike this solution. It renders the "poor man's wide screen process" to be a true wide screen process, therefore making television release as difficult as the release of any other movie shot in other wide screen formats. I always go to see one of my films, or any other film, that I know was shot with the "poor man's wide screen process," knowing that I'll be seeing portions of the image on film that were not intended to be seen. The audience rightfully considers such things as microphones or lights in the shot as major mistakes in photography. How do I safeguard against this? I just don't photograph anything in those two zones of the negative that are not supposed to be part of the frame. Even if the composition suffers, at least there are no unwanted objects, crew members, or equipment to be seen.

The 1000-watt to 2000-watt lights, for example, in the rafters above the regular light bulbs in the dance hall of the Cajun Village, could never be seen, as they were placed safely out of any portion of the frame that was photographed. But I knew that their effect would be seen. What I had to come to terms with was how badly this would affect the shot if it were misframed in projection. Though there is no completely acceptable answer, I decided that this little imperfection wouldn't be noticed by most moviegoers. Obviously, this is not to be excused as good photography, it is just part of life in the fast lane of making movies.

There are many other aspects of film production, though not necessarily part of photography, that a cinematographer has to live with. Each film dictates its own requirements. In the case of *Southern Comfort*, we had to learn how to spend days working in freezing water. On some mornings we would arrive at the location to find a thin layer of ice covering the water. We had to devise new ways of building dolly tracks in and under water, of mounting

Figure 1.7 Dolly track in swamp

cameras on barges, or of building camera towers and parallels without fear of them sinking and toppling in the muddy bottom of the swamp (see Figures 1.7, 1.8, and 1.9). The unusual qualities and demands of our swamp location also called for unusual methods and equipment—that did not exist. To accomplish certain shots, new methods and equipment had to be devised. We affectionately called one such piece of equipment the "Aqua Dolly" (see Figure 1.10). It was the brainchild and creation of my key grip, Tom May, who made it from inner tubes, speed rail, and a small trolling motor of the type used in bass fishing, driven by a battery. It worked well, giving us smooth dolly shots of the cast making their way through the water (see Figure 1.11).

Creating the images in a film cannot be done by one person alone. The crews surrounding the director of photography play a major part in what culminates in the images of the film. In selecting crew members who are experts in their fields, one must also take into consideration their personal qualities. Living with a

Figure 1.8 Cameras set up on barge

crew, at times for months on end, isolated in a remote part of the world, can be very difficult and can create huge problems if the personalities clash. A good crew, on the other hand, becomes one's family, forming friendships for life (see Figure 1.13).

Of course, there is always the unexpected. The prime portion of the day for a certain shot may be first thing in the morning. That is when the magical colors, hues, and shadings happen, as the sun slowly rises and golden reflections dance on the surface of the water. There have been many nights in my career spent sleeplessly, anticipating such conditions, only to find that for some reason the shot could not be made at the designated time. A cast member might be late, or spend too much time in makeup. Or, as in the case of *Southern Comfort*, our Cajun musicians might have to be bailed out of jail. They were a happy bunch who did a wonderful job for their part in the film, but they also partied hard, got drunk, and on a few occasions, as I heard, spent the night in jail, holding up the production the following

Figure 1.9 A multiple camera set up on a parallel. Note silk panel and smoke

morning. When something like that happens, the much-anticipated shot never comes off as planned. A "second best" shot takes its place, making the cinematographer feel that he has just lost something wonderful. Adding insult to injury, all other shots scheduled for the day will have to be speeded up to make up for lost time, with equally detrimental effects. At least that is the way the director of photography feels. Very few people on the set will know how the shot should have been photographed, and none of

Figure 1.10 "Aqua Dolly" in action

Figure 1.11 Shooting while towing

Figure 1.12 Three camera set-up in swamp

the audience watching the film in a theater will ever know that the shot they are seeing was not photographed the way it was planned. But shots made under adverse conditions and technically less than perfect, in some cases, may nevertheless be labeled by film critics as the work of genius for their unusual qualities. Chapter 2, "*The Warriors*," will illustrate many such examples.

Though audiences consciously or unconsciously analyze, like, or dislike films, I learned long ago that in most cases they accept films as they see them. Some film critics occasionally offer

Figure 1.13 Walter and I with camera crew

suggestions about how a film should have been made. Though they might be right sometimes, when the film in question is one I was a part of, I can see when the criticisms are far off target and the critics have no idea what they are talking about. But I am delighted if a film I photographed is well received, if the look of the film is favorably commented on, and I can sense that the images I created played a part in the favorable reactions of viewers. I am delighted, even if it took "bad/good" photography to produce those results.

Much of what I have covered in this chapter will keep cropping up again and again throughout this book, though involving more complicated and difficult techniques and conditions of filmmaking. The next plateau of cinematography leads us to the opposite of Point and Shoot, where not a single shot could have been accomplished by just pointing the camera and shooting. *The Warriors* is such a film. Like *Southern Comfort*, it was photographed entirely on location—but all at night, which necessitated lighting every shot for exposure and effect, and, most importantly, to create interesting, unusual, and memorable images.

Q&A *Southern Comfort*

ANDREW QUICKE: Early in the chapter you described some students who thought a cinematographer needed tons of equipment to shoot a movie with. How did they react when you showed them *Southern Comfort* and explained how little lighting you used for the movie?

ANDREW LASZLO: I honestly don't know. I hope they saw my point and learned something about the importance of lighting or the lack of it. At times it's hard to convince people that lack of success or ability can not always be blamed on lack of equipment.

AQ: Can you tell me a bit more about black dot filters? Have you used them since *Southern Comfort*?

AL: Black dot filters are very unusual, not often used, in fact disliked by many of my colleagues. Some, as I was at first, are afraid of them. Yes, I used them again, but only for a small section of the film *First Blood*. It had similar photography to *Southern Comfort*, and I thought that the black dot filters would enhance the look of those scenes in *First Blood*.

AQ: When you met the DP (director of photography) on the Disney set in the swamp, the chap who complained about his contrast problem, did you advise him about the black dot filters?

AL: I did, but he was skeptical. As I pointed out in the chapter, the black dots enhanced the style of my film because it added to the look of the bleak, monochromatic winter swamp without sunlight. My colleague was shooting his movie calling for a different style, during the summer in intense sunlight.

AQ: When you got the message from the lab, that your footage was not usable, did you really think of killing yourself?

AL: Of course not! But one must not take anything that affects one's work lightly. Filmmaking has been the largest portion of my life, and I take it very seriously. In fact, anything that goes wrong in front of my camera, even though it may have nothing to do with my part of the production, I feel responsible for. I did feel very badly about the problem.

AQ: How involved does a DP get in preproduction?

AL: It depends on two factors: one, how complicated the photography will be, and two, money. Generally, there are different financial considerations for preproduction; that is, some of the preproduction period is compensated for at a reduced rate. More often than not, because of these two factors, the preproduction period might vary from between three to six weeks. Of course, there are exceptions.

AQ: What do you mean by working at a reduced rate during preproduction?

AL: Because the workload during the preproduction period is not as intense as during production, a director of photography at times agrees to a reduction from his normal rate of pay during that period.

AQ: You mentioned that in case of a creative, or an artistic difference between two creative people on the set is at times decided arbitrarily by one. How does that work?

AL: I didn't exactly say that such a difference is decided arbitrarily. What I did say was, that after careful consideration and discussion, the decision should be based on what's best for the film. For instance, if the decision is made on the basis of ego, let's say by the director, without consideration for the other point of view, it will, in my opinion, be detrimental to the film.

AQ: How is preproduction different between feature films, TV, and commercials?

AL: Feature film preproduction is generally longer and more involved. But there are TV projects, such as *Shogun*, which required a very long preproduction period. Some TV commercials may be prepared during one meeting, while others may require round-the-world trips.

AQ: How much influence do you have in postproduction?

AL: Very little. In most instances a DP's involvement is restricted to the timing of the print. That means that as the first lab print is completed, a DP spends several sessions at the lab with the color timer, the person who adjusts the color and the densities of the print.

AQ: How often have you been a lighting cameraman, meaning being your own camera operator as well as lighting the sets?

AL: At no point in my career have I functioned on a film, feature, or TV project fulfilling both of those capacities. Motion picture photography is a team effort executed by several people. A director of photography has too many areas to be concerned with, and if he operates his own camera, he won't be able to concentrate on aspects other than framing the shots and the camera moves. Yet, in my opinion, he can't relinquish his involvement in the operation of the camera. In some countries, England for example, lighting the set and operating the camera were two isolated functions for a very long time. In Japan, a DP would always operate his own camera. I find fault with both of those approaches and don't subscribe to them. Each of my cameras has always had its individual operator—except in certain cases where the operation of a certain camera might be too dangerous, in which case it is remotely controlled or locked off, requiring no operator. Of course, there are certain instances when a DP prefers to operate a shot himself, rather than try to describe what he wants and then, after the shot is made, interpret his operator's description as to how the shot worked out. This is not too common any more, because of the addition of video tap in the camera, showing the frame on a monitor, to view shots as they're taken. In certain instances when a shot might be fun to make, a DP might elect to operate the camera. I did operate my camera on documentary films. On documentaries, the demands of the assignment and the ground rules of crew structure are totally different, and having a camera operator in most cases would not make sense.

AQ: You mentioned that during one of the lunch breaks you got lost in the swamp and understood the soldiers' predicament. What did you mean by that?

AL: As the movie points out, the soldiers were hopelessly lost in the endless swamp. The day I went looking for nice images to photograph, I got so engrossed in the beauty of the swamp that I found myself separated from the rest of our group. As I realized that the swamp looked the same in all directions, I had no idea where I was or where our base camp was. Of course, I didn't have any Cajuns gunning for me, but it was a bit scary that I had no idea where I was or how to get back to the set. If the situation of *Southern Comfort* had been real, and I had been part of it, I would have known how the soldiers must have felt.

AQ: You talk about the beauty of the sunset shot in the film, and the shots you photographed during your lunchtime forays into the swamp. How do you equate that with the harsh environment, the harsh look, you wanted the film to have?

AL: First the sunset shot. If you look at this shot, its beauty is not the standard, picture postcard type. It does have, certainly within the context of the film's story, an understated, almost threatening quality. Very few of the other shots were used in the film. I took them because I found them interesting, and because I like to take pictures.

AQ: What is a four perf per frame film format?

AL: A perf, a commonly used film term, means a perforation, or the square holes on both sides of the filmstrip. Most film formats use four perforations per frame. There have been several other formats experimented with, such as two or three perforations per frame, but very few of these formats survived as the rest of the industry is locked into the four perf per frame format. The Vista-Vision system, which is much used in special effects photography, uses eight perforations per frame, to take advantage of the sharpness offered by a large negative.

AQ: You mentioned mixing and editing anamorphic footage with standard equipment. What did you mean by that?

AL: Mixing is a term that denotes the process of combining the various elements of a film soundtrack. Certain wide screen processes, such as 65mm photography, require special postproduction equipment, while anamorphic photography or films shot in the 1.85:1 ratio can be mixed with standard equipment.

AQ: What is the difference between a slow and a fast lens?

AL: A slow lens cannot transmit enough light needed for proper exposure under low-level light conditions. It requires more light, natural or artificial, than a fast lens, which is just the opposite.

AQ: How much does knowing about carpentry and building—being a "Mr. Fixit" guy—help in being a cinematographer?

AL: Truly a lot. Understanding construction helps solve problems and helps create solutions. Being handy with tools is another big help. A cinematographer should really know every craft on the set. A basic knowledge of electricity, for example, is very important, but understanding the functions of the different crafts helps the cinematographer to communicate with and be helpful to his crew.

AQ: If fog machines are so much trouble, why not stick to just using the silks?

AL: Using silks on a large scale is very complicated, time-consuming, and expensive. Besides, in some cases, using silks is just not possible, particularly at the spur of the moment.

AQ: Do some shots need silks *and* smoke?

AL: Silks and smoke are often used in conjunction with one another (see Figure 1.12). The choice is generally dictated by the needs of the story. If the script describes a foggy, overcast morning, but the shot has to be made in sunlight without fog, silking the set coupled with minimal underexposure will create an overcast effect, and smoke will provide the fog.

AQ: Describe this handheld 35mm camera sitting on the car seat. Was it an Arri?

AL: Yes, it was a Panavision-converted Arriflex, using Panavision lenses and accessories. It had a 400-foot magazine as well as a number one black dot filter to maintain the continuity of the deteriorated image. When one operates alone, it is important that the camera be as small and as easy to handle as possible.

AQ: How could you start working on a second film like *Southern Comfort* while you were still working on a previous film?

AL: As I mentioned in the chapter, I did location scouting for *Southern Comfort* on my weekends and shot tests whenever the opportunity came up and I had some spare time on my hands while shooting the film in South Carolina. The conditions were similar to what I expected for *Southern Comfort*. This is not very unusual in film production.

AQ: Describe the camera crew hierarchy. You often refer to your assistant—is he the camera operator, the first ac (assistant cameraman), or second ac?

AL: A standard, basic camera crew on the types of pictures I describe in this book generally consists of the Director of Photography, Camera Operator, First Assistant Cameraperson, and Second Assistant Cameraperson. The Director of Photography is completely in charge of the design and execution of photography. All of the others work under the Director of Photography. The Camera Operator, or Operating Cameraperson as he or she is sometimes referred to, executes the handling of the camera during the shots. Panning, tilting the camera, maintaining a proper and pleasing composition, and smooth camera moves are the responsibility of the camera operator. His job is more artistic than technical; he works very closely with the Director of Photography, making suggestions in areas of lighting, camera moves, composition, and so on. He also works very closely with the director of the film. The First Assistant Cameraperson is perhaps the most important position on a camera crew. He assembles and tests all the camera equipment prior to shooting and is in charge of making sure that all equipment is on hand and operating perfectly during the shoot. During the photography, his primary concern is to keep the shots in sharp focus, have the T-stop properly set, and have the correct filters in front of or behind the lens. The maintenance of the equipment is entirely his responsibility, in which he is assisted by the Second Assistant Cameraperson and other additional members of the camera crew. If the film in question is a multicamera operation, each camera has its own Operating Cameraperson and First Assistant Cameraperson. In the case of a multicamera operation, there may be many additional Assistant Camerapeople on the project as would be needed for an efficient operation.

AQ: What is the secret of photography?

AL: Hmm . . . that's a big one. I know I opened this chapter by talking about the secret of photography, but giving a definition, well . . . I think I'll save that one for the end of the book!

2
THE WARRIORS

By this time in my career, 1978, I was in a fortunate position of getting more and more calls for projects. I was an up-and-coming New York cinematographer, who was fortunate to land some plums. My first feature, *One Potato, Two Potato* (1964), had been a Cannes Film Festival winner. Because of the controversial subject matter of that film for the time—an interracial marriage—it received lots of publicity, which is always a good way of getting one's name batted around in the industry. My second feature was Francis Ford Coppola's first major film, *You're a Big Boy Now* (1967) and *The Night They Raided Minsky's* (1968), Billy Friedkin's first major film, followed. Both of these films drew great attention from the industry and the box office. The reviews singled out the photography of these films, labeling them as new wave cinematography. The look of these films was much imitated in television commercials, which was by then, and is still the best testimonial a cinematographer can get. *Minsky's* was a star-studded, relatively high-budget movie for the time, but it had lots of problems during production, not the least of which was the unfortunate death of the legendary actor Bert Lahr, best known for his portrayal of the cowardly lion in the *Wizard of Oz*, in the middle of the shooting. The film was finished with doubles, voice mimics, and clever cutting, but nothing could really do the job Bert Lahr would have done.

The stature of these films brought with them high visibility and credibility for me as a mainstream player among the better regarded cinematographers of the day. *Popi* (1969) with Alan Arkin and Rita Moreno, *The Out of Towners* (1970) with Jack Lemmon and Sandy Dennis, *The Owl and the Pussycat* (1971) with Barbra Streisand, and other highly successful features followed, all receiving good notices for photography. In between these films I shot for television for a time, but no longer accepted running series. As in features, television was also a very fertile area for me. Having started on *The Phil Silvers Show* (1954–1958) ("Sergeant Bilko") as a camera operator, I worked on some notable series, mostly for Herb Brodkin's company Plautus Production. He was a very highly regarded New York producer of quality television with such filmed television shows as *Brenner*, *The Defenders*, *The Doctors and Nurses*, and others. I worked on most of those shows in the capacity of camera operator. After my break came on *Naked City*, which was the first series where I worked as director of photography, I moved up to director of photography on *The Doctors and Nurses*, one of Herb Brodkin's shows. To fill the gaps between feature films and television, I shot a never-ending stream of television commercials.

It was the spring of 1978 when the phone rang, the voice on the other end sounded almost like a recording, which I was beginning to hear with more and more frequency, announcing the possibility of a new project. "Hi, Andy," the voice said this time, "I'm Frank Marshall. My partner and I are in town from L.A. prepping a project for Paramount, and we were wondering about your availability and if you would be interested in looking at our script."

The task, on occasions like this, was to somehow conceal my excitement, not to sound terribly anxious, yet friendly and interested enough not to frighten away the caller. I had no idea who Frank Marshall was, nor did I ever hear of his partner, director Walter Hill. I was promised the script the same day, to be delivered by messenger, and we set up a time to meet the following morning in New York City.

The appointment was to take place in one of the Central Park South hotels, in a top floor suite overlooking the park. It was somewhat disheartening to see one of my colleagues, a well-known New York director of photography, leave the suite with a script under his arm, ushered out by a very friendly young man who turned out to be Frank Marshall. As the two of them parted on what seemed like very friendly terms, I was led into another room in the suite, believing that the cinematographer who just left had the film all locked up and that my interview was no more than a formality now.

I was introduced to another man, Walter Hill. Walter looked somewhat different from what I had expected. I grew up in a generation of filmmakers who still wore suits with pressed shirts and ties held with gold tie clips. In fact, as a camera operator working on various projects with the well-known New York director of photography Bill Miller, had I ever shown up on the set not wearing a freshly pressed pair of slacks with a sports jacket, dress shirt, and tie, he probably would have sent me home to change. Now here I was facing a director who looked very different from all that. Walter was a youngish man, a bit overweight, sitting—or sprawled, I should say—on a high bar stool, wearing dark glasses and a cloth cap with a visor. He had a full beard and chewed on a toothpick, which, I learned later, was his trademark. His weight was somewhat exaggerated by the undersized black T-shirt he wore, which didn't quite meet the top of his equally undersized blue jeans. Frank, on the other hand, looked clean-cut, had short hair with no beard, and wore a pressed red-striped shirt, but without a tie. These two were "new generation" filmmakers.

We talked for a while. The day before, as I started reading the script, I wasn't really a 100 percent certain I liked it. It was about a Brooklyn street gang. Though the dialogue was generously peppered with four-letter words, I found the story line more interesting as I read on, and in spite of the rough language, the script addressed some highly principled philosophies. Following the success of my first features, *One Potato, Two Potato* and *You're a Big Boy Now*, I wanted to build my list of credits and would have jumped on just about any bona fide feature project by any of the "Majors." Besides, I needed the work. Of my four children, two were still in private schools and two had finished college but were not established enough to be entirely on their own.

The interview, I sensed, went well. We talked about the script, the story's popular theme as well as its classical overtones, and discussed some of the difficulties of production in New York City. I answered questions about how to get from one location to another in a hurry in New York City traffic, how difficult crowd control was in the city, whether the Police Department was cooperative, and so on and so forth. My background in fast-moving New York TV production amply qualified me to answer these questions. Walter didn't say much. He grunted now and then, but I learned later that this was his style and when you didn't hear much from him, it was generally good news. I liked him!

The next appointment, another New York cinematographer with many good credits to his name—and much better known than I was at that time—was waiting as I left. But much to my surprise, later the same evening, Frank called to let me know that the picture was mine if I wanted it.

And that's how it started. Frank, Walter, and I became good friends. This book is, in part, a testimonial to that friendship, as of the five films I talk about in this book, three of them were done with Walter. Let me tell you how *The Warriors* proceeded from here on.

The Warriors, like *Southern Comfort*, was to be an action film shot entirely on location. I filmed *The Warriors* before I filmed *Southern Comfort*, but for the purposes of this book I discussed *Southern Comfort* first because it represents a more basic type of filmmaking. The principal difference between the two films is that although both were filmed entirely on location, *Southern Comfort* was photographed mostly during the day with little or no lighting, and *The Warriors* was photographed mostly at night, which required tremendous amounts of lighting. *The Warriors*, therefore, is the next logical step in the order of the five films I talk about, each representing a higher plateau, a more complex level of filmmaking.

Because of my background in photographing New York City locations under all kinds of conditions, I knew that I was heading into many areas that would represent a constant stream of artistic, as well as technical, difficulties. But before I tackle the problems and challenges of this production, let me give you a brief synopsis of the story. The story has always been my guide in determining the style, or the "look," of the film.

Though this has no direct bearing on the photography of *The Warriors*, it may be interesting to note here that the story, as in so many of other Walter Hill films, is an updated version of ancient Greek history and mythology. In this case, the story is a modern version of Xenophon's retreat from Persia. The film tells the story of one night in the life of a Brooklyn gang. They, along with nine other members of each of the New York gangs, are invited to attend a meeting organized by Cyrus, the leader of New York's most powerful gang. The purpose of this meeting is to organize most of the City's gangs into a single, coordinated unit under the direction of Cyrus in order to take over the control of the city. But Cyrus is shot and killed during the meeting. The actual murderers accuse *The Warriors*, whose leader is also killed in the ensuing melee, of killing Cyrus. Like Xenophon and his soldiers, *The Warriors* must make their way back to the sea and their home on Coney Island through the hostile turf of the many gangs bent on revenge—while also being pursued by the police.

My strong belief in having the photography support the story, having it enhance the story to the point that it subconsciously manipulates the emotions of the audience, has always been the starting point in my search for the "look" of any of my films. Sometimes, however, the look of the film, any film, may not turn out as the cinematographer plans it. Many factors come into play. First and foremost are the elements of the exterior locations themselves, which may impose certain conditions on the cinematographer and can at times dramatically affect and change the final look of the film. Political, budgetary, and various unforeseen conditions will impose their demands also, as will the contributions of other creative (and noncreative) people connected with the film. Add to this all the other elements—an actor getting sick, a location suddenly becoming unavailable, equipment breaking down, and so on—that a cinematographer must deal with in a manner that is consistent with the dictates and best interests of the final product, the movie.

In the case of *The Warriors*, the most immediate problem I anticipated was the many nights of photography in the seedier, mostly underlit areas of the City. The photography on moving trains in and out of the tunnels of the New York City subway system also presented me with previously unencountered situations. My number one problem in this regard was the only kind of negative film stock I was familiar with at the time: Kodak 5247. It was a very good film, but having used it over the years I knew it would be woefully inadequate for this project. Its speed, ASA 80-100, was far below the level I needed, but there really wasn't any choice. This was the best negative stock available among the film stocks with the same sensitivity that were on the market in 1978.

Some time prior to the start of the photography, even before the first production meeting, I went into the City one evening and took light-level readings at key positions in areas where I knew we were going to work. The light levels under street lamps, taken at eye height, ranged between 6 and 12 foot-candles, far below the level of sensitivity of the film stock. The lenses and the laboratory processes at that time were also below today's standards. The fastest prime lens in 1978 was a T:2, but it was rare. I was fortunate enough to get one, a Panavision 55mm, I believe, but as you went to longer focal length lenses, the lens speeds diminished dramatically to such levels as T:4.5, T:5.6, and worse. I knew that I could and would supplement the light coming from the existing street lighting, but I also knew that by doing so the background in the distance would suffer, losing detail to underexposure. In most instances, it would be possible to light the foreground and some limited background, but in situations where large portions of the City were visible, I knew this technique would not work.

I also knew that the depth of field was going to be very shallow at the very low light levels, because of photographing with the lenses fully opened. I partially remedied the shallow depth of field problem by the use of split diopters. While "diopter" is usually a definition of the power of a lens, these diopters, usually a single element attachment to a lens that alters its focal length, are also generally referred to as "diopters." These diopter lenses come in strengths of ½, 1, 2, 3, and so on. They are also available in what are called "split diopters." This means that a diopter lens is cut in half, one half is removed, and the remaining half, when placed in front of a lens, alters the focal length of only that half of the lens that it is in front of.

I had a big problem on my hands: I was faced with either inferior results, or extra expense and production time spent on lighting vast areas of the City. This would have been money the budget didn't have. Although it is hard to describe the exact reasoning behind my thinking, I slowly gravitated away from the standard, studio-type lighting of pretty, pleasant images, and towards a technically imperfect, at times rough photography. Because of the conditions imposed on me by the locations, I knew that this was going to happen to a certain extent anyway. This being the case, I also began to sense that in presenting a story such as *The Warriors*, the imperfect photographic approach would probably be preferable to those achieved by studio-type lighting. I made a calculated decision to accept "inferior results" rather than attempt the use of conventional techniques that, in my opinion, would have been difficult and may not have worked at all. I believed that if I could somehow present an image that showed and gave the feel of the environment of the City—which I considered to be one of the stars of the movie—it would help present the rough situations of the story in an interesting way. Even if the photography wasn't perfect, "good" photography, it would be preferable to making the "look" of the film fall in line with convention.

In the early days of production I had a lot of explaining to do to most of the Hollywood members of the production team, who were used to slick Hollywood images. But as rough assemblies began to emerge from the editing room and *The Warriors* was taking shape, it became increasingly clear that the look of the film was right for the story. I must admit, though, that even with my artistic resolve, there were moments when I would worry over shots and sequences that I photographed, knowing that the results were going to be way below what at that time was considered good photography. For example, we needed and photographed a bunch of shots for the opening sequences of the movie, which were not scripted. We did this throughout the filming whenever the opportunity presented itself. I had cameras set up in various parts of our train and rolled the cameras as the train hurtled through the tunnels and stations under the City on the way to location. At times I ran the cameras at high speed, or undercranked without any attempt to correct color temperature or exposure. None of these shots were "good" photography, but they were interesting enough to make up most of the opening sequence of the movie.

The night I shot the train slowly pulling into a station, one of the opening shots of the movie, caused me a lot of anxiety and loss of sleep. The camera was set up on a bridge over the tracks, shooting the train approaching from a distance. There was no way I could have lit even the smallest portion of the area the train approached from, as there were no buildings, structures, or anything to light. Even if had I wanted to, I could not have corrected the color temperature of the lights in the train, or those over the platforms of the station. Instead, I decided to shoot the shot just as it was: underexposed in the dark areas and overexposed in the lit areas such as the platforms, which were directly in front of and below the camera. I knew the contrast would be drastic and the color temperature of the fluorescent lights would result in anything but good color. This was "bad" photography at its worst—or should I say *best*?

The dailies the following afternoon were, in a strange way, not as bad as I expected them to be. The footage had a quality that in some respects was new, even interesting to me. I wasn't exactly sure how to explain, interpret, like, or dislike it. To my surprise, there were no negative comments in the screening room. I wasn't sure if I should interpret this as a sign of approval, or a signal that I'd be imminently fired. I knew the dailies were not "good" photography as I thought good photography should be until then, and watching the dailies made me uncomfortable. Perhaps that is the way the audience should feel, I consoled myself. Later, as we came out of the screening room, somebody cornered me and told me he thought the footage was very "unusual and interesting." I learned then that as the cinematographer of the movie, I will never be the sole judge of the photography, though I would be the only person held responsible for it. But, obviously, I still looked for approval and welcomed kind remarks and encouragement from others.

Fortunately, we were deeply into the picture by then and had seen footage photographed in subway stations where the situation was similar and, in some respects, even "worse." In addition to the built-in fluorescent lighting of the subway cars we worked in, some areas in the stations were lit with florescent tubes of different color characteristics, and these lights were different again from fluorescents in other parts of the station. Even that is not the end of the story.

Our particular station, the one at which most of the film's action takes place, also had incandescent bulbs, designed and built into its structure as far back as when the station was first constructed. The bulbs were old, producing a red or warm tone, and none of them could have been replaced. At the time the New York City subway system was put into service, it was wired with low-voltage lighting, for reasons of economy, but mainly because low-voltage bulbs, if stolen, could not have been used in homes. To further deter thieves, these bulbs had left-handed sockets, making them even more difficult to remove and impossible to use in the home. All of this meant that I had to live with these bulbs, without any possibility of correcting them.

At this point I no longer even considered trying to correct existing lighting to 3200 Kelvin, or to correct my standard 3200

Kelvin motion picture lights to match the color of the fluorescent and incandescent lighting of the location. I wouldn't have known how or what to correct to achieve a proper balance. The result was a mixture, a hodgepodge of color. At least three different kinds of fluorescent and incandescent sources were mixed with neons and motion picture lights, all of which melded into an image that couldn't be classified as "good" by the standards of the time. Yet after the film came out, most of the reviews called the photography of *The Warriors* a cinematic masterpiece. A little blurb on the jacket of the VHS cassette and the laser disk concludes with the following sentence: "This intense and stylized film is a dazzling achievement for cinematographer Andrew Laszlo."

Let me talk a bit about photographing this "intense," "stylized," and "dazzling achievement," starting with photographing inside the moving train. This was relatively simple, once I discarded the idea of attempting standard lighting in favor of rarely lighting at all. As I mentioned earlier, the cars were illuminated by built-in fluorescent lights. These lights were manufactured for the NYC Transit Authority, and even if I could have found equal size, photographically correct tubes, we would have had to dismantle the cars to replace the lights. This might have given us good results in one car, but would have mismatched the light in every other car. I did manage to borrow some replacement tubes from the Transit Authority and have my gaffer jury-rig a few floor units to be used as fill lights, rim lights, or whenever additional light was needed. The film company had a train completely at our disposal. We rigged it so the view through the windows was lit in a realistic fashion, though most of the time it was underexposed, except when outside objects, such as bridge girders, tunnel walls, and so on were close enough to the train to produce proper exposure. Even this irregularity—the never-ending fluctuation in densities—added an ever-changing quality that, although it wasn't "good" photography, turned out to benefit the film's look. It proved the points I made in the Introduction and Chapter 1 about "bad/good" photography. I'll keep coming back to that oddball description again and again, in connection with *The Warriors* as well as the subsequent films I will be discussing.

Let me digress for a bit and touch upon another aspect of working on this film, another aspect of the cinematographer's life—what I call studio politics.

The overwhelming and number one consideration of studios and production companies on all films is the budget, that is, how to bring the film in within, or under, budget. While the budget and a good final result should go hand in hand, the front office, particularly at the beginning of a production, sees nothing but numbers on paper, and is unable or unwilling to consider the final result on which the success or failure of a film hinges. Most films are budgeted by highly capable experts with vast experience who can, and usually do, come very close to the final cost of the film. But even these experts can't think of all eventualities and all necessities, and at times they can overlook or don't allow for important items needed for the production. It wouldn't be fair to say that they undercut their own films, but, as in the case of *The Warriors*, the production company had to move within a studio-imposed figure. Although I can't claim absolute accuracy, it is my understanding that the film would not have been green-lighted (i.e., made) if the budget could not have been brought under $4.7 million. Apparently, the original estimate of the film was much higher, but after many reworked budgets it was brought below the rumored, studio-designated figure of $4.7 million and the go-ahead was given. Perhaps $4.7 million was all the money Paramount had at the time, I really don't know. It is my understanding though, (again, I don't know this to be a fact) that the film came in substantially above the projected figure, which is not unusual for a location picture.

Whatever the actual facts, I was trying to consider all eventualities from my very first reading of the script, and I decided to find out what the company's policy was in case we found ourselves under conditions we could not work in. One such condition was heavy rain, which was a strong possibility. After all, it was not unreasonable to expect that in sixty some odd nights during the summer it would rain a few times. But behind my question about the company policy of standing down or not due to rain was an ulterior motive: I knew that this film had no cover sets. For the benefit of those who might not be familiar with the term "cover set," let me explain what they are. Cover sets are alternatives to the scheduled, assigned work for any given day. If for any reason something interferes with the execution of scheduled work, there are always alternative scenes and work that the company can switch to on a moment's notice. For example, on a studio lot the company may abandon a set due to any number of reasons and switch to a "cover set" to continue working with as little time loss as possible. In the case of *The Warriors*, since the film was to be photographed all on location, we had no cover sets. Besides, I knew that moving to an unprepared location at night and starting from scratch on a film like *The Warriors* was not an option.

I posed my question at an early production meeting, wanting to know the company policy in case of rain (do we continue working in the rain? do we stand down? do we go home as we used to in the old days?). But I knew that getting someone to stick his neck out with a hard-and-fast answer was not likely. As invariably happens, someone wanted to know if I had any suggestions. Would it be possible to photograph in a way that wouldn't show the rain, using filters, for example, and other inane questions and suggestions that one hears from even the seasoned veterans of the business in such a situation. The answer was negative to all of the above, but I did have a suggestion that would, I told everybody at the meeting, solve the problem.

I had spent enough time in the film industry to know that almost anything is more preferable to a production company than the loss of production time. My suggestion was that we introduce a new scene, to be written and added to the existing script, of a brief but intense summer thunderstorm to take place early in the story. It would be, I explained, very dramatic, and it would ensure continuity, because we would wet down all the streets to be photographed following this rain scene in the story. I explained that this would ensure and preserve continuity and would, I conceded, also enhance the photography of drab, dark night shots. There would be little or no production time lost, and we wouldn't have to stand down in light rain or wait till the streets dried. I knew that wetting down the streets was an expensive proposition, but I also knew that it would enhance the look of the film tremendously. Water would turn drab pavements into shiny, black mirrors, which would reflect the lit elements of the shots and enhance the look of the movie. At the same time, my stated concern about continuity was also valid, for the story was continuous, all of it taking place in the time span of one night. But in the final result, it was the look of the film that benefited most. It might even have helped production by requiring less time for lighting and therefore fewer extra crews.

I learned more than a few lessons on this film, technical, artistic, and political lessons that I used over and over again in my half-century long career. I learned, for example, that even though I usually like to imitate reality, as I mentioned in Chapter 1 regarding my later film *Southern Comfort*, I must not hesitate to enhance reality. Imagine, for instance, that we have a stretch of wide New York street in front of the camera, with an elevated train structure overhead (this shot is in the movie), but in the center of the shot the pavement is dark, without detail or interest. There are many streetlights reflected in the pavement, except in the center of the frame where detail is most needed. It is easy to correct such a situation by hanging an additional light from the elevated train structure, or even putting a light on a stand right in the shot, some distance away and pointing at the camera, so that its reflection produces a bright streak at the right spot in the pavement. This is both enhancing reality, as well as a providing a quick and effective remedy for the shortcomings of a shot. Under certain conditions, a color gel on such a light adds to its qualities and further enhances the image. The old taboo against seeing a light in a shot clearly does not include a situation such as this. There are many other legitimate lights in the shot, none of which will be individually examined or justified by the audience. Seeing one more light, provided it cannot be positively identified as a piece of filmmaking equipment, would not matter, nor should putting it in the middle of the frame prove a deterrent.

I had all sorts of signs made up prior to the beginning of photography, some of which said Hotel, Bar, Garage, Park, Eats, Diner, Restaurant, and so forth. These signs were of various sizes, cut out of thin plywood, and covered with 3M Scotchlite, the material used for front projection screens. Any of these signs could be positioned at any portion in the shot, usually some distance from the camera in order to render the stand invisible. The stand could also be made invisible by covering it with black fabric, "blackwrap," or black tape. A small light placed right next to the lens would illuminate these signs, which, when they reflected the small light, would appear as brilliant as real neon or incandescent signs. The signs could easily be positioned to fill in an otherwise blank or uninteresting portion of the frame, and they could be precisely positioned, moved from side to side, and raised or lowered to enhance and complement the composition and structuring of a shot. In some cases, the signs could be made to flicker, pulsate, or turn on and off at regular intervals as an old-fashioned hotel sign would, or be given a color simply by slipping a color gel into the small light next to the lens. By alternating two or more lights with different color gels in them, the Scotchlite sign in the distance could create all sorts of effects—and create the illusion of detail that would not otherwise exist. For some time prior to *The Warriors*, I used this technique to create distant roadblocks, simulated train semaphores, and harbor lights where there were none. These lights also do wonders in situations where one has wet pavement without detail, by adding detail, color, and brilliance.

The Scotchlite technique brings to mind a "war story" that happened in connection with filming another movie. I was setting up a night shot in Georgetown, Washington, D.C. The camera had to be in a certain place, pointing in a specific direction, but, unfortunately, almost the entire right one-third of the frame area was dark without detail. There was a building there, even some bushes between the wall and the sidewalk, but the windows were not lit and the entire building, occupying a large portion of the frame, was dark. I told my grip to get two standard-size show-cards (the white on one side, black on the other side variety) and staple them to a 1" × 3" brace. I then attached the cards to "C" stands and covered them with 3M Scotchlite material. Two-inch black tape, simulating the crossbars of standard windows, and some crudely fashioned curtains made out of cheesecloth completed the "windows," which were then set up some distance from the camera alongside the unlit wall. A small, 1000-watt light with a straw filter, to add the mood of a warm glow of incandescent lighting, was placed as close to the lens barrel as I could get it to illuminate the "windows."

In the final shot, the "windows" were slightly soft, beyond the depth of field of the shot, but to the unsuspecting viewer they appeared quite real and believable. In fact, just before I was ready to turn on the small light alongside the lens, I asked the director, Gary Nelson, to look through the camera, and fibbed that I had just talked with the people who lived in the unlit building and that they were about to turn on the lights. At that point I switched on the small light next to the lens and two windows lit up in the frame. The director was amazed. But he was even more amazed when I called out to my grip, as the director was still looking through the camera, to move one of the windows a couple of feet to the left. The lit window moved, as if by magic. In a way it was magic, "movie magic," as we like to call it in the business.

What makes this technique so workable is the ability of Scotchlite to return light. The properties of Scotchlite must be understood to successfully apply this technique. Scotchlite will return all but a fraction of the light it receives, but unlike a mirror, it returns the light to the light source—in other words, to the light itself. If the light is placed in the optical axis of the lens (and this is possible with a prism or one-way glass), a small light can overpower the biggest unit on the set and appear extremely bright, as it would if one looked straight into the light. Yet the effect of this small light would not be visible, much less exposable, on any other surface in its path. For the application of this technique it is not necessary to put the light in the optical axis of the lens, but it is important to place the light as close to the lens as possible. Placement that is even a few inches from the lens can drastically diminish the reflected intensity of the light.

This and other innovations and new techniques became the order of the day on almost any given night while photographing *The Warriors*. Convention and established practices went by the wayside, as the situation demanded. I set out to produce unusual images by whatever new and unorthodox way I could; none of them could have been at that time considered standard "good" photography, but they became the important consideration in creating the visual style for *The Warriors*. I kept pushing the limits, sometimes because I had to, sometimes just because I had learned to love it.

One such time came one night as the work was interrupted by a torrential downpour, the type I had suggested we write into the script, except that this was real and we had to take cover inside the El Station at the end of the Coney Island Line. The building was a multilevel structure, with not much passenger or train traffic at that hour in the night. It was a dark and drab place, which soon got on everybody's nerves. Walter was as annoyed as I was at losing valuable production time, and he soon suggested we shoot something. I agreed, but asked him, "What?" "Why don't we shoot the kids," he said, referring to *The Warriors*, only a few of whom were much younger than he was. "OK," I agreed, waiting for his suggestions. He chewed on his toothpick for a while, then suggested I set up some close-ups and tight two-shots of the guys, and he would write some lines for them. Walter is an accomplished writer with a number of well-known original screenplays to his name (*48 Hours, Hickey and Boggs, The Getaway, Mackintosh Man, The Drowning Pool*), and, in fact, he shares screenwriting credit with David Shaber on *The Warriors*.

One of the most difficult tasks is to light something for a movie without knowing what the scene is about. I had hoped to get a clue from Walter, but I think he was waiting to see the images to inspire him. He told me he would just have the kids say a few words, one-liners, and thought that the lighting should be very sketchy. This comment was a help from another point of view as well. The place, a large area just below the platforms but above street level, was dismal. The cement walls probably hadn't seen a paintbrush for decades and were crumbling. It didn't take a genius to know that the less we saw of it the better. Besides, these shots weren't part of the script and weren't supposed to fit into any specific part of the story. I had the camera set up and asked two of the actors to stand in for themselves as I placed a single light directly overhead, so only a minimal amount of the light reached the faces and none of it reached the wall behind the actors. It was an interesting idea and produced an interesting image, but it did need a background that wasn't there. I had my gaffer set up a light behind the actors, shooting directly into the lens of the camera. As we made shot after shot with different actors, I put different color gels and diffusion in the lights and moved them into slightly different positions to fill in the background, either to obliterate what was there or to create a background where there was none. This technique worked, allowing the audience to catch a quick glimpse of an actor's face for just long enough to hear the actor ask, "What do you know about Cyrus?" "He is the one and only," the other answered, and we cut.

In one form or another, that same question would be rephrased and spoken by other actors in similar size cuts, with very little change in the lighting. All of these cuts were improvised, none were scripted, and, as far as I know, never got into any revised version of the screenplay. But almost all of the shots became part of the final cut. I didn't think then that the type of lighting I used for those shots could be sustained in longer cuts or scenes, but since *The Warriors* I have used similar techniques for longer and longer cuts, until the technique metamorphosed into a style—one which I'll talk about in connection with the photography of the film *Streets of Fire* in Chapter 4, much of which was shot using this technique.

In *The Warriors,* this technique was subsequently used in other parts of the film, where the existing background could have been improved, or needed to be partially or totally obliterated. By this time in the production I had come to learn—and be convinced—that problems, foreseen and unforeseen, were not necessarily detrimental to the film. In fact, if the problems were handled creatively, the disadvantage could turn into a plus for the movie. In the case of *The Warriors*, the idea was to make the images different and unusual, without losing track of the story's dictates. Some of the conditions that were imposed on me, and therefore on the movie, dictated that even in the cases where no unusual look was created by necessity, such as the train coming into a station, I could and did make the images different. By doing so, they became more unusual and interesting. This is how the film's comic book qualities materialized, at times by necessity, but as the film progressed, more and more often by conscious decision. Had this picture started as a standard studio production, shooting on the back lot or on the soundstage, its look probably would have been very different. Standard studio practices and techniques, perfected and polished over the years, would have made this picture just another film, without the visual impact that evolved out of existing conditions and necessities. Instead of creating and controlling every aspect of the lighting, most of the time was spent conforming to and working creatively with existing conditions, which set the standards as far as light levels and the mood of the shots were concerned.

With this new technique came a kind of artistic freedom, which allowed me to discard lots of stale techniques and practices of previous years, work with what I had to, and add the touches, all of which made the imagery of the film different from almost anything I had done before. It also made the film different from other contemporary films. Conventions, "dos and don'ts," went by the wayside, allowing and encouraging me to use previously unheard of techniques, particularly as solutions to problems.

Frequently, opportunities popped up unexpectedly. One shot called for Swan, the leader of *The Warriors*, played by Michael Beck, and Mercy, the only female member of a second-rate gang called The Orphans, played by Deborah van Valkenburgh, who forsakes her own gang and attaches herself to *The Warriors*, to walk through a subway tunnel. The shot was an interim shot in the sequence involving these two characters, who, having been separated from the rest of the gang, are trying to get to Coney Island. Having shed their pursuers, the two are walking through one of the subway tunnels under New York City. It was to be a simple shot, but when I got to the location in the tunnel, an unusual image confronted me. The camera was already set up on legs in the middle of the tracks, waiting to be moved into position. Usually the action is rehearsed first, on the basis of which the camera position is determined. But when I looked through the camera I was struck by an extremely beautiful image of the dark tunnel with the highly polished curved tracks reflecting the lights of a distant station. I was amazed by how different this image was in comparison to seeing it without the camera: as the camera framed the scene, which was enhanced by the long focal length of the zoom lens, it emphasized the strong graphics of only the crucial elements of the shot.

Prior to seeing this image, I had had no idea how this particular shot of the two cast members was to be accomplished. I figured, as I usually did in similar situations, that I'd wait till Walter rehearsed the shot with the actors, and then I would frame it, light it, and add whatever additional elements I thought would help the shot. But in this instance the extraordinary beauty of the shot was handed to me. I introduced some smoke-and-steam atmosphere into the background of the shot, added light coming through this atmosphere, and let the silhouettes of the unlit actors walk between the shiny, gracefully curving tracks to the camera as they went through their dialogue. It turned out to be one of my favorite shots in the movie.

Another favorite shot (which, interestingly, is part of the same sequence) also came about without design. Shortly after the tunnel shot and some philosophical dialogue between Swan and Mercy, the script called for the two actors, suddenly and unexpectedly, to kiss passionately. While shooting in the tunnels we were interrupted time and again by the thunderous noise of trains passing in a parallel tunnel, from which we were separated by a wall with large openings. As the trains roared by, I was fascinated by their highly polished stainless steel skin reflecting our lights and creating a machine-gun like effect of flashes. I suggested to Walter to move the kissing couple in front of one of these openings and time the kiss as a train went through the adjacent tunnel. I then had my gaffer place lights in other, nearby openings, aimed at the mirrorlike sides of the trains at such an angle that the passing train would reflect these intense lights right into the lens, resulting in the kissing couple being silhouetted by the resulting fireworks. The intensity of the reflections, the flares the lights produced in the lens, and the earsplitting roar of the train made the kiss a very intense moment in the otherwise quiet, almost tranquil setting of the dark tunnel. When our editor, Dave Holden, saw the shot in dailies the following day, he called me to tell me that this shot alone was, as he put it, "worth the price of admission."

The sequence in which *The Warriors* are chased through the park by The Baseball Furies (another gang in the story) was photographed in an area of Central Park in New York City that was close to a mile long. The gangs ran long distances, as the camera car pulled in front of, ran abreast to, or followed the runners. The entire park was visible. The only way to light it, according to conventional methods, was with powerful lights from a distance, which, in my opinion, would have been very unrealistic and ugly or from the camera side along the path of the camera car, which would have been flat, overlit, unrealistic, and ugly as well. Instead, I placed hundreds of "Gator Clip" lights in tree branches along the path of the runners, most of which are visible in the finished film, but which don't look like lights in tree branches. Running rapidly by them with the camera car, they quickly pass beyond the depth of field of the cameras and become out-of-focus, bright balloons, as if they were distant lights of the City. The exciting sequence keeps the audience focused on the action, rather than allowing them to wonder about how the scene might have been technically accomplished.

By the time the shooting schedule brought us to the old cemetery in Brooklyn, where the scene just after the break-up of the meeting in the Bronx takes place, I had no fear of placing park-light-type lights right in between the graves. The lights allowed me to brighten areas, which otherwise would have gone totally black, to add visual interest; and, most importantly, they justified the rest of the illumination of the images, which was provided by standard, off-camera motion picture equipment. The light—or the lack of light—on an actor's face, for instance, would have been disturbing to any lay person in the audience, if it weren't for the visible park lights in the shots, establishing the legitimacy of the illumination.

At this point, I should say a few words about lighting in general: why it is done and how it evolved. Historically, photographic lighting goes back as far as photography does, but for a reason other than to create an artistic image. Light was the overwhelming necessity for recording an image on film or on paper. Without light—without an overwhelming amount of light—photography would not have been possible. In still photography, time exposure was the answer, even if the subject, as in so many Civil War still photographs, had to be immobilized by being tied to a chair or leaning against a solid object. In the case of early motion pictures, the lack of sensitivity of motion picture film at the beginning of the twentieth century, coupled with slow lenses and primitive processing techniques, relegated film photography to instances when bright sunlight was available. Because daylight was limited, even after the industry moved to California to take advantage of more sunny days per year, artificial lights had to be created to supplement daylight. Light was the one overwhelming element needed to allow proper exposure and the recording of a satisfactory image.

It is beyond the purpose of this book to try to follow the evolution of lights used for photography. Let me just say that early lights were primitive, crude devices, to say the least, but they did make photography possible when daylight alone was not enough. It is true that some of the lights, particularly open-faced arc lights that used two sets of carbon arcs burning in a simple metal housing, emitted so much ultraviolet radiation that they literally sunburned and blistered the actors and in some instances caused temporary or even permanent eye damage. But as these lights were improved and became more controlled and plentiful, cameramen of the day recognized their value as creative tools of photography.

The word "modeling," adding character to the image, became a part of the photographic jargon. Indeed, the films of Fritz Lang and others became known and successful, at least partially, because of their unusual imagery—which was created by unusual dramatic lighting. As film technology evolved, lighting equipment became more refined, and film stocks and lenses became more sensitive, so the necessity of more light on the subject for the sake of exposure alone diminished. Modeling took over as the more important element in the creation of an image by lighting. The realization that withholding light was as important to the creation of the image as adding light became obvious, and in most cases became an overwhelming element in the creation of the image. The great master painters—Rembrandt, van Eyck, Hals, Vermeer, and many others—all taught us that less light, used in a realistic and artistic manner, made the images more interesting.

When *The Warriors* was photographed in 1978, the necessity of a specific light level was still very much a consideration, as without it the negative could not have been satisfactorily exposed. But by that time I had also discovered that I could overlook certain standards of what was then still considered to be good photography, and not only get away with it, but achieve certain artistic results by discarding convention and adding elements that produced the unusual images of *The Warriors*.

Sitting in the screening room watching dailies, even I cringed at times, finding certain images difficult to accept on the basis of the standards of past experience. It is not easy to unlearn practices and standards acquired and used over the years and suddenly replace them with untried, unproven, and, in some instances, known-to-be-bad techniques and procedure. Hearing from the labs almost daily that my negative was not strong enough, or that the colors weren't true, I realized how restrictive and detrimental established practices such as lab procedures can be, holding back an art form by restricting it to their interpretation of the state of the art.

At this point let me take a moment to talk about a process known as "pushing." It was suggested more than once, mostly by lab personnel, that I push the film, forcing the negative in development. "Forcing," as this technique is also called, did not make sense to me in connection with the night photography of *The Warriors*. Forcing the negative simply means that the negative is developed for a longer than normal time period, therefore allowing some of the detail to mature a bit further than it would with normal developing. But this can't be done without a detrimental effect to the image. Forced processing will not put detail into the negative that was not photographed in the first place. Night sky or a dark wall will appear without detail in the print as it had no detail in the negative. Pushing the film cannot help in this sort of situation. It will increase the density of the well-exposed or overexposed areas in the negative, therefore extending the difference between black areas and highlights and making the image more contrasty. At the same time, the overdevelopment destroys the underexposed, dark areas in the negative and degrades the richness of black areas, which will become a greenish grey swirling mass of grain. I am not a proponent of forced developing, and never have been, and today, with the faster negative stocks that have just about eliminated the need for forced developing, I wouldn't have to be. In certain instances where the results of forced developing, such as increased grain, may be desirable, it is a technique that can still be seen occasionally in TV commercials and in some dramatic films, but used only as an effect.

Back to where I left off. The state of film art (even my interpretation of it) in 1978 would not have allowed me to place lights, which were visible in the shot, in tree branches or to put park lights between graves in a cemetery. So blatant was this process that every time I see the film even today, I wonder why no one seems to see those lights, or question or criticize why they are there. And that brings me to another revelation that came to me while I was filming *The Warriors*.

Audiences see what they want to see, not just in the case of *The Warriors* but in the case of any film. The theory that audiences do not remember the previous cut is in most cases true. Watching the dailies of *The Warriors*, but not seeing some blatant irregularities, was as surprising to me as to most of us. I wonder how many readers of this book, who saw *The Warriors* in its initial release or have looked at it since, spotted the two camera cranes smack in the middle of one of the shots, following the killing of Cyrus? During the seminars I give for Kodak, I prepare my audience to look for these two cranes in the finished film. One is a Titan Crane, the biggest camera crane at that time, and the other is an Atlas Crane, which was the second biggest. Both of them are in the middle of a shot in the chaotic action of the sequence after Cyrus is shot. I point out to my audience that they have the advantage of being forewarned, which people coming to see the film in theaters do not have. I also point out that most of my seminar audiences have some background in filmmaking, which average filmgoers do not have. I forewarn my audience to look for unusual lighting techniques before showing them this film segment. Even after having been forewarned, it is amazing how few in the audience see the lights in the tree branches, the park lights between graves, or two of the biggest pieces of motion picture equipment in the middle of a shot. Indeed, audiences see what they want to see. Very few people question lighting techniques as long as the story holds and the action and the imagery are interesting enough to divert attention away from those aspects that are unimportant to the audience.

Now that the point of what the audience does or does not see has been made, one might rightfully ask, "Why are the two cranes in the shot in the first place?" The reason underlies an important aspect that exerts an influence in the cinematographer's life and affects his abilities to produce images exactly as he had planned. The shot containing the two cranes was the last to be photographed during the nights scheduled for the sequence involving the big meeting in the Bronx and Cyrus' killing. It was, as most of the shots in the chaos sequence were, a very difficult shot to accomplish. The cameras had to be transported to and set up at the designated positions, while the actions of a thousand extras were choreographed and principal actors and bit players were positioned and rehearsed. I knew that the two cranes were smack in the middle of the shot. I also knew that removing them would have taken hours, as the area they were in was a fenced portion of the scene and putting the cranes into this area had taken an entire day—the day before the shots were scheduled. The camera cranes had had to be lifted into position by a large construction crane, which was available, but removing the cranes would not have been possible before daybreak.

A night shot of this scope could not have been accomplished in daylight. Holding the shoot over to the next day would have necessitated adding an extra day to the shooting schedule and recalling a thousand extras. The potential added expense could have resulted in cutting the shot from the movie. It was an important shot in the sequence, and we had to do everything possible to get it before daylight. Orders were given fast and executed immediately. It must be added that in situations such as this, every member of a good production team pitches in to accomplish very difficult tasks.

First, the shapes of the cranes were broken up and camouflaged by placing branches and other nondescript objects between them and the camera. The action of the shot was then designed so as to draw attention away from the area the cranes were in. While all this was going on, the clock kept ticking. As the eastern sky over New York City was showing the first signs of daybreak, the cameras were raised to minimize seeing the sky. A large tree branch with thick foliage and extra added branches was placed in front of the master camera to mask most of the sky. Graduated, neutral-density filters were added to both cameras to darken the sky in the top portion of the frame. A police cruiser took up most of the left side of the frame, its blinkers going. The action, taking place directly in front of the camera, kept the audience occupied and further masked the two strange objects in the middle of the shot.

This was the kind of situation I generally refer to as "pulling a rabbit out of the hat." Suddenly, one is faced with a situation that has to be dealt with. One knows it cannot be done well, but it must be done as well as possible under the circumstances. This is the time when all eyes are focused on the cinematographer, expecting him to come up with a solution. A production manager, or a line producer, suddenly materializes on the set and stands near enough for his baleful expression to be clearly visible. The director and the cinematographer scamper to accomplish the shot, somehow, not because production is putting on the pressure, but because the shot is very important to the film. Although production and the cinematographer are sometimes at loggerheads, it's not hard to understand the concern over adding an extra day to the schedule and calling back and paying a thousand extras—all of whom will also have to be fed a meal and put into wardrobe.

And that brings to mind another war story, one that is not terribly important as far as cinematography is concerned, but is worth mentioning as part of the cinematographer's life—and every part of the cinematographer's life, I should point out, affects his cinematography.

A thousand extras are not easy to work with, particularly when a large portion of the thousand extras are nonprofessionals, as was the case while filming the large-scale gang meeting in the Bronx. In a situation like the crowd scene in *The Warriors*, the Screen Actors Guild at times grants permission to use a certain percentage of non-Guild members, particularly when definite types are needed. In the case of *The Warriors*, we used hundreds of extras, of which quite a few were actual New York gang members. On the first night of the shooting the level of excitement was very high among both the professional and nonprofessional members of this crowd. Most of them thought it was going to be fun to be in a movie, especially if they were in a real gang and the movie was about gangs.

But the excitement was short-lived. Very few of the nonprofessionals knew that filmmaking was hard work. The crew and cast slept all day, coming to work in the evening and working till daybreak the following day. The nonprofessional extras had been up all day before the shooting, and by midnight most of them started to fade. Some just dozed off where they were, or found a nice grassy spot and went to sleep. Others decided that Hollywood wasn't for them and went home. Night after night this scene was repeated, and we had to change our shot order to shoot the shots requiring the largest crowd scenes early in the night and concentrating the remaining extras into smaller and smaller shots as the night wore on and the crowd diminished. This meant lots of repositioning of the cameras and relighting of the shots, which wouldn't have been necessary if the extras had stayed and we could have proceeded with shooting in sequence as planned (see Figures 2.1–2.4).

There were other problems, too, which affected the production. When some of the extras decided to go home, some took their costumes with them. In some cases the clothes were better than their own, or looked more like gang-fashion. Paramount Pictures had to keep replenishing the wardrobe. To ensure the return of hard-to-replace items of clothing, all extras were given a ticket when they changed into wardrobe. When they returned the wardrobe the following morning, there was a raffle, giving away a color TV set to the lucky extra holding the winning ticket. This system worked well until the third or fourth morning, when the winner, happily carrying his new color TV set, was mugged within eyesight of the location. Incidents like these are fond memories now but weren't quite as amusing then.

Some of the difficulties and hard work that were needed to film *The Warriors* are contrary to the popular beliefs of some fans regarding the "glamour" of the industry. Yes, we all know that there is glamour, and lots of it, but more often than not, it isn't found in the front lines of filmmaking. Sure, it's glamourous and nice to be where news cameras flash, but it does not diminish the hard work necessary to bring a screenplay to the screen. Being in the film industry extends certain opportunities. Not many people will ever have an opportunity to see the extremely interesting world under New York City. Not many people might want to. After all, spending night after night in the subway tunnels surrounded

Figure 2.1 Shooting crowd reactions at the big meeting in the Bronx

Figure 2.2 Shooting crowd shots at the big meeting in the Bronx

Figure 2.3 A typical three-camera set-up while filming the big meeting in the Bronx. Camera "A" is on the crane, cameras "B" and "C" are on the parallel.

by the world's largest rats might not be everybody's cup of tea. After my first night in the tunnels, in oppressive heat and humidity, I was surprised to discover black dust running off my body as I showered. An inch-and-a-half, maybe two-inch layer of this black dust covers the bottom of the tunnels, which we churned up as we walked. The dust is finely ground bits of steel, produced by wheels grinding on the rails since the day the first train went through the tunnel. Glamour! But not the same glamour as depicted in fan magazines.

Turning one's life literally upside-down applies to another aspect of the cinematographer's life. I slept through the entire summer of 1978 while filming *The Warriors*. Saturday mornings came slowly. There was always "just one more shot" to be squeezed in before we wrapped for the week, just as the eastern sky was getting brighter. Since I live on Long Island, east of New York City, I

Figure 2.4 Filming Cyrus with three cameras, before he is shot

would be driving home looking straight into the rising sun, and by the time I arrived, my wife and children had already started their day. I was ready for a quick shower and bed. In order not to miss too much time with my family, I had my alarm set for one o'clock in the afternoon and made myself get out of bed, but for the rest of the day I was a zombie. By about eight or nine o'clock in the evening I was again ready for bed and wouldn't wake up till about nine Sunday morning. Sunday was a bit better. I was more rested, more or less back on the normal clock. I played with my children, spent time with my wife, and in the evening went to bed at a more or less normal time. The problem was that I woke up at a normal time Monday morning, with nothing to do but wait until four or so in the afternoon to go to dailies, and from there to work. Monday, when the cycle started again, was always a twenty-four hour day for me. I slept through most of the summer that year. Glamour!

Of course, not every second of filmmaking is hard work. Spending most of one's time with a closely-knit group of people, all with the same interests, is very enjoyable. Good friendships and close associations develop. As work on a film progresses and it becomes obvious that the film is coming together according to hopes and expectations, the insecurities wane, the intensity of work eases up, and lighter moments happen more and more often. One such incident happened on *The Warriors*.

Early in the filming, Larry Gordon, the film's producer, wanted to know what happened to a scripted and scheduled shot of a loudspeaker, which in one of the scenes was supposed to be making an announcement on one of the elevated train platforms. It was what at times is referred to in filmmaking as a "throw-away shot," meaning that it was not a terribly important one to get, certainly not if getting it would have been at the expense of not getting a more important shot. So, as we put it off night after night, Larry kept asking about it just about every time we looked at dailies. "The Loudspeaker Shot," as it became known, was listed on all call sheets, and, indeed, wherever we went, we carried a loudspeaker with us, made-up to look like it fitted in on any elevated platform as standard equipment. Every time we arrived at a new location, the loudspeaker would be set up on some nondescript structure to be photographed at any time we had a few minutes on our hands with nothing else to do. But weeks went by without an opportunity to shoot the loudspeaker. None of us were terribly concerned, as we knew that eventually the shot would be done. But Larry continued asking about the shot and his concern seemed to have intensified with each day.

One evening we were standing down for some reason and I decided to shoot the loudspeaker. Larry wanted several shots, mainly because neither he, nor anyone else, had a clear picture as to what this shot should look like, or how it was to be used. Regardless of how it was shot, as long as the audience clearly understood that they were listening to words coming from the loudspeaker, the shot would work for the few seconds it was going to be on the screen. As a gag I set up a camera on the platform, some distance from the loudspeaker, and shot about fifteen feet of film at the widest focal length of the zoom lens. The loudspeaker was in the shot but totally invisible, as it was too small, in the middle of a very wide shot and way in the distance above the platform. I then made progressively tighter and tighter shots, slowly making the loudspeaker become visible as we got closer and closer to it. All of these shots were clearly identified by the proper script number, in addition to the word "Loudspeaker" in large letters on the slate.

When the first shot came on at dailies the following evening, Larry was puzzled as he read the slate but couldn't see the loudspeaker. He asked where the speaker was. Nobody answered. Some didn't know, and others, who were in on the gag, kept mum. There were no comments. I was wondering if I might have overstepped the boundaries of light humor. But slowly, as the gag became obvious, there were a few chuckles, which grew into uproarious laughter. Larry, being the good-natured person he is with a larger-than-normal good sense of humor, enjoyed that evening in the screening room most of all, I think. He never failed to bring up the "Loudspeaker Shot" every time we saw each other after *The Warriors* was completed.

There were other incidents as well that turned into great moments of filmmaking. Paramount Pictures became increasingly uneasy about the film going over schedule. Several studio executives came in from Hollywood to visit the set and to get the company back on schedule, by whatever means. They all failed. But they did report to the home office that some of the changes they instituted would help the company speed up its operation. One such innovation was to work longer days, even though as the summer was slowly giving way to fall there was progressively less daylight to work in each day. By this time we were on a day schedule, doing the daytime scenes of the story in and around Coney Island. We would report to work at six o'clock in the morning and fumble around in total darkness, trying to locate the catering truck in hopes of getting a cup of hot coffee. Shooting anything in the dark was, of course, out of the question.

One morning, as I was standing on top of a sand dune looking out at the ocean, I noticed the brightening of the eastern horizon. Soon, the colors were turning to every shade of orange, yellow, dark red, all set off by the rich, still deep blue sky in the west. Within seconds, I knew, we were going to have a rare and probably incredible sunrise. I called for a camera, but none were ready yet. By the time I had a camera on its way to where I was, the sun was high in the sky and one of the most beautiful sunrises I've ever seen was a thing of the past. Not getting a shot of it was a great loss to me, even though the script did not call for a sunrise shot. It also saddened me to believe that it would never be repeated, certainly not to match the beauty of the sunrise I had just witnessed. Perhaps out of frustration, I told my first assistant that I wanted three cameras set up, each with different focal length lenses, ready to go on the same spot the following morning, just in case there would be a repeat performance. I didn't think there could be. But as it turned out, the following morning three cameras rolled as a brilliant flash over the horizon announced the sun's imminent appearance, which turned out to be more beautiful than the day before. As an added attraction, a flight of geese and some wispy, golden clouds, exaggerated by the long focal lengths of the lenses, crossed the huge red ball of sun as three thousand feet of film went through the cameras and the sun was high enough to start the day's work. If nothing else, I thought, the Paramount Film Library will have some footage to add to their considerable inventory of sunrise shots, which I thought would all have to be inferior to what I had just shot. The shots drew lots of "Uhhhhs," and "Ahhhs" at dailies the following day, and a short segment of one of the shots became the bridge between the night and the day portions of the movie. It was a tremendously satisfying experience! Since then, I have always tried to be ready to shoot when the conditions are right, or to be ready to shoot at unexpected moments like the sunset shot during *Southern Comfort*, which is one of the secrets behind successful location photography.

Now, let me say a few words, as I always do when I talk about *The Warriors*, about the power of the film medium. We have all experienced the power that presents a story in a way that entertains, holds the attention, creates lasting impressions, manipulates the emotions, and exerts an influence over the audience. In the case of

The Warriors, this influence was extreme. If someone had canvassed all the creative members of the production team of this film, all those who had a part in bringing the film to the screen, I don't believe a single person would have been able to predict the enormous and unbelievably dramatic reactions this film created. Disturbances broke out at almost all the theaters where the film was shown. I went to see it with my family the day after it opened in one of the theaters in my area. The manager of the theater suggested that if I came to the six o'clock showing on Saturday evening, which generally did not draw a large audience, I probably wouldn't have to stand in line in the severe winter cold. She was right, and I was terribly disappointed as I sat among some sixty people in an almost empty theater. All of us, my wife and children and I, wore Warrior jackets, similar to the gang jackets the actors wore in the film, but the dismal attendance dampened my enthusiasm.

This mood changed, however, as the six o'clock showing was over and we came out. The lobby was filled with people, six abreast along the wall, all the way back to the doors and out into the street. The line went around the block in the severe cold, and I wondered if everybody was going to get in. I decided to go back into the auditorium to see the film again with a large audience. It was a totally different experience with a theater full of people reacting to the film. In fact, some time before the film was over, some of the teenage and younger members of the audience started to tear up the seats and trash the theater. People flocked to this movie, even though this scenario—and worse—was repeated all over the country. Nobody could figure out why.

By the time Paramount agreed to discontinue TV ads, posters, and other forms of advertising, the ads were no longer needed as news about *The Warriors* had moved to the front page of papers across the country. I don't know how much of this reaction was due to copycatting other violent reactions to the movie, but I do know that when I witnessed it, it had to be spontaneous, as the film was only in its second day of release. I also know that guards, placed in some theaters and paid for by Paramount Pictures, did not help. The violent reaction to the film intensified across the country. More and more lawsuits were filed against Paramount, and when two people were killed, allegedly as a reaction generated by the film, Paramount had no choice but to pull the film from release. It has been estimated that the film would have been a very large financial success had it not become necessary to discontinue its release.

In spite of this misfortune, the film was an artistic success, as attested to by the many favorable reviews, the best of which was Pauline Kael's review, reprinted by Paramount as a full-page ad in various newspapers. During the production phase, neither I nor anyone else who worked on the film could have predicted the extreme reactions the film generated. In fact, most of us thought that the choreographed fights in the film were too mild and weren't as spectacular as we thought they should have been. Besides Cyrus and Cleon, no one is killed and no one is maimed. In fact, there is only one sequence in the entire film that shows blood, and then the blood is but a trickle on the lips of Ajax, one of the gang members, as he is arrested by a woman decoy police officer.

The Warriors helped me focus my attention on the power of the film medium as an extremely important factor that we filmmakers, and future filmmakers, must be aware of and respect. Besides being entertaining, film has the power to instruct, sway, and sell, and it can be a most formidable weapon of propaganda for good or evil. I often speculate whether the Nazi Party of Germany in the thirties would have succeeded as well—or if, indeed, World War II with its devastating consequences would have happened—without the spectacular, powerful propaganda imagery of Leni Riefenstahl, the documentary filmmaker of the Third Reich.

If made today, *The Warriors* would probably be an altogether different movie. The availability of fast and more sensitive, more forgiving negative and positive film stocks, faster lenses in all focal ranges, smaller, more powerful lights, electronic postproduction—all would add up to different photographic techniques, which would negate the need for the same ingenuity in dealing with the difficulties of cinematography in 1978. The film, if made today, would have few or no technical shortcomings. The contrast, color temperatures, depth of field, as well as all the other elements of photography on location at night would be near perfect. There would be far fewer challenges and, in my humble opinion, far less need to come up with unconventional, imaginative solutions. Today, the challenges could all be easily handled with state-of-the-art techniques, equipment, and materials, and there would definitely not be a need for "bad/good" photography.

The Warriors continues to be quoted in many publications and cited often as an early example of the type of image creation it became known for and for which it was much imitated. Today, over twenty years after its release, *The Warriors* is still around and has a surprisingly large cult following.

Q&A *The Warriors*

ANDREW QUICKE: The park lights you say you placed in between the graves in the cemetery scene, what sorts of lights were they? Also, what is a park light, another kind of HMI?

ANDREW LASZLO: Park lights are what exist in real parks, providing night illumination. We carried with us a truckload of replica park lights of the sort found in New York City parks. These lights were made to look like the real, existing lights and were used to provide illumination where there were no real park lights, or where the real park lights did not provide enough illumination.

AQ: Explain f-stops and T-stops.

AL: For all practical purposes, both of these designations mean the same thing, but they are arrived at according to different scientific formulas. Simply put, f-stops were calculated on the basis of a relationship between the focal length and the diameter of the lens. T-stops simply mean the amount of light transmitted by the lens at any designated setting. The numbers denoting these settings were retained from the older f-stop system and are still used today for setting the exposure, even though an F:4 may not necessarily be equal to a T:4. T-stops, however, assure a more exact

Figure 2.5 Walter and the author with the camera crew. Note the unusual camera set-up. Three cameras are shooting simultaneously in the middle of a room as an unrehearsed free for all is going on all around.

light transmission match between lenses. F- or T-stops are designations to set the iris of the lens to control exposure.

AQ: You mentioned *The Phil Silvers Show* and Sergeant Bilko. Was he not one of the central characters of the show?

AL: He was. In fact, he was the star of the show. The conniving but loveable Sergeant Bilko was played by Phil Silvers. Originally the show started out with the name *You'll Never Get Rich*, and as it became successful the name was changed to *The Phil Silvers Show*.

AQ: You mention the "Majors." Who or what exactly are the Majors?

AL: The industry jargon refers to major studios in Hollywood—Universal, MGM, Warner Brothers, Paramount, and others—as the "Majors."

AQ: Why was wetting down the streets an expensive proposition?

AL: Wetting down a street for a shot is not a particularly difficult or expensive proposition, but wetting down every street for every shot of an entire picture is time-consuming and expensive. Time is money, and on a hot night the wetting down has to be repeated before each take or before the pavement dries. As some of the shots are large, at times two or three tankers are used, so it is an expensive proposition.

AQ: How did this save time and why did it eliminate extra crews?

AL: Because of the reflections that the wetting down gave us, we needed to light less areas in a shot that did not require the extra crews for lighting.

AQ: What was the movie you refer to in connection with the Scotchlite window effect in Georgetown?

AL: Actually, it was a television mini-series called *Washington behind Closed Doors* (1977).

AQ: Is there a way to learn to make good instinctual judgments while on the set?

AL: I believe instinctual judgment is exercising one's own power of logic and the interpretation and evaluation of situations. It is entirely self-taught, and I'd be hard put to define a formula as to how to learn it.

AQ: Do you really mean that you put an actual film light smack in the middle of the frame? Surely, while a streetlight does not matter, a film light does.

AL: It really doesn't, but you are right: it must not look like or be recognizable as a film light. With all the lights in the shot, as I explained in the chapter, one more light does not matter. The audience will not critically try to identify each light, unless the action or the story bores them—in which case it wouldn't matter, as the film will fail anyway.

AQ: You said that you "pointed a light at the lens": wouldn't that give you a flare?

AL: Pointing a light at the lens will produce a flare of varying intensity, depending on the relationship between the optical axis of the lens and the axis of the light beam. The intensity and the quality of the light are also considerations. A hard light, for example, with a mirror and a lens, that is focused to spot and is shooting directly into the lens will produce a blinding flare, but a less intense, soft light might not. So altering the direction and intensity of the light will effectively control the flare.

AQ: What did you mean by having lights "off camera"?

AL: The expression "off camera" means anything that is just outside of the frame: a light, a stand, anything that might have something to do with the photography of a particular shot, but is not visible in the shot.

AQ: Are there any reasons today to force the negative?

AL: Only if the effect created by the force development process is desirable. Such an effect might be excessive graininess. With all the new high-speed negative stocks available today on medium- to high-budget productions, there really shouldn't be any need to force-develop the negative for the purpose of supplementing exposure.

AQ: About the Loudspeaker shot: did you intend this as a gag from the start and was it your idea?

AL: The loudspeaker was a scripted shot, but as we kept putting it off and as Larry kept asking for it, it became a running gag on the set. Shooting the shot as I described it in the chapter was my idea.

AQ: Do you feel regrets or responsibility for the violent reactions to *The Warriors*? Would you not have done the film if you had known what the response would be?

AL: First, I most certainly would not have done the film had I known for sure the extent of the reactions. Second, as I explained in the text, none of us working on the film had any idea that the film would generate even mild disturbances.

AQ: You said that because of better film stocks and equipment today there would be no need to seek out or use "bad/good" photography. Couldn't today's filmmakers use "bad/good" photography anyway?

AL: An excellent question! They could indeed. May I add at this point that there really is no such a thing as "bad/good" photography. If it is good for the picture it is good photography!

3

FIRST BLOOD

While I was finishing the photography of *Southern Comfort*, it occurred to me that I would probably never have another picture that would be as physically tough as *Southern Comfort* was. Considering the difficulties and hardships of shooting in the swamp, I don't know if this was simply wishful thinking. But as it turned out, it was not to be true.

I was winding up a visit with film students at Dartmouth College in New Hampshire when a message was handed to me that a Mr. Andy Vajna had called me in New York about a film project. The message said that I was not to return the call, as Mr. Vajna was visiting the locations with the film's director and would call me again in two days. I'd never heard of Mr. Vajna, but I recognized the name as being Hungarian, which raised the question of whether he had called me because of my Hungarian name and background. Two days later I was lounging poolside behind my house when he called again. As is the norm in cases of first contact, he explained who he was: he was a film distributor but was about to produce his first feature film. Having seen some of my films, such as *The Warriors* and *Southern Comfort*, he thought I would be the best qualified cinematographer for his movie. He was interested in my availability.

Up to that point the call was not unusual, but he also wanted to know if I could come to British Columbia the following day to meet with him and the director of the film. I asked who the director was. Mr. Vajna told me it was Ted Kotcheff. I had to admit I didn't know him and asked Mr. Vajna about Mr. Kotcheff's credits. Mr. Vajna mentioned *The Apprenticeship of Duddy Kravitz*, *Who Is Killing the Great Chefs of Europe*, and a few more. Unfortunately, I had only heard of *Who Is Killing the Great Chefs of Europe*, but had not seen it. Mr. Vajna assured me that Mr. Kotcheff was a very good director, a Canadian citizen who now lived in Hollywood and was absolutely the best choice for the film.

By this time in my career, though I was still not completely independent, I was more careful about selecting my projects. I had a string of successful films to my name and was fully aware of how important one's list of credits is—particularly the film completed last. This project sounded to me like an independent film, without major studio involvement, for a first-time producer I'd never heard of, with a director whose credits, rightly or wrongly, I thought were less than impressive. I can't say that this kind of appraisal is always fair or reasonable—after all, Francis Ford Coppola, Billy Friedkin, Larry Peerce, even Walter Hill, were almost or completely unknown when I worked with them for the first time. I asked about the film, and Mr. Vajna, in turn, wanted to know if I was familiar with the book, *First Blood*, by David Morrell. I was not. I asked about the cast. The star of the film was to be Sylvester Stallone—*I knew of him!*

The following morning I was getting into the car to go to the airport when a messenger delivered the script, which I was going to read on the plane to Vancouver. The meeting with Mr. Vajna and Mr. Kotcheff was scheduled for the same evening, and the following day I was to return to New York.

Mr. Vajna was a man about my age, with a sense of humor, easy to talk with, and not at all affected or egotistical as some Hollywood people I knew. We even spoke a few sentences in Hungarian and within a short time were on first name basis, pretty well acquainted. Ted Kotcheff also turned out to be someone, I knew instinctively, I would be able to work and get along with. Of course, the important thing was whether he also thought that he wanted to work with me. It is always the director who picks, or at least approves, the cinematographer and not the other way around. He very openly told me about himself, his background, and his films, and I was surprised about how well informed he was about my films and me. I must admit I was a bit embarrassed, as I was not at all familiar with his work. (Since this incident I have always made it a point to research and learn as much as possible about the people I am to meet for the first time in connection with a possible project.) By the end of our meeting, I had no doubt that all of us felt we were on the same wavelength and that we would make a good team.

During dinner Ted asked if I could visit a few of the locations with him the following day. Even though I hadn't planned to stay, I had nothing else scheduled and told him I could. When we met in the lobby the following morning I knew I was a bit underprepared. He was wearing heavy boots, field pants, a parka, and a hat—all items that I did not have with me. I bought some clothes in Vancouver, for by the third or fourth day of my extended stay my relatively new dress clothes, the only clothes I had with me, were showing serious signs of wear. They weren't right for climbing up steep mountainsides, or stepping over huge, wet logs. On one occasion, one of my loafers came off as I sank a bit too deep into the mud. Other than that, I did manage to get along well. By the time I was on my way back to New York, almost a week after I arrived, a deal was worked out with my agent, and that's how *First Blood* got started. A couple of days later, I headed back to Vancouver for the duration of the filming.

Doing *First Blood* was an outstanding experience on all levels. It was a story I could identify with, though I knew that once again I was in for a great deal of hardship. And that is one of the reasons I selected this film to be part of this book. It has elements that are highly unusual and unorthodox as far as filmmaking is concerned, certainly as compared to studio or backlot films. Some of the lessons I learned while doing other films, particularly the two movies I have already discussed, I applied in the filming of *First Blood*. But new experiences mounted as well, as I experimented and was forced to learn new tricks of the trade.

I'll be talking mostly about what takes place during the last half of the movie, so it will be helpful to go into the film's story a bit. It is the story of a Medal of Honor winner Vietnam veteran. He is about to visit the last remaining member of his squad, somewhere in the northwest United States. He hitchhikes, walking most of the way, only to find that his friend is also dead, having died as a result of having been exposed to Agent Orange in Vietnam. John Rambo, as our hero is called, portrayed by Sylvester Stallone, wanders into a nearby small town where he is stopped by the local sheriff and arrested for vagrancy.

In the course of the interrogation, one of the deputies decides to get rough with Rambo, badly mistreating him and triggering Rambo to recall his POW experience. This sets off a violent reaction in Rambo, who escapes from the police station and heads for the mountains. The sheriff and his deputies are unable to capture Rambo, who by this time has been accused of killing one of the deputies. The State Police as well as the National Guard are called in to help with the pursuit. This is the point in the story where the film contains most of the material I'll be talking about.

The first such element deals with the technique of matching the portions of a scene photographed on location to those photographed in the studio. Unless the climatic conditions of the location are well known and reliable, in most such cases it is imperative that the location portions of a scene are filmed first. The conditions of the location cannot be matched otherwise. The scene in this instance takes place in a first aid tent at the command center of the pursuit, as the sheriff, having been roughed up by Rambo, is being patched up by a first aid specialist. Army vehicles, troops, ambulances, and State Police cars are moving around throughout the staging area surrounding the command center. A helicopter lands and the captain of the State Police enters the first aid tent. He and the sheriff have a heated discussion, as they are joined by a deputy and a Colonel Trautman, John Rambo's ex-commanding officer, who comes to claim Rambo.

This is a relatively long scene, mostly dialogue, during which the camera covers the interior of the tent, front and back. We see lots of activity through the large opening at the front of the tent. These are the shots that were shot on location. All the other cuts, particularly the ones shooting towards the back of the tent, were photographed in the studio many weeks after the location shots were completed. The reason behind this is very straightforward. The scene in the tent involves three principal players. Outside the tent are hundreds of extras, a Canadian Army unit dressed in American National Guard uniforms, actors dressed as State Policemen, trucks, jeeps, ambulances, helicopters, not to mention the film crew of about a hundred. Having all these people on payroll, while three actors are being photographed, would not have made sense.

The question comes up: Why not go back to location after the shots involving all the people and equipment outside the tent are made—the extras having been released, the equipment returned to the rental agencies—and then photograph the three actors in the tent without showing any of the outside? This is a reasonable question, which has a reasonable answer. In this case, the location was about two hours from our base, and returning would have cost the company four hours of travel per day, involving the transport of cast, crew, and filmmaking equipment, not to mention having catering on location and possibly having to deal with the elements—all of which would have been costly and unnecessary. Besides, by the time the photography of the tent interiors was scheduled, the company was working in the Vancouver area in a studio, and everybody knew that shooting the tent interiors would not be difficult in the studio. (In fact, it wasn't really a studio; it was a large warehouse, which served as a studio. But I'll be talking about that later, so for now I'll call it studio.) At any rate, the purpose here is to discuss how I went about the deception of making the tent interior scene shot in the studio match the original interiors shot on location.

It took a certain amount of studying the look of the tent interiors on a Moviola (a piece of equipment that was used at that time for viewing and editing film), analyzing that look, and recalling the conditions as they existed on location. On the days the command center activities were photographed on location, the weather was overcast and damp. The light was not bright, but was diffused and soft, particularly as it illuminated the interior of the tent. When we set up the same tent in the studio, the first order of the day was to create the same kind of illumination—meaning having an identical quality, direction, and source—that came through the open end of the tent. At the location, as in the studio, there was no other illumination in the tent other than what entered through the tent's opening. I had a silk tent built in front of and over the entrance of the tent in the studio, and surrounded this silk tent with a large number of powerful lighting units, all having extra diffusion in front of them. The extra diffusion in the lamps assured me of no hard, directional light reaching the interior of the tent. Blue gels added to the lights simulated the high color temperature of the location, which dictated the use of the No. 85 filter in the camera even in the studio. Lighting the tent interior in this manner resulted in a quality of light and light levels that were very close to what existed on location, assuring the same exposures, and therefore the same qualities such as depth of field. When a procedure such as this is called for, the technique of how to accomplish it should be decided well in advance. It is advisable to keep accurate notes of such factors as light levels, color temperature readings, filters used, exposures, focal length of lenses, and so on, while still shooting the location segments.

Beyond lighting the tent as close to the original as possible, certain other factors were also introduced to round out and complete the deception. Through the openings in the back of the tent (one of which was created knowing that extra elements of deception would be needed in the studio), we see some exterior activity of soldiers walking by in wet ponchos as a mild breeze gently moves the open window's flaps. The kerosene lamp, hanging from the tent pole overhead, gives off a warm glow, which would not have been possible if we had photographed the studio portions with normal, 3200 Kelvin studio lights and without the No. 85 filter in the camera. The tent flaps also move occasionally, as though someone walking alongside it brushed it, or just as the wind would have made it move on location. The wind in the studio was produced by "E" fans, standard motion picture equipment, made for just such a need. The illusion worked. The matching of studio photographed images to location photography in this film turned out to be quite seamless. Even when I prepare my audience during my lectures and ask them to look for and expose the deception, most are hard put to find faults that would give the technique away and render it useless. Completing such work is always very satisfying, but it works only if the audience does not see it. If it were detected, it would destroy the effectiveness of the deception, and affect the credibility of other aspects of the film.

Another example, an infrequently used technique, is also illustrated well in *First Blood*, and that is the use of unusual light sources for motion picture photography. This film contains many scenes and sequences that were photographed either exclusively or partially with unusual light sources. For the benefit of those who have seen this film recently, or will look at it after reading this book, let me list some of the light sources I used in connection with *First Blood*: Coleman lanterns, a match, a torch, a camp fire, large explosions, and fires.

The first of these unusual light sources that I want to talk about are Coleman lanterns (the type used in camping), which burn a fuel similar to white gasoline and give off a very bright, greenish-yellow light. In Chapter 2, "*The Warriors*," I talked about some of the "dos and don'ts" of filmmaking. For some time, using a Coleman lantern as a light source would have been a "don't," simply because it was not a bona fide light made for motion picture photography, and because its color would have imposed a greenish-yellow hue on the image, which would have been considered "bad" photography. But it was this greenish-yellow hue that attracted me to the use of these lights. It was an unusual "look," and the lanterns realistically would have been the sort a military unit might use in the field.

I was fascinated by the quality of the light these units produced and decided to use them exclusively for filming the interior of the communication tent, without the addition of any other type of light. The entire interior of the tent was lit by Coleman lanterns. Once again I cheated a bit, by adding off-camera Coleman lanterns, to raise the level of the illumination, but I made no attempt to correct the color temperature of the lanterns. Two little tricks were used to make the effect more believable. In one of the shots, the sheriff lifts one of these lanterns hanging from a nail and places it on a table, on a curved map that was used as a reflector to help illuminate him. As the light moves the illumination changes, adding reality and credibility to the shot—therefore, to the whole situation in front of the camera. A bit of action such as moving a light points out the reality of the situation, but it must be very subtle, as flaunting it would undoubtedly diminish its value.

Another trick used was a dark spot on the glass cover of one of these lanterns, which sits on the hood of a jeep. The lantern illuminates the radio operator and his equipment in the jeep, as well as the sheriff, the State Police Captain, and Colonel Trautman. This black spot makes the lantern look used, real, and believable, but the real purpose of the black spot was to eliminate the "hot spot" of the burning element, which, if allowed to reach the lens, would have flared. In this instance, such a flare would not have been desirable. This is a much-used technique, particularly for taming the filament of electric bulbs. It is usually achieved by spray-painting the camera side of light bulbs, as was the case in the Cajun party scene in *Southern Comfort* (see Chapter 1). In this case, the camera side of a Coleman lantern was spray-painted. By doing this, only the camera flare of the lantern is controlled, without affecting the light output as it illuminates the actors huddled around it. The added touch of the reality of the black spot affects the audience's interpretation and acceptance of the scene.

I generally use hairspray for this purpose. Inexpensive, water-soluble hairspray is available from many sources, in many colors. My preference is black or brown, though on some occasions and for other purposes, I have used other colors as well. I keep several cans of these near at hand during a shoot for just such occasions. In my opinion, the use of the lanterns in this instance added great value to the image by producing an interesting and unusual result that until this time was rarely, if ever, seen in films. By using lanterns, subliminal qualities of the shot, such as the greenish color, added interest to the scene. Although I believe the audience probably enjoyed it more than standard photography, I don't believe that they were consciously aware of or cared about the technique. The qualities achieved by the use of the lanterns were not noticed for their own sake, but were an important element in creating the total impact of the image.

At this point, before I continue with my discussion about the use of other unusual light sources, I'd like to digress for a moment and tell another "war story." This one has nothing whatever to do with the use of lanterns, torches, or matches to light scenes with, but it involves an example that did affect the execution of this film and is very much part of the filmmaking process.

To begin with, it was my understanding that *First Blood* was to be filmed in British Columbia because that region of Canada had the climate the story called for. What about Oregon or Washington, you may ask. As it was pointed out to me, it never snowed in the part of British Columbia where we were going to film in and the type of weather the story called for was assured, as was the visual continuity of the film. In fact, I was told that the City of Vancouver didn't own a snowplow. I suspected that the exchange rate of the dollar and the lower production costs in Canada also had something to do with us being in British Columbia. Be that as it may, much to the surprise of all, it started snowing gently one day as we started the photography of the command post scenes. The locals assured us that this was very unusual. It hadn't happened in many years, and they were sure the snow would soon stop and melt quickly. At first the property men made a valiant effort to try to sweep the snow out of the shots, which didn't work. It kept on snowing, and more powerful measures were called for. Backpack leaf blowers were brought in, but they couldn't do the job either. The snow was accumulating. Water hoses and high-pressure steam could not remove it, and the use of big equipment like snow plows or bulldozers would not have worked because of the uneven, difficult terrain. We decided to wrap and go back to Vancouver while the going was good.

By the time we reached Vancouver late that evening, the City was a mess. The citizenry of the city was not used to driving in snow and there were huge pile-ups at the bottom of sloping streets. (The City of Vancouver probably has snowplows now.) We had a huge problem on our hands. The rental of large amounts of military equipment, the extras contracted for the shoot—all had to be put on hold. The shooting schedule of the film, having been thrown off track, had to be dealt with. Even after the snow stopped and we could return to location, a big problem still remained—continuity. There was about three feet of snow in some parts of the location, which was inconsistent with the film's story and the footage photographed till then or to be photographed after the snow melted. The solution to this problem turned out to be very simple.

There was a television crew from one of the Vancouver stations who were filming us filming the scenes at the command center. I suggested that we put the TV crew, a reporter, a camera person, and a producer in our shots, give the news reporter lines about the snow that explained it in such a way that the presence of the snow would no longer be a problem of continuity. That's exactly what we did. As the camera follows a landing helicopter, it brings the newsman into our frame just as he talks about the " . . . fugitive Rambo, who is hiding somewhere in these rugged mountains, possibly high above the snow line . . . " The "snow line" was the key word, and once it was said, seeing snow in some of the shots was no longer a problem. We resumed work, disregarded the snow, and overlooked all the problems created by it, which normally would have been considered unacceptable from the point of continuity. In fact, when you view the film again, you'll see the most blatant disregard of continuity. For instance, the chopper, in one scene, lands in snow, and the people who just got out of the helicopter are seen in the next cut with not a snowflake in sight. Once again, many rules thought to be hard and fast, inviolable bastions of filmmaking, turned out not to matter. For some reason, these kinds of mistakes seem to matter only if they are the result of not knowing that they are wrong, but somehow one gets away with them when they are made by consciously disregarding convention.

I would also like to talk a bit about the use of "magic hour," that absolutely wonderful part of the day just before and shortly after the sun sets and the sky is still a rich blue color and there is a bit of daylight left to make a few shots. Because of the low light levels, the lenses are set to wider openings, allowing brighter objects—tail lights, for example—to overexpose a bit and become rich, bright rubies, while all the other parts of the shot are a little blue and subdued. "Magic hour" is usually very short-lived. The sun ducks behind the horizon and in a short time daylight gives way to night. But "magic hour," in the case of shooting the command center in *First Blood*, lasted all day long. The sky wasn't blue, but because of the cloud cover and the damp atmosphere, the color temperatures, coming from the overcast, were way up, while the light levels were low. Most of the time I shot with close to wide open lenses, which opened up the darker portions of the shots and allowed the tail lights of the vehicles to become saturated, slightly overexposed, bright and beautiful jewels. As we look at the exterior portions of the shot from the communication tent, the higher than normal, bluish color temperatures of the outside mixed well with the greenish yellow hues of the lanterns in the tent. It is a beautiful shot, as the sheriff, Colonel Trautman, and the State Police Captain approach the communication tent and enter. Most people in the audience do not consciously evaluate or even see this bit of a light play, only sensing it. Nevertheless, it is immensely satisfying to the cinematographer as he creates the image.

Now, let me return to the use of unconventional light sources, in this case the flame of a match. The overzealous National Guardsmen blow up the entrance to the cave, and Rambo is trapped in the dark. That was the way the scene was described in the script: he is in total darkness. I have been in total darkness, in photographic darkrooms, in caves, and I know what total darkness is like. But in movies, total darkness was, for a very long time, one of the taboos I talked about earlier. In most similar situations in the past, it was important to create an illusion of darkness, by presenting the action in sketchy, underlit shots. In this instance however, an illusion of darkness would not have worked for me. I wanted total darkness shattered by the flare of a match. I wanted to see the match slowly burn itself out, turning the screen back to total darkness again. That is what Rambo's situation was, and that is the way I wanted to present it. For various reasons, many people connected with a film, producers mostly, worry about not always lighting a big star so his features are clearly visible. In this instance I had no problem. Even if Andy Vajna and his partner Mario Kassar didn't like the shot, I knew I could reshoot the short clip later, perhaps adding some artificial lighting. But everybody liked the effect of the match in dailies. Here is how I did it.

The shot was a close head-and-shoulders shot of Rambo. I explained to him where to strike and hold the match, in relation to his face. The flame had to be a certain distance from his face in order to be correct for exposure. Before I go any further, I have a confession to make and need to let you in on a little secret. As they say, I stretched the truth a bit, and instead of using one match I used two. The matches were the large, kitchen variety, and I taped two of them together. The head of one was slightly higher than the other. As the first match was struck, before the flare would start to fizzle, it ignited the second match. The duration of the flare was thus doubled and the exposure provided by the combined flares was almost twice that of what a single match would have produced. I experimented for some time before this shot was made, by lighting one, two, and more matches, but settled on using two for the shot, which I thought gave the best, most natural and effective results. I determined the exposure during the testing of the matches by holding a light meter at my face and striking the matches at the distance I knew they would have to be in order to be in the proper place in the composition of the shots. After I knew what the light levels were, I decided not to use the proper exposure when the flare was at its highest point, but instead opted for a slight overexposure at the height of the flare.

In sequence, here is the way I'd describe the results. The screen is totally dark as the match is struck. The flare shows Rambo's face, brighter and brighter, and as the flare grows in intensity the flame becomes white in overexposure. The face is also a little hot, overexposed, but only for a short time, as the flame fades, flickers, and Rambo's face disappears into darkness again as the match goes out. Imperfections, such as under- and overexposures of Rambo's face during the life of the flame, without any other parts of the frame having properly exposed detail, became the strong element of this image. It was real, believable, true to the situation, and helped focus attention on Rambo's predicament. Do you recall those shots in movies of a bygone era, when a character carrying a candle walks through the dark hallway of a castle, and there are ten shadows of him and the candle on the wall? Of course we all do, but for me that sort of technique, dictated by the need to increase light level for exposure, would not have worked.

By this time in the practice of cinematography shooting with the light of flames was not unique. Stanley Kubrick's film, *Barry Lyndon*, got a lot of publicity mileage out of shooting with candlelight, seven years before *First Blood*. That film might have been the first to use a then-brand-new lens, which I believe was a T:0.95 or close to it. It is a very fast lens, indeed, a rarity even today. This was a milestone in motion picture photography, one that I was delighted to see, as it broke with convention and was not afraid to experiment with radical, new approaches. Looking at those scenes today creates a somewhat different reaction, as one sees a tremendous number of candles all over the set and wonders why all those candles are necessary. And that brings me back to one more comment about Rambo and the match. When I read the script for the first time, I immediately saw the opportunity and decided to shoot this shot of Rambo with no lighting other than a match. Instead of hundreds of candles, as in *Barry Lyndon*, this shot would be made by the light of a single flame. The rest you know.

The continuation of the shot, as Stallone quickly improvises a torch by wrapping a strip of cloth around his knife and lighting it with another match, was photographed the same way. The light of two matches worked as before, and so did the light of the torch, though its flame was more powerful than the match. But Stallone knew where and how far to hold the flame from himself for the shot to be realistic and the exposure to be correct. During the continuation of the sequence, Rambo finds some kerosene left over from when the mine was active (as good an explanation as any), and in the light produced by his makeshift torch he fashions a real torch with strips of cloth from his shirt, wrapped around a stick. From here on, the photography of the cave sequence became very interesting, though not without trauma. (See Color Plate III.)

The script depicts Rambo trapped in the mine and the cave, and the torch is the device by which he finds his way out of the cave. The flames are driven by a draft of air, and as long as he follows the draft, he knows it will lead him to some sort of opening, a way out of his trap. Besides the scripted reason for the torch, I saw another, for me, much more important opportunity: lighting an entire sequence with the flame of a torch. While selling the match shot and not lighting the star of the movie by any other means was not particularly hard, selling the idea of lighting the cave, a very large set, with the flame of a single torch turned out to be very difficult. I didn't want to start shooting this very important sequence without letting everybody know of my intention. This was going to be a radical departure from the then-current, established practices, and I felt I needed approval prior to the shooting. Without approval and cooperation, I could have faced extensive reshoots and caused a great financial loss to the company. When I brought up the issue, many of the production team thought it was foolhardy. Andy Vajna's point, rightfully so from his perspective, was that he paid a very large sum of money to have the three-story cave set built (which, incidentally, was very realistic and beautiful), and he was concerned whether spending all that money would pay off in the best interest of the movie if the audiences would only see it in the light of a torch.

I was convinced it would. The audience, in my opinion, should see the cave exactly as Rambo sees it. I stated during one of these discussions that I could light the cave in the conventional, well-established manner of a studio picture, but pointed out that we would miss out on a very great cinematic opportunity, and in the end, the cave was going to look like the *Pirates of the Caribbean* ride in Disneyland. What finally sold the idea was that Stallone and Ted Kotcheff both saw the opportunity and backed my idea. There was, of course, lots of anxiety until the first day's dailies were shown, and even after seeing the dailies not everyone was convinced.

Let me say a few words at this point about dailies. I hate them! One sits, at times for as long as an hour, watching take after take after take of a shot, which, when cut, might represent less than a couple of minutes of the finished film. But as one sits in the dark screening room, concentrating on the same shot over and over again, they become torturous: one ends up seeing nothing but mistakes and what could have been done better. There were some sections in the cave footage, which, judged individually, were not particularly good photography, yet, as in the case of some of *The Warriors* footage, even they looked interesting in the finished film. Viewing such footage convinced me that one must, at times, be impulsive. An image, the result of impulse, might not look great in dailies, but almost invariably be right when the film is assembled.

Choreographing these shots was very important, in order to have the light-play of the torch pay off, and in order to see the set and feel Rambo's predicament. Stallone was a big help in choreographing the shots. Going through the cave, at times he would hold the torch in front of him as he faced the camera, in which case he was totally exposed and visible, but the background was swallowed up in darkness. At other times he would turn his back to the camera, lighting the background, against which he became silhouetted. The sense of suspense from being in the cave—what lay in a shroud of darkness, beyond a turn or a rock; the dripping water; the rats—all paid off better, because the audience wasn't forewarned, because there was more mystery to the shots, and, most importantly, because the look of the shots were ever-changing and never conventional. (See Color Plate IV.) Shooting this sequence with the torch was tremendously enjoyable, and is one of the most fondly remembered experiences of my career.

When one goes to work every day and does the conventional, predictable, established routine, the days can become long, repetitious, boring. In the film business, I don't think I spent a single day in over fifty years when something did not break the routine, when improvisation and ingenuity were not called for. I have been asked many times how the dolly shots were accomplished in the cave. Movie fans, film students, even some professionals sometimes believe that on a big budget film, all you have to do is snap your fingers and whatever might be needed immediately appears. That is definitely not the case. If it were, it would be boring, and the opportunities for improvisation and ingenuity would be missed. When I decided to make the dolly shot in the cave, I knew I could not use any of our dollies, or cranes, because of the way the cave was built and because of the water we worked in. My grips and I decided to improvise a dolly by attaching a high hat to a slab of Styrofoam, which is very buoyant and is used in the construction of docks. We put the camera on the high hat, and as my dolly grip guided this contraption through the water, my camera operator made the shots of following Rambo, torch in hand, going through the cave, hip deep in water. By this time the smell of rats and rat feces were sickeningly strong in the set. Though the rats were tame white laboratory rats with dyed fur, some got away from their handlers and within days reverted to a wild stage, rearing up on their hind legs and biting the handlers as they tried to recapture them. I've always hated rats, but since this incident I've learned to hate them with a passion. But the photography in the cave had to be done: it was part of the job, part of my life, rats and all.

Two situations in particular called for inventiveness during the filming of this movie. We had to have close-ups of the Deputy in the helicopter shooting at Rambo, as Rambo is hanging from the sheer cliff wall of the canyon. The helicopter is in flight and, of course, there was no way for me to get into position with the camera to shoot close-ups and to shoot the scene between the Deputy and the pilot just moments before Rambo hits the bubble of the chopper with a rock. In the film story, the shattering canopy makes the pilot sway the helicopter, causing the Deputy to fall to his death.

I knew there was a piece of flat ground near some abandoned railroad tracks (I had spotted it during one of our scouting trips) high up at the lip of the canyon. I had a very sturdy platform built, roughly ten-by-ten feet square and two feet off the ground sitting on large, inflated inner tubes to simulate the rocking motion of the chopper, on the lip of the canyon. This platform had an additional top layer, sitting on about a thousand tennis balls that acted as ball bearings, turning the platform into a giant lazy Susan. The helicopter was to sit on this platform moving side to side as grips pushed, pulled, and turned the turntable right and left and the camera dollyed in and out, arming up and down and tilting side to side, to create a sensation of the helicopter's motion in real flight (see Figure 3.1). Because we were at the edge of the canyon, there were no reference points, or any visible features of our side of the canyon, and the chopper appears to be in mid air, as these shots are edited into footage showing the helicopter in actual flight.

Of course, Rambo, on the reverse of these shots, hanging on for dear life from the sheer granite wall of the canyon, had to be photographed in close-up, as well as in "over the shoulder shots" showing him in the foreground on the rock wall, and the helicopter, with the Deputy firing at him, in real flight in the canyon. We had a very large slab of artificial rock wall built and put into position at a spot from which the artificial rock appears to be a part of the actual rock wall of the canyon, which is visible in the background of the shot. Rambo is hanging by his fingernails, and as the bullets (squibs) strike all around him, he falls out of the shot, to the ground, no more than a foot below. This shot is the first in the stunt sequence of Rambo jumping from the cliff.

This sequence would not have been complete without the shots actually photographed from the chopper in flight, shooting

Figure 3.1 Helicopter on "lazy Susan"

over the shoulder of the Deputy as he leans out of the bubble and fires at Rambo (a photo-double stuntman, hanging from the real rock wall).

For some reason, the Canadian camera crews would not do helicopter work. I know it wasn't a question of money, but I believe they considered helicopter work dangerous. Of course, they were right. After I imported a helicopter expert from Hollywood, whose work turned out to be unusable, I ended up doing the shots myself. Wearing a kind of safety harness, I stood with one foot on the runner of the chopper, camera on shoulder, and held on to the chopper with my left hand as I made shot after shot of the Deputy firing at Rambo. One aspect of doing these shots that I could not have foreseen was that the collar of my windbreaker was flapping so violently in the downwash of the rotor, that by the time we landed half my face was pretty badly cut up and covered with blood. And that wasn't the worst.

When the production stills came back, showing me shooting from the chopper, they clearly showed the tail rotor of the helicopter being dangerously close to the rock wall behind us. A cameraman, looking through the viewfinder of a camera, soon forgets the real world, and becomes involved with only what is visible in the frame. While adjusting and composing the shot, I gave directions to the pilot to go a little higher, lower, to the right, and to the left. The pilot, complying with those directions, forgets at times that by doing what the cameraman wants him to do, the chopper may be brought into dangerous positions. Safety first is a good thing to remember! And that reminds me of another shot I had to make for this sequence.

We needed some shots (see Figure 3.2) that accentuated Rambo's peril, showing the enormous, sheer rock wall and the rocky, turbulent river way below him at the bottom of the canyon. This could only have been seen from the top, away from the rock wall, looking down at Rambo's photo double hanging on and the helicopter way below us. We rigged a sort of a yardarm at the top edge of the cliff, with a bosun's seat dangling from it. In these pre-videotap days, it would have been difficult to tell a camera operator exactly what sort of a shot I wanted. So instead of trying to explain it, to the relief of my camera operator, I decided to do the shot myself. Once I was strapped into the bosun's chair (in reality nothing more than a plank of wood) with camera in hand, the rig was swung out over the canyon, and I proceeded to make a series of shots of the stunt double working his way on the sheer cliff and of the chopper hovering below me. It is absolutely incredible how scary a situation like this can be. To be hanging in midair over an enormous chasm, from a jury-rigged Rube Goldberg contraption, is frightening beyond description. But it's even more amazing how quickly the feeling of danger dissolves as one looks through the camera and starts concentrating on the shot. After doing these types of shots, I usually make a strong resolve never to do another foolhardy, stupid thing like this ever again—a resolve that quickly falls by the wayside as the need, or the excitement, of other challenges surfaces.

Figure 3.2 Chopper in flight in canyon. Camera crew on ledge. Note safety ropes.

Back to the cave. The end of the cave sequence provided me with another opportunity to play with light. As Rambo's last torch is about to fizzle, burning with a very red and anemic flame, Rambo finds himself at the bottom of a shaft, brought to this "stairway to heaven" by the flame of his torch driven by the draft. He looks up the shaft at the sky (simulated in the studio) and drops his torch. The red light produced by the torch, which, incidentally, the audience has become very accustomed to by this time, drops from his face like a veil, and is replaced by minimal amounts of blue hues of daylight, creating highlights of his sweat-covered dark face, arms, and shoulder.

As long as I'm talking about photographing with the light of flame, let me back up a step and say a few words about shooting the campfire shots in the cave. These were relatively easy. There was little action and few camera moves during these shots. Rambo sits by the campfire and eats pieces of the boar he has killed, which is roasting by the fire. In this case, unlike the rest of the cave scenes, the fire did not provide the only illumination. There was one additional light, a "Junior," shooting through the flames of the fire at Rambo's face for no other reason than to illuminate his eyes. This is an important scene in the story line, and it was necessary to see his expression, particularly his eyes. The light does not give itself away. One would be hard put to realize that the gentle flicker of the campfire is supplemented by the addition of this light. The light from the "Junior" is shooting through the flames, projecting the very natural effect of fire flicker, but its real purpose is to see its reflection in Rambo's eyes. Its direction is straight from the source, the campfire, and therefore does not conflict with the qualities of the shot. The mild reflection of the light in Rambo's eyes is barely visible, but it accentuates the emotional impact of the shot. (See Color Plate V.)

Throughout my career, like all other cinematographers, I have experimented with various fire and flame effects. We have tried rotating drums covered with aluminum foil and orange gels, and strips of cloth attached to a stick dangled in front of a lamp, among many others. But for me, the only way of producing a good fire effect is to use actual fire in front of lights. The projected image of the flames looks real, and the only thing the motion picture light does is to increase the light level for exposure.

When shooting with the light of a match, and with the flame of the torch in the cave, I had no problem determining exposure. I experimented to determine the exposure and accepted the red hues of the flames as an unavoidable and, for me, essential and desirable part of the photography. I could not have done any color correction of real flames with photographic methods, such as gels on lights, as I could in the case of incandescent or other electric lights. Changing the color of flames is possible by the use of certain chemicals, or during the printing process in the lab. But correcting the color of flames in printing is not desirable, as the correction will also affect the color of everything else in the frame.

In the case of the torch-lit shots, I could have removed some red color from the flames, but not without also affecting the skin tones and the backgrounds of the shots.

When we were shooting larger shots, such as the exploding and burning sporting goods store and the gas station in *First Blood,* no experimentation was possible. For one thing, no one, not even the special effects people, could accurately predict the extent of the explosions and the fire. Beyond having an idea, we could only guess, but we had to be prepared and ready for all eventualities. There were some "givens" at the sporting goods shop, as well as at the gas station. Both of these places were illuminated by standard lighting for the portion of the photography that preceded and followed the explosions and the fire. Both of these sequences were what I usually describe or refer to as "one-time events." By that I mean that the event will happen once, and unless it is photographed while it is happening, there will be no "take two," no second chance to shoot it. In such cases, perhaps the best protection against all eventualities is the use of multiple cameras. This is always a must when shooting one-time events, such as fights, concerts, political rallies, and so on. By using multiple cameras, one not only has backup in the case of a mechanical problem affecting one of the cameras, but the coverage of what happens in front of the cameras is sure to be accomplished as the event is going on. This technique is also very useful when one works with small children, animals, or boats on water, where actions cannot be completely controlled, or predicted, and no retakes of the same action are possible.

I decided to use five cameras to photograph the gas station as Rambo sets it on fire and it blows up. I would have liked to have more, but for many reasons, five was my limit. The cameras had to be very carefully assigned to cover what I thought was going to happen, but I didn't have a clue about such detail as the extent of the explosions and the resulting fire. To start with, I knew that I needed a camera that would start the sequence by photographing the gas station prior to the fire, as Rambo's truck smashes the gas pumps and the fire engulfs the station. This was to be my number one camera, designated as "A" camera. Its exposure was set for the pre- and post-explosion segments of the sequence. Because it was too close to the explosions, it was to be remotely operated. This camera covered the gas station with a wide-angle lens, which was fast enough for the necessary pre-fire exposure. There were no moves planned for this camera, so it didn't require an operator nor the use of a remotely operated head. It was to be a "tied-off" camera, which is turned on remotely before the sequence starts and turned off once the sequence is over. I knew that portions of this camera's footage, when the flames were the most intense and the explosions were the largest, were going to be overexposed and unusable. The additional four cameras were located in strategic positions to concentrate on important facets of this sequence and, at the same time, provide backup and coverage.

Photographing flames and explosions, as opposed to certain other "one-time events," offers additional opportunities to enhance the photography. The use of long focal length lenses will compress the distance between the subject and the camera, therefore making the flames and the explosions more concentrated and intense. "Overcranking" these cameras, or having the film go through the cameras faster and producing slow motion, adds a poetic quality to the explosions, as well as extending their screen time. But using long focal length lenses, particularly at fast film travel, is not without a price. Long focal length lenses are slower (though not as much these days as they were then), meaning that their widest setting may not be enough to produce acceptable exposures. Slow motion is also costly, as every time the film's travel through the camera is doubled, the exposure is cut in half, requiring twice as much light. Normal camera speed, as we all know, is 24 frames per second. If the exposure calculated at that speed is, say T:4, it would have to be reset to T:2.8 as the camera speed is increased to 48 fps. In the case of long focal length lenses, which have settings of T:4 or higher, such an adjustment is not possible. In this instance, pushing the film one stop might be justified, even recommended, but only if the camera were not expected to produce usable footage of those portions of the explosions that would provide adequate and higher exposures. That was the case as we blew up the gas station in *First Blood*. (See Color Plate VI.) The complication that I did not know, and could not have guessed, was the extent of the light levels the explosions would produce. Here is how I handled it.

I had five "walkie-talkies" taped to a board and set up at my command post, a vantage point from where I had a good view of everything the cameras were to photograph. The "send" buttons of these walkie-talkies were taped down, so as I talked everybody manning the cameras could hear me, but they couldn't talk to me. Actually, I didn't want them to talk to me. I only wanted them to hear my instructions, which were going to be limited to exposure, or possibly something unforeseen. Beyond that, there was nothing to talk about. If any of the cameras had a problem once the sequence started, I considered the camera a write-off and did not need to know anything further about it. If the crew could fix the problem quickly, and bring the camera back on line before the sequence was over, that was fine with me, but as the rapid-fire events started to happen, I knew I would not have time to discuss anything. As the "Roll cameras" was given, "A" camera rolled, followed quickly by "B," "C," "D," and "E."

Once the flames grew, after the explosions, it became necessary to reset the lenses to the proper exposures. I constantly monitored the intensity of the flames and the explosions with a spot meter, refigured the exposures with a calculator in my other hand, and called out new corrections to each of the cameras by their designation letter. In this way, only the camera instructed made the basic exposure changes, on the basis of which the assistant cameraman further calculated and adjusted the exposure, taking the camera's speed into consideration. This was a very hectic portion of the filming. I knew that in most cases my instructions would be lagging and obsolete by the time they reached the assistants as they took the time necessary to reset the T-stops. I could only hope I would end up with enough good footage to have complete coverage of the event. As it turned out, I did. Not because the exposures were always correct, but because they weren't. In most cases, by the time the cameras were reset, the exposure would no longer be correct and needed resetting again. Yet, some of the footage that was not exposed correctly seemed to produce the more interesting results. Once again, "bad" photography became the desirable choice.

The footage of such a one-time event should also be protected from other possible harm. Whenever the event takes place away from home base on distant location, as in British Columbia, the exposed, undeveloped negative should not be shipped all at once, nor in one package. Though its loss in a plane crash, for example, would pale in comparison to human losses, rephotographing the event would necessitate rebuilding the set, waiting for identical weather, and transporting, housing, feeding, and paying the crews for the reshoot. This would not only be a very expensive proposition, it could also delay the completion and release of the film. The negative of such a shoot should be shipped in separate packages, per camera. If one package were lost, the loss would amount to no more than a camera not functioning during the shoot. If the packages are shipped one package a day, the likelihood of two or more packages being lost or damaged is dramatically reduced.

It must be said at this point that not all the shots of the gas station sequence were photographed at once. Many shots, such as Rambo starting the fire by throwing his lit Zippo into the gasoline, the police cars arriving at the scene, the burning billboard in the background, and a number of others, were photographed long after the blowing up and burning of the gas station were completed. The important consideration here was the same as in the case of the first aid tent at the command center: to match the later footage seamlessly to the original. The advantage in this instance was that all the additional shots, though photographed later, were done at very similar locations to where the actual event was photographed and not in the studio.

A word of caution. Fires and explosions, though created for a movie, are nevertheless real and potentially dangerous. I've witnessed, and have been part of, many an unforeseen and unexpected mishap with serious results. One cannot be overly cautious. Some of the townspeople, who came to watch the gas station being blown up, were surprised and frightened by the unexpected violence of the large explosion, as fragments of burning wood and other debris were raining down over a very large area. No movie is worth the loss of a single life, or even the slightest injury.

This reminds me of a war story (there really is no end to these) that happened early in the production, before the photography started, as soon as I returned to Vancouver and started working. I found myself on a scout again, this time clothed in proper garments, with a rope tying me to a tree as I was looking over the edge of a cliff, high up over the deep canyon, searching for possible camera positions. Below me, at the bottom of the canyon, was a group, part of our scouting party, who seemed to be frantically waving at me. I noted that they did not stop waving as I waved back at them. Some of them were pointing at something near me, others were shouting, but I couldn't make out what. When I joined them at the bottom of the canyon later, they pointed out that at the point where I had been standing on the edge of the cliff, the rocks fell away from under the very thin layer of topsoil I was standing on. The topsoil was held together only by the roots of the shrubbery growing from it and could easily have collapsed under my weight at any moment. They weren't waving a friendly "hello," they wanted me to get away from where I was before I could have fallen.

More war stories later, but now back to the movie. The original script called for Rambo to reenter the town in search of the sheriff. On his way to the police station he shoots out all the lights in the small town with his newly acquired M-60 machine gun. But the actual town, where these scenes of the movie were made, turned out to be much larger than the town the writer envisioned. Rambo could not have shot out all the lights individually. New shots and scenes were written, such as Rambo shooting out the transformers on power poles that turned entire sections of the town dark. Obviously, the transformers were ours, rigged with appropriate pyrotechnics. The blackout was not particularly difficult to accomplish. Each building had a production assistant or other crew member standing by the main switch of the building's power supply, walkie-talkie in hand, pulling the switch on command. By this method, section after section of the town went dark—except for one Chinese restaurant. The owner didn't want his lights turned off, or to close the restaurant, in spite of compensation offered. We had no choice but to park one of our biggest trucks, covered with black fabric, in front of the restaurant, blocking it from view of the camera—another simple solution for what could have been a very serious problem.

This film incorporates most of the elements we discussed in the previous two films, *Southern Comfort* and *The Warriors,* and introduces additional elements of filmmaking. I already talked a bit about working in the studio, an element of filmmaking that had been totally missing from the previous two films. Now I'd like to spend a little more time on some of the studio techniques that we used in conjunction with the completion of the first aid tent interior scene. First, as I promised when I discussed filming those shots, let me explain what I meant by saying that the studio was not really a studio. It was, in fact, a very large warehouse where the City of Vancouver stored broken-down and obsolete equipment, such as old buses and streetcars. A very large area of this warehouse was empty and made available to the film company. This is where we built the cave/mine set, and this is where I was to shoot additional close-ups of Rambo as he drives the Army truck before coming into town and wrecking the gas station.

Driving a vehicle with cameras mounted on it is very difficult. Imagine that you are supposed to drive a car or a truck at high speed on a winding, bumpy gravel road, with a good size camera directly in front of you blocking your vision, another camera just slightly to the side, and possibly one or more cameras looking through the side windows. In between the cameras are powerful lights blinding you, and all you have to do is drive the vehicle while also acting the part. No wonder there are accidents, and that most of the time studios frown upon letting their stars do this kind of dangerous driving. There are all kinds of equipment available for mounting cameras and lights on just about any sort of vehicle. In the case of the Army truck, we used Speed Rail, which is an

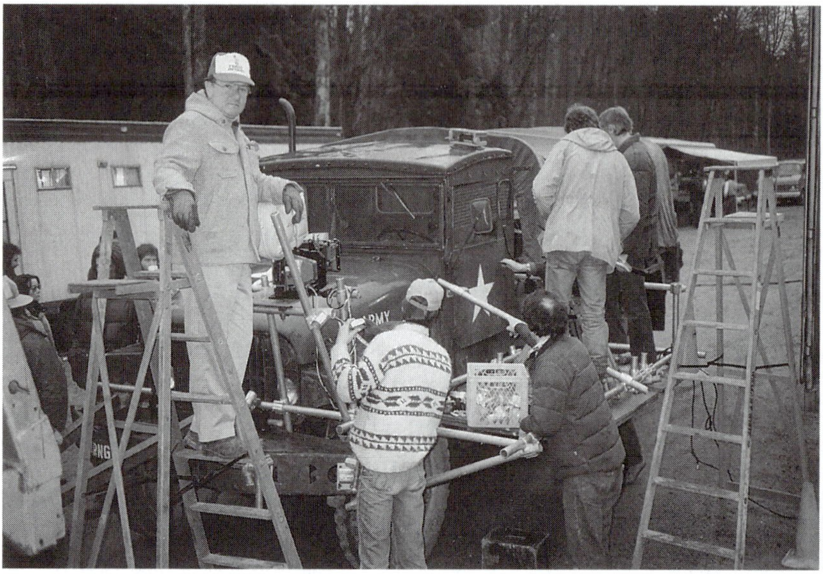

Figure 3.3 Rigging Army truck on location

erector-set type of system for putting the mounts together. Suction-cup devices, clamps, straps, and more are all available from rental houses (see Figures 3.3 and 3.4).

The sequence of Rambo driving the truck, smashing a police car, and ramming through a police barricade was already "in the can," but the editors and the director felt we needed additional close-ups of Rambo driving the truck. Going back to the actual locations for a couple of shots was out of the question, and it was up to me to make these shots so they would fit seamlessly into the cut sequence of Rambo driving to town. This sort of deception, as I sometimes call it, always appealed to me. It was an in-camera special effect, a rabbit to be pulled out of a hat in an emergency. I knew how to do it.

First, we brought in the same Army truck that Rambo had commandeered and placed some blocks under its frame, so that grips could rock it by operating long two-by-four levers. This was

Figure 3.4 Rigged Army truck on location

the beginning of achieving the deception: giving the truck one aspect of motion. But besides the up and down motion, as the truck ostensibly bounces over rough roads, I needed to simulate forward motion. I resorted to one of the oldest tricks, an in-camera special effect known and used by filmmakers as far back as *The Great Train Robbery* (1903), the countryside speeding by the train, as seen through the open door of the mail car. Something moving by the truck could not have been accomplished in the warehouse. There was no road, no countryside, no trees, no mountains in the distance—nor did we really need any of that. What we needed was the illusion of some motion, something that suggested motion. The trick was to see something, a reflection, moving across the windshield—all that was needed to make the quick cuts believable. This technique has been long replaced by rear projection, front projection, blue screen and green screen processes, but where cost or the lack of state-of-the-art equipment is a factor, the technique is still used often. Even less sophisticated, "primitive," methods still work, if they are accomplished with finesse. One has to be careful, however, as too little of the technique will not be enough, and too much of it, well, will be too much.

The first and perhaps most important element is to create a lighting environment that matches the light of the footage shot on location. In this case, the location portions of the sequence were shot on cloudy, overcast days, which, as in the case of the first aid tent, was not difficult to duplicate. The next important element was a device that was going to provide the motion reflected in the windshield. The shot itself was a relatively tight, head-and-shoulder-size close-up of Rambo. He actually drove the truck in some of the location footage, but during the stunts the truck was driven by a stunt double. That was the reason why we needed additional close-ups.

The device was a large, crudely made paper and wood drum, held up by a "C" stand, on which it could be slowly rotated (see Color Plate VII). The rotation motion did not have to be smooth, and the image, painted on the grey, seamless paper drum, did not have to be perfect, or even remotely realistic. In fact the image was a primitive rendition of the countryside, as executed by yours truly, made up of trees, a distant mountain range, and some clouds in the sky. I did the painting, which normally, and rightfully, would be frowned upon by the Union painting crew. But if I'd asked them to do the painting, in all probability they would have painted a beautiful rendition of the countryside, which would have taken too long, would have been unnecessary, and would have been totally wasted.

As all the elements became available, one more problem had to be dealt with. The warehouse, which we used as our studio, did not have the conveniences of a real, standard, major lot studio. It was not designed for motion picture photography. The old warehouse had lots of space, but it also had huge windows three stories high along the entire length of its walls. These windows allowed uncontrollable, intense daylight and direct sunlight to enter the building, which we couldn't live with. There were two possible solutions. One, to cover as many of the windows as possible near our work area; two, to shoot the scenes at night. The second solution was the more practical of the two, and the shots were accomplished by the "poor man's process" technique.

Normally, in a studio environment, "process" photography would be used to make similar shots of a star performer's close-ups as he drives a car. "Process" is the name for rear projection, front projection, and many other methods that combine actual photography with additional elements, such as a background. When real "process" techniques are not available, "poor man's process" is the next best thing—and in some ways it is preferable to the real thing.

In our case, as we got ready to do a "poor man's process" shot, the truck was located in an area where I had enough room for lights, the drum, and the camera. Next, the camera was placed in front and slightly camera right of the truck, at just slightly below eye height of the driver. The frame showed a portion of the windshield around Rambo, and the frame of the windshield around the glass. Military trucks of this type have a flat windshield, which was a blessing. If it had had a curved windshield, as regular cars do, I would have had a very difficult task of keeping unwanted reflections out of the curved windshield. I chose a longer than normal focal length lens for these shots as I wanted a shallow depth of field. If the focus had reached all the way to the rotating drum, we would have seen the crudely painted image, which would not have worked. The shallow depth of field of the long focal length lens, in this case a 150mm, allowed me to see a moving image from the drum reflected in the windshield, which was so diffused that identification of any of its detail was not possible. Nor was it really necessary to clearly identify any of the detail. We see the detail of the countryside and the mountains in the long shots taken on location, and when we cut to these close-ups, all we really need is a suggestion of motion. With all the elements in place and Stallone in the cab, we rolled the camera as the grips on both sides of the truck rocked and occasionally jolted the truck with long two by fours and the large paper drum slowly

Figure 3.5 Stallone in truck in "studio"/warehouse. Note windows.

rotated in a counterclockwise direction (see Figures 3.5 and 3.6). The footage was better than some of the close-ups taken on location. It showed more motion and detail then the location close-ups, and the added motion, produced by the rotating drum, introduced an extra element of reality and excitement.

There is no end to how far one can go to embellish the illusions within this process. Lightning effect can easily be simulated, and actual lightning bolts can be created with Scotchlite. Let me elaborate on how this can be done. Take a wire hanger, or similar wire, and cover it with Scotchlite tape, which is available in most auto parts stores. Bend the wire in the shape of a lightning bolt and hang the wire a good distance behind or to the side of the car, as seen through the rear window from the front, shooting backwards, or through the car from a side angle. Put a small light, as much as possible out of view of the camera, but as close to the line of the optical axis of the lens as possible, pointed at the Scotchlite-

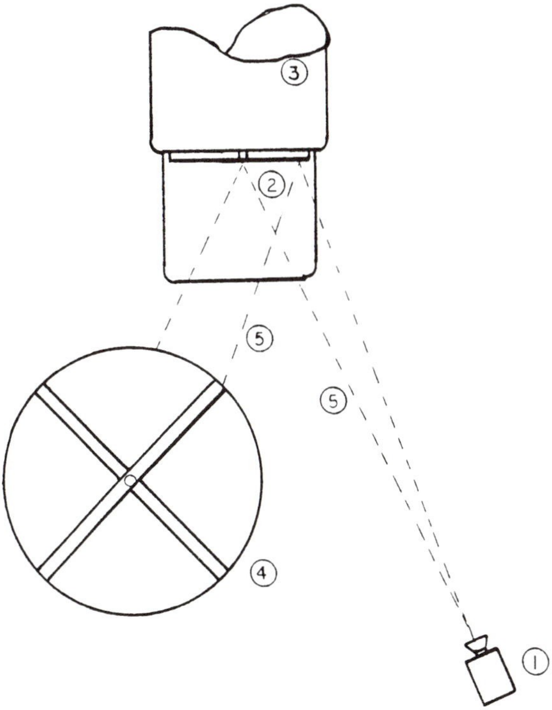

Figure 3.6 "Poor Man's Process." Shooting Rambo's close-up in truck. (1) Camera; (2) windshield; (3) truck; (4) paper drum; (5) camera's view.

covered wire. This light can actually be in the shot, if it is camouflaged with "blackwrap" or in some way made invisible by a flag or any other material that would blend it into the background. When the small light is turned on, it will illuminate the Scotchlite covered wire, which, because of its ability to return most of the light it receives, will appear extremely bright, as a distant lightning bolt would. Turning this light on and off for varying durations of time will simulate flashes of lightning. One can go as far as bypassing the light switch and jury-rigging a bare wire, which, when rubbed on a rough metal surface and connected to the hot

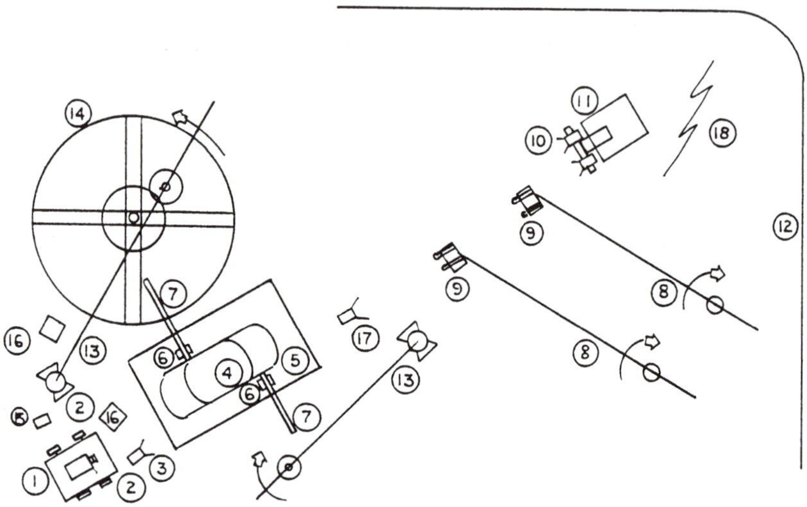

Figure 3.7 "Poor Man's Process": (1) camera; (2) dolly; (3) light to simulate on-coming headlights; (4) subject car; (5) water tray; (6) rocker blocks; (7) lever 2x4s for rockers; (8) arms for swinging simulated taillights; (9) simulated taillights; (10) simulated headlights; (11) dolly for simulated headlights; (12) black studio drape; (13) overhead swinging lights simulating passing streetlights; (14) paper drum; (15) water hose; (16) fog and lightning arc generator; (17) light for lightning in background; (18) simulated Scotchlite lightning.

side of the power supply, will produce the sizzling effect of the lightning bolt. Multibranched lightning can easily be created by adding additional wires, also covered with Scotchlite tape, to the original stem of the lightning bolt (see Figure 3.7).

For side shots, the rotating drum can simulate the nearby roadside speeding by, or the distant countryside rolling by gently. Tiny dots of Scotchlite applied in a row on the rotating drum will simulate a row of distant lights, while a cluster of many Scotchlite dots will give the illusion of a distant town. Cutouts of cars and trucks, taken from advertising posters and automotive magazines, will speed by in the opposite direction, if pasted to the rotating

Color Plate I Beautiful summer swamp

Color Plate II Sunset

Color Plate III Rambo with torch in cave

Color Plate IV Rambo with torch in cave with rats

Color Plate V Rambo in cave with campfire

Color Plate VI Joe Lederer's photograph of burning gas station

Color Plate VII Author with drum, lit truck, and camera ready to go

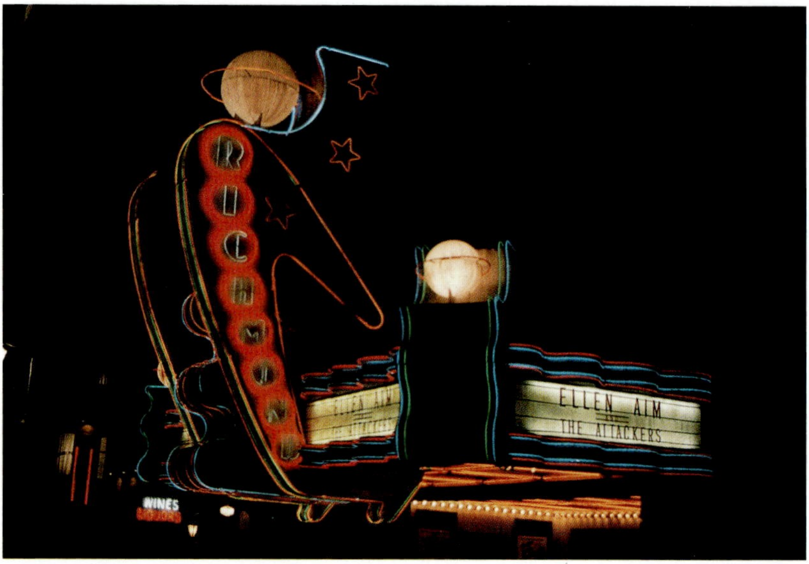

Color Plate VIII The marquee partially lit up

Color Plate IX One-man submersible with camera operator Jeff Laszlo

Color Plate X Fiona Lewis and Kevin McCarthy in suitcase

Color Plate XI Phone booth with cast

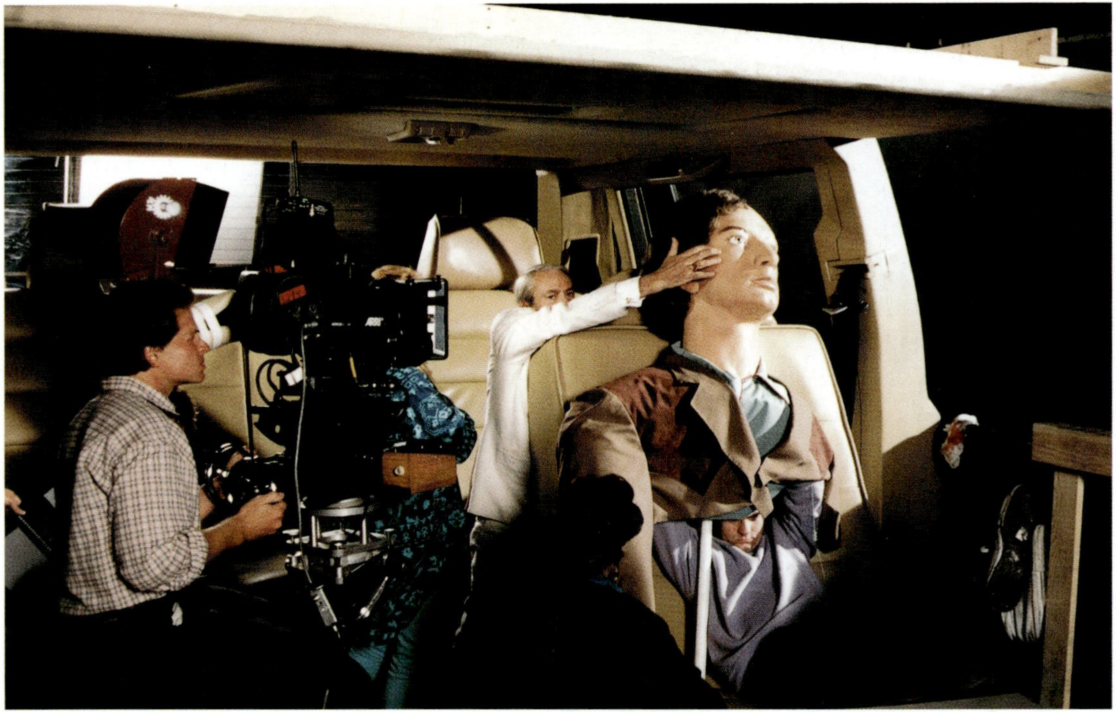

Color Plate XII Portion of fight being filmed. Kevin McCarthy fighting with a double-size puppet of Martin Short. (See puppeteer in "Marty's" stomach.)

drum. The back sides of eighteen-wheelers, illuminated in the simulated head lamps and seen from the inside of the subject car, will sustain for a second or two, making this process as productive as its creators want to make it.

But the most important element to round out this bit of deception is a pair of headlights behind, as seen through the rear window of the subject car, as if a car or a truck is following. The "headlights," two small "inky" type units, are attached to a bar or a one-by-three piece of lumber. The lights may be attached to the arm of a crab dolly, which is covered with black fabric and is operated by a grip, also covered with black fabric. If the production does not have a crab dolly available, the light bar can be held by a black-fabric-covered operator sitting in a wheel chair, or on a cart of any kind. As the cart is moved closer to, or away from, the rear of the subject car, the operator of the light can move the light bar up and down gently, perhaps side to side now and then, to simulate the effect of the headlights of a car following. If there is rain or snow in the shot, it will help mask unwanted detail. If there is no rain in the shot, a bit of baby powder on the rear window goes a long way to mask whatever we don't want to see through the rear window of the subject car.

This is a process, proven by time, that has been in use since the earliest days of filmmaking. It is readily available to film students, as well as to major studios. I had an occasion recently to demonstrate this technique at Montana State University in Bozeman, at an advanced cinematography class. After the demonstration I showed segments from a relatively high-budget MGM film, *Poltergeist II*, which I shot at MGM studios employing the same technique.

If you have the need for a shot of this nature but can't go on location with lots of equipment and a large crew, or if you don't have the money for expensive special effects, you can still make the shot the way I described it here and it will be as good as, perhaps even better than, if it had been shot on location. For one thing, the creation of rain, snow, wind, or lightning is much easier in the studio than on location.

And now I'd like to cover yet another aspect of location photography. Location interiors, or photographing inside a real building, is an ongoing practice wherever a building suitable for the purposes of the script is available. If no such building can be found, the production company usually builds one. Such a building does not have to be complete, or completely finished, as long as the shots designed in and around it can be made with as little expense as possible. In the case of *First Blood* we needed a police station, with extensive photography planned in and around the building. Furthermore, according to the story, Rambo trashes this building by shooting it up with his M-60 machine gun, which would not have been possible if a real building had been used. The town of Hope in British Columbia donated the land to build this building on, in return for the building once the photography was completed. After we were finished with it, the company repaired and refurbished the building, and it is now one of the municipal buildings in Hope.

For our use it was a well-designed and well-built structure, containing all the elements of a police station as dictated by the story. The roof had to be designed and built to accommodate scripted scenes, as did the interiors, which were used during Rambo's initial arrest, his escape, and the finishing scenes of the movie as Rambo shoots up the building, enters the shot-up building and shoots the sheriff, has it out with Colonel Trautman, and surrenders. We had an enormous amount of work planned in and around this building. Knowing that, I had the idea to design and build as much of the lighting for the shots into the building as possible. Following my principle of imitating nature and reality where and when reality is important, I thought that photographing by the light of fluorescent fixtures built into the ceilings, by lamps on the desks, or by windows during the day and at night would go a long way toward making the building and the action in and around it more believable. In this case, unlike the subway stations in *The Warriors*, I had no problem with the color temperatures of the fluorescent lights. They were all ours and were made for photography. This allowed me to supplement them with either additional fluorescent units made for motion picture photography, or with any other kind of motion picture lights, all of which are color balanced to 3200 Kelvin. As the ceiling units were carefully calculated to be located where we figured most of the action would take place, I had very little actual lighting to add—and in my opinion, the shots appear very real and believable.

The place has the looks of an ordinary police station. The area surrounding the building is real and clearly visible through the windows during the day and night shots. Important elements of the story, such as the gas station burning in the distance, can be seen through the windows, or from the roof as the Sheriff is surveying the town, expecting Rambo. When Rambo does arrive and spots the Sheriff on the roof, he shoots up the building, in one of the most exciting sequences of the film. As he enters the building, all the lights having been shot out the building is supposed to be completely dark. In this instance, I had to fall back on a technique that I had rejected in connection with shooting the cave interiors, that of creating an "illusion of darkness." Because we had to see and understand the action, every important aspect of this sequence had to be visible to some extent. In the best interests of the story, I created the illusion of darkness by using sketchy lighting, unexplained light that came from here and there as the shots needed it, without regard to what the source of these lights might have been. Remember, by this time in the story all the lights in town were out, and the town was completely dark. But we needed light to see the action, and the "illusion of darkness" was the right way to go. As Rambo enters the station—well, let me take a small side step and tell you what happens from this point on in the form of a war story. It is amusing, but also contains a lesson, which should be of interest to all cinematographers, particularly those who are just entering or are on their way to the profession.

As was the practice on this shoot while we were on location in and around Hope, we saw our dailies every evening in the only theater in town, after the last show let out around ten. This particular night I settled into my usual seat, about ten rows back from the screen in the center, which I found to be the best vantage point to see the footage from in the huge old theater. The theater dated back to the heyday of movies and the palatial splendor of theaters. But the splendor was gone, and there weren't any good seats, as the screen was yellowed by age and here and there was patched up with white cloth. The projector no longer projected bright, steady, sharp images, as it was as old as the theater, and its lens probably hadn't seen lens tissue in decades. The condenser lenses might have been broken, or covered with dust trapped by oil, and the arc advance mechanism needed constant attention and nudging by the projectionist. But it was the only game in town. I still wonder why the company did not have a portable, state-of-the-art, double-system projector for us. The bottom line was that we didn't have one, and we had to look at dailies in the old theater, without sound, at ten o'clock at night after long, backbreaking days. That night, I was totally engrossed in watching the footage and hadn't realized that Stallone and his entourage (which by this time had grown very large, including his friends, hairdressers, make-up and wardrobe people, a couple of bodyguards, and his agent, who incidentally received credit as one of the film's producers) had come in sometime after I had and sat down in the back row.

In one of the many shots, after he shoots up the building, Rambo enters the police station. This shot was photographed inside the wrecked, dark, station house, looking down a corridor. In order to see Rambo in the dark interior, I had had a portion of the wall at the end of the hallway replaced with a floor-to-ceiling frosted glass panel that was lit from the outside—a bit of "artistic license," as there wasn't supposed to be any light in town. But we had to see Rambo and the action at this very dramatic point in the story. In the foreground of the shot we make out the folding ladder, leading to the roof, and a now dark fluorescent light fixture, shot out of the ceiling and dangling from its wire connection. The muzzle of Rambo's M-60 emerges cautiously from behind the corner of the hallway, followed shortly by Rambo, silhouetted against the frosted glass panel. He cautiously advances into the dark building and stops in front of the camera in a large close-up.

His face is dark, and we can hardly make out his eyes as he surveys the situation.

As this shot of Rambo entering the station came on and Stallone walked into his dark close-up, from the back of the old theater, Stallone's inimitable, throaty tone and delivery broke the silence: " . . . Eyy, Ah can' zee mah facce . . . " (translation: I can't see my face . . .). I turned around, went back to where he was sitting, and explained that in the best interest of the story, the shot, in my opinion, could not and should not have been photographed in any other way. I explained that this shot was going to be on the screen in the finished cut for no more than ten, maybe twelve seconds. I pointed out the fact that he, as Rambo, had shot out every light in town and the whole town was dark. I told him that by this portion of the movie audiences would know who Rambo is, what he does and how, and that if we glamour-lit him in every shot, the whole movie would have been relegated to a style of filmmaking of a long-gone era. I pointed out that without radical lighting, the film would have no ups and downs and would be boring. Besides, I added with a smile, his public already knows how handsome he is. All the while I was talking, Stallone was looking at the screen as additional takes of the same shot were repeated, and as the rest of the dailies followed, but offered no further comment. I knew this was silent understanding and approval of everything I had said, and I went back to my seat to look at the rest of the dailies.

By this time in the production a very good working relationship had developed between Stallone and me. It was based on mutual respect as we worked together and got to know one another as professionals and individuals. Contrary to some preconceived notions that Stallone, perhaps due to the part he played in *Rocky* that catapulted him into fame and stardom, is a beef-punching moron, I can tell you that nothing could be further from the truth. The opposite is true. Though Stallone may not be right to play every part, no actor is, he is uniquely qualified as a filmmaker on many levels. Think about it for a second. He is well qualified for certain roles (case in point, Rambo), is a good and accomplished screenwriter, and a better-than-average director

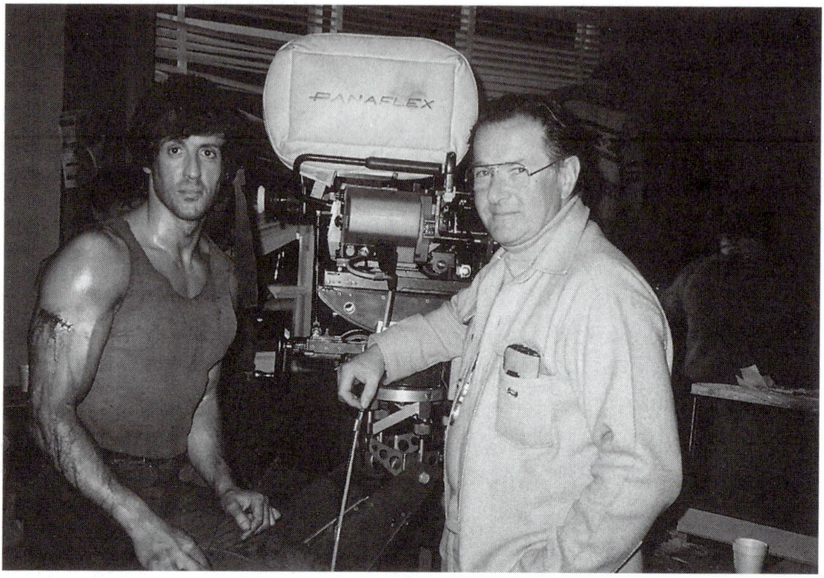

Figure 3.8 The author with Stallone by camera

who also produces some of his films. I have the highest regard for him (see Figure 3.8). We worked well together, even at times when we didn't see eye-to-eye, as in one particular instance that I'll relate later. But before I go into that incident, let me get back to this war story and give you my reason for telling it.

Let's assume that you are a cinematographer contracted to direct the photography of a film called *First Blood*. You read and re-read the script, make endless notes on the margins and blank page backs, prepare and prepare, and finally the first day of the shoot is on hand. Your first shot is the shot I just described above, which the script describes as "Sc. 371, INT. Police Station, Night. Rambo enters dark Police Station, walks into close-up." That's it. By this time you have visualized this shot a hundred times, scouted the location many times, and came to the conclusion to shoot it exactly as I shot it and be absolutely thrilled with the result. But the following day, when you go to dailies, with everybody from the company and some studio executives present, someone, during the viewing of this shot, will call out from the back, "Andy, this shot will print up, right?" The question is a veiled paraphrasing of, "The studio just paid millions of dollars to Stallone, because he has a huge following who want to see him, but we don't, because his face is too dark. The movie," the speaker's tone indicates, "will probably be a disaster, and you, the cinematographer, are the reason."

You know the shot will not "print up." If it were brightened in printing, it would look washed out and awful. But producers and studio executives are fearful people full of anxieties, and no matter how impressive your credits may be, shortly after dailies someone will come up to you and tell you that you are fired, removed from the picture. None of the explanations I gave Stallone the night we viewed this shot in dailies would convince the studio executives or the producers of the film to see this shot your way—especially if it is only the first day of shooting. In my case, we have been in production for a couple of months by this point, and even though not seeing his face clearly might have been a shock at dailies, Stallone and all involved clearly understood the story of the picture, have seen similar shots in dailies, and therefore could not argue with the look of the shot. The case is different if your shot will be seen at the very beginning of production, when anxieties over how the film might turn out are still very high. Seeing sketchy, underlit shots, particularly of the star's close-up, and viewing it in dailies take after take, is not what fills studio executives with confidence. And that is the point of this war story.

Should you be called upon to shoot Sc. 371 as the first shot of the production, I would advise you to put more light than I did on the star's face as he stops in front of the camera in a large close-up. Make him look as good as he does in his publicity shots, as good as his fans are accustomed to seeing him. Add a little backlight to separate him from the dark background, and don't hesitate to increase the eye lights a bit to make his eyes sparkle. Make him attractive, and you will hear a few very nice comments and congratulations the next day at dailies. Then, a few weeks into the photography, as rough assemblies of scenes start emerging from the cutting room, and as confidence for a possibly successful film is slowly replacing the anxieties, one day, probably on a Monday, the director will corner you after dailies, put his arm around you as you walk out of the screening room, and say something to the effect: "Andy, my friend, I spent the entire weekend in the editing room and I can tell you, we have a movie. We are going to have a great movie! The assemblies are coming together great, and I just wanted to tell you what a super job you are doing. The look of the footage is sensational, it is f—ing marvelous!" You beam and say a modest "thanks," as the director continues: "In all the footage there is only one shot that I, the producer, and the star feel is a bit overlit, and we have decided to reshoot it sometime this week." You ask innocently, "Which shot is that?" The director will explain that it is a shot of Rambo coming into the police station. When he stops in a large close-up, "the consensus of opinion," the director goes on, "is that this shot is a bit too bright. Not bad, mind you, and probably could be printed down," he assures you, trying not to upset you. "But," he continues, "I'm sure you'll agree it would be best if we reshot it." He will then offer you his understanding and his explanation that you couldn't possibly have foreseen how dark the rest of the shots in that sequence were going to be, which is probably why the shot was a bit overlit. You nod your understanding, suppress a smile, and continue shooting the film exactly as you planned it. Of course, the chances of this happening to you, as I described it here, is very remote. The remake of *First Blood* is not going to happen for a while yet, but as sure as I'm typing these words, something like this will happen to you at some point in your career. When it does, you will remember this war story.

Now, about the other incident I hinted about earlier that brought Stallone and me closer together at a time when his relationship with some other members of the creative team was not as good as it could have been. The occasion was the shooting of the scene in which he is mistreated by the Deputies at the police station. Rambo is reminded of a very painful, unpleasant memory of mistreatment by the Viet Cong, which triggers a reaction of superhuman strength as he takes out the Deputies and escapes from the police station.

We were rehearsing the fight, which Stallone started to choreograph himself. He is a trained boxer and an advanced expert in martial arts. His refined movements indicated this as he went through the motions of taking out the Deputies one by one, but I didn't think that this fight should be an exhibition of martial arts skills. My expression must have indicated my thoughts as I walked away from the set. He saw me and followed me. "Wattsa madder?" (Translation: "What's the matter?") he asked. I told him exactly what I thought and explained that audiences, in my opinion, would enjoy this scene more if Rambo overwhelmed the Deputies by having something snap inside, something that gives him power in his blind rage, than because he is such a smooth martial arts expert. Once again, as was his style, he said nothing as he walked away. One of the line producers (whom I have to say I didn't care a great deal for, and I knew that the feeling was mutual) saw this and came over to tell me that because I had infuriated Stallone, he would probably stay away from the set the rest of the day and that we, having nothing else to shoot, would lose a half a day of production.

But that is not the way it worked out. Stallone was back on the set shortly, a cup of coffee in hand, indicating that he only left to get coffee. Of course, that may not have been true, with ten or so PAs ready to run for coffee for him, but he was back, and within minutes the first shots of the fight, minus martial arts moves, judo chops, karate kicks, etc., were in the can. That is how it ended up in the final cut. After the shooting he came over to me and said, "You were right," and that was the moment when Stallone and I started a wonderful working relationship, which continued throughout the rest of the photography.

Now, getting back to the photography of *First Blood*, I would like to say a few words about the importance of shadows, or the removal or withholding of light from shots, to create images of the proper mood. As Rambo breaks down in the police station in the final scenes, after shooting the Sheriff, he is comforted by

Colonel Trautman. As Trautman listens, his face is fully visible because of the headlights of hundreds of police and army vehicles outside. But for me, the mood of the scene did not permit an overlit look; instead, it demanded a subdued look, dominated by shadows. As the Colonel faces the windows, I felt that his face was too bland in the flat light and decided to superimpose a shadow. It could be explained and understood as a shadow of the window frame, which appears either as a vertical shadow, or, as he moves, a horizontal one.

The interesting thing about this shadow (look for it the next time you view this film) is that the shadow moves as Colonel Trautman moves. It's not exactly as though the shadow was painted on his face, but if you look carefully, the shadow almost imperceptibly follows him. I know, because I created the shadow by clamping a long, narrow piece of wood in a stand, and gently moved the stand on its casters as the Colonel moved. Not too many people see this, and those who do, I suspect, don't really care. It's a shadow on the Colonel's face; it belongs there because the situation, quite reasonably, put it there. That is all there is to it. I brought it up because I love shadows. I love shadows as much as I love light, which produces shadows, all of which are part of creating the image.

So much about the photography, at least some of the highlights of shooting *First Blood*. Of course, there is a lot more to the experience, i.e., the life of a cinematographer. The hardships of the daily work don't show in the film, and for that matter, neither do the enjoyable moments. Being away from one's family is not easy. At times, being on the other side of the world, on a completely upside down clock, in inaccessible places without daily telephone calls, strains the strongest marriages and relationships. There are great gaps in seeing one's children grow up. And when a long project is over, there is always a time period of serious readjustment. An understanding spouse is perhaps the most important element behind one's success as a cinematographer.

Although most of the film's crew were housed in area motels and hotels, I was fortunate to have an entire Swiss-Chalet-type house as my residence. It had two floors, a living room, several bedrooms and baths, and a kitchen. Every night, as I got back and stripped out of my wet and muddy foul weather gear, I would start a fire in the fireplace, drape the wet garments over chairs by the fire, shower, and start to cook dinner. My gaffer and good friend of many years, Rusty Engels, would come over sometimes and we would cook up a steak, usually soaked in Napoleon Brandy. I did go out to eat occasionally, particularly when Rusty's family visited, and we went to one of the area's few good restaurants. Sometimes Ted Kotcheff and I would get together, and at other times I'd join groups of crew people to let off a little steam at the end of a hard week's work. Even though one is anxious to finish and go home by the end of a shoot, in retrospect, one tends to remember only the good, interesting, and pleasant experiences. The life offered in this profession has many, many compensations, as well as interesting and unusual opportunities, which I don't believe exist in too many other occupations.

There was one other very interesting aspect connected with *First Blood,* and that is the way the film was marketed and sold. I should repeat that the producers Andy Vajna and his partner, Mario Kassar, were in distribution, but on the basis of the very limited information that reached me, I don't think their business was among the top distributors in Hollywood. I've heard that they distributed films that other companies would not, and that they distributed them in countries such as Hungary and some of the other then-Soviet-block countries.

By late summer, following the completion of photography of *First Blood,* though the film was far from finished, Andy assembled an eighty-minute-long, roughly-put-together version of the film from daily prints, all scratched up by the editing process and containing white leader slugs where shots had not yet been inserted. The soundtrack was mostly original recording from location, unbalanced and in some cases containing elements that would be eliminated in the final editing and mixing of the soundtrack. There were no titles, nor opticals, but the assembly contained most of the spectacular action sequences and shots of the film, including the stunt that cracked several of Stallone's ribs.

It was the week the foreign film buyers were in Hollywood, filling their slates for the next year. Andy booked one of the best theaters in Westwood for one showing and invited every film buyer in town. The screening was followed by a reception and dinner for several hundred invited guests in a three-story restaurant on Pico Boulevard. There was quite a bit of enthusiastic reaction at the screening, which was a good sign, as this audience was made up of professional, hardened veterans who did not applaud out of courtesy. After my wife and I got to the restaurant, before we had even sat down to dinner, Andy brought us a glass of champagne and told us that the entire foreign distribution of *First Blood* was sold, and that his fledgling little production company, Carolco, was in the black by a huge margin. Remembering the few occasions when Andy or Mario would disappear from the set, and everybody knew they were trying to find more financing so we could continue the shooting, this was good news indeed. The rest is history, except for one thing: this film also caused riots, but for entirely different reasons than those that caused the riots in connection with *The Warriors*. I've heard that in Rome, during the initial run of the film, the theater oversold one of the performances. Those who didn't get in rioted, and by the time the police arrived, I understand, scores of rioters were injured.

The enormous success of *First Blood*, as is the case for many highly successful films, inspired the creation of sequels. The assumption, besides the promise of financial gain, might be that all who saw the first film will come to see the sequel, and the ones who missed the first one will come so as not to miss the second one. A sequel, perhaps because of that great interest, sometimes generates higher revenues than the original did. Though asked, I didn't do any of the sequels but I will not hesitate to say that *First Blood* was a very good movie and a very enjoyable one for me to work on and look back on.

Q&A *First Blood*

ANDREW QUICKE: Could not knowing Ted Kotcheff's or someone's credits in an interview cause you not to get the job?

ANDREW LASZLO: Possibly. In a business where egos have been known to reach ridiculous levels, not getting a job for not knowing someone's credits could happen. Though it did not happen in my case, as I mentioned, the better one is prepare for an interview, the better off one might be, not just about credits, but almost anything regarding an individual or the project. For instance I didn't know about the book *First Blood*. I probably should have.

AQ: What year was *First Blood*?

AL: 1982.

AQ: You seemed skeptical about doing *First Blood*, because it was an independent film. How do you feel about the current popularity of "Indie" films?

AL: Personally, I welcome independent films. It removes the counterproductive studio meddling and allows the filmmakers to do their best, rather than justifying some middle-level executives' existence in the front office.

AQ: So when Andy Vajna first called you, was it Stallone's participation that convinced you to take the picture?

AL: To a great extent, yes. Stallone was well known by then, though the Rambo series is what I believe made him a superstar.

AQ: You said, you "could identify with the story." What do you mean by that?

AL: First, the story was a physical, outdoors-type story. I am a physical, outdoors-type person. I like mountains, the woods, adventure, exploration, and the like. *First Blood* was also the story of a mistreated Vietnam veteran, whose plight and situation I understood and sympathized with.

AQ: What were the "unusual" and "unorthodox" elements of this film and would they be unusual and unorthodox today?

AL: Well, the film really didn't have elements that were exclusive to it. Many films in the past have been shot on distant, rugged locations all over the world. I had done a number of them even before *First Blood*. But *First Blood* was not a studio picture, and that is what appealed to me.

AQ: Yet you say that the tent interiors were easier to shoot in the studio. Why? Was it cheaper?

AL: Yes, as I pointed out in the chapter, it was less expensive to shoot the scene without going back to location with the entire company and to do the interiors of the tent in the studio.

AQ: Regarding the continuity problem because of the snow, would there have been a problem if you had just held up shooting until the snow melted?

AL: There would not have been a continuity problem if the company could have stood down, waiting for the snow to melt, but the expense would have been enormous, and prohibitive.

AQ: You mentioned some shots from older films, of people going through an old castle at night by candlelight. What were the elements in those shots that made the old process unacceptable to you?

AL: As I emphasize throughout the book, I am a committed proponent of reality, of imitating nature, and so on. Seeing people in a night environment where the illumination is provided by one candle, or one candelabra, but seeing multiple shadows of the people as they move, is totally unreal and, for me, unacceptable. I am convinced that even those people in the audience who are not well-versed in film production techniques would notice, or at least be disturbed, by such an effect.

AQ: Why did you work in water in the cave? Was the warehouse you used as a makeshift studio, flooded?

AL: No, the studio wasn't flooded. I was referring to the scenes in the portion of the cave that were flooded. It was our own making, for the scene called for Rambo to wade through water. We flooded a portion of the cave for these shots and needed a dolly with which to make camera moves. Standard equipment did not work, because of the narrow and irregular passageways, which is why we had to make an improvised dolly.

AQ: You mentioned that you would have liked to have had more than five cameras to shoot the gas station fire with. My students are understandably envious. Why more than five?

AL: We cinematographers are a greedy bunch. We always want more, you know, just one more shot! We are also fearful. What if two, three, even four of the five cameras should break down as the gas station is burning to the ground? Wouldn't it be good to have more cameras? More coverage of a one-time event also means more opportunities to get additional, interesting shots.

AQ: Was this a real gas station or a set?

AL: It was a set, built for the movie.

AQ: Could you have found an old gas station to blow up?

AL: Possibly, but a real gas station would have been built in a way that would have made it difficult to blow up and burn down, and it probably would not have had the elements the film called for.

AQ: How prevalent is the practice of shooting cutaway shots at a different time?

AL: Picking up cutaway shots, after the actual sequence is completed, is a very common practice. When a sequence is edited, the need for cutaways becomes obvious, and these shots may be picked up while the film is still in photography, or even after photography is finished. In fact, additional dialogue shots might be photographed on a rebuilt or simulated set. In some cases, entire sequences might be added to already existing scenes long after the original scene was photographed and even after the picture wrapped.

AQ: Why did you use your orange 85 filter in the studio portions of the first aid tent if the lights were blued? What was the stock balanced for?

AL: The stock was tungsten balanced for 3200 Kelvin. The lights had blue gels added to simulate the daylight of 6000 Kelvin. Without the 85 filter the footage would have looked very blue. Shooting the set without the filter but with the lights also balanced for 3200 Kelvin would have been correct, but it would not have given me the same feel of the light as it existed on location, nor would I have had the warm glow of the kerosene light hanging in the back of the tent. The color of its flame would have been much closer to the tungsten balance of the negative stock and the lights, diminishing the color difference of the light.

AQ: How important is note-taking in the preproduction and/or the production phase?

AL: The importance of note-taking cannot be overemphasized. I'm sure you recall my remarks about reading a script over and over again and constantly making notes. But note-taking should not be restricted to the reading of the script only. At every phase of the production, during meetings, scouting locations, for example, copious notes should be taken. During the production phase, note-taking and record-keeping are extremely important. In fact, the production notes I have my assistants take are more often than not supplemented by Polaroid shots, or other still photography, videotape, and even film clips from actual shots. We just talked about making pick-up shots, or cutaways to sequences already photographed. Without notes, one would have a difficult time remembering the focal length of the lens used during the photography, what sort of filter(s) the lenses had, and every other detail that might be important to the shot. I very strongly advocate and recommend note-taking.

AQ: How often do you use the "magic hour"? Is this different from the "golden hour"?

AL: Photographing during "magic hour," though it is always beautiful, may not be applicable to certain shots. Where it is applicable and desirable, it should be carefully planned, as the time available for photography is usually very short. Under all conditions the widest shots should be completed first, as tight shots can be effectively faked. "Golden hour," or "golden time," as it is sometimes referred to, is a phrase meaning an overtime period on top of already existing overtime hours, usually three times the normal hourly rate. It has nothing whatever to do with "magic hour."

AQ: Is it true that Terence Malik, when shooting *Days of Heaven*, shot entirely during magic hours only?

AL: I really don't know the exact answer to that. Talking with Nestor Almendros, the cinematographer of *Days of Heaven*, it was my impression that a very large portion of the film was shot during magic hour. It is a very beautifully photographed film, but, unfortunately, photographing a more commercial film exclusively during magic hours would result in nothing but golden hours for every cast and crew member, making that practice prohibitively expensive and therefore not feasible.

AQ: Viewing *First Blood*, I noticed that the rotor blades of the helicopter seemed to be turning slower than they should. What is the reason for this?

AL: This phenomenon is a shortcoming of motion picture photography. By accommodating one facet of a shot, other facets may be adversely effected. In the case of the helicopter shots, as the Deputy is firing at Rambo hanging from the cliff, I used slow motion to enhance Rambo's fall. The slow motion (the film running faster in the camera) not only slowed down Rambo's fall, which was desirable, but it also slowed down the rotors of the helicopter, which was not.

AQ: Did Stallone really break his ribs?

AL: I don't know if there is a difference between breaking or cracking ribs, but as far as I know he cracked his ribs while we shot the last shot of the sequence of him jumping from the cliff, through the tree branches. Of course, the fall from the cliff and the smashing through tree branches was done by his photo-double stuntman, but the last shot, as we see him falling out of the tree onto the ground, was done by Stallone. It was a pretty nasty crash. It's in the film, and when you look at it again, you'll see him wince as he crashes onto the tree branch.

AQ: How important is safety on the set? Who is ultimately in charge of safety?

AL: Safety should be the most important consideration of everyone on the set. Though studios place more and more emphasis on safety, my belief is that this is only done for liability and insurance reasons. For instance, it is now the practice that at the beginning of the workday the assistant director gathers the crew and reads a very carefully worded statement about safety. At times this session is even videotaped. I always considered this an annoying bit of the studio covering its back, as within minutes after hearing the safety notes one might find oneself in a dangerous situation. Accidents do happen, particularly in an industry that is not routine oriented. Every shot is different, done under new and different conditions and circumstances, and danger always lurks close by. But as I stated in the text, no film can justify the loss of a life, or a limb, or other injuries. Ultimately, one is in charge of one's own safety and should be concerned with the safety issues all around.

AQ: There are many mismatches in *First Blood*. How do you justify them?

AL: You and other trained film professionals see these mismatches, and I can't really justify them. But I hope that most average moviegoers don't see them, or ignore them if they do. If the mismatches are not blatant, or can be explained somehow, they are really not important. Snow on one portion of the mountain, followed by a shot without snow in another portion of the mountain, is not worth wondering about if the action and the story makes no point of it. Let me ask you if you saw a mismatch that most people don't, when Rambo cuts up the piece of tarpaulin that he makes a tunic from. He is in a rush, just steps ahead of his pursuers, and as he unsheathes his knife he throws the sheath away. Did you notice that, and did it bother you that in the next cut, when you see him use his knife, the knife is back in its sheath? Very few do!

AQ: How was the night close-up of Rambo driving into town in the Army truck photographed? Did you use "poor man's process"?

AL: Yes. It was a simple matter of relighting the day close-ups. You might have noticed the rain on the windshield and the wiper going. It helped me obscure what would have been real reflections if we had photographed these shots on actual location.

AQ: What is the color temperature of normal, non-motion-picture fluorescent lights?

AL: The color temperature of commercial fluorescent lights is subject to age, voltage, the covering on the light fixtures, and many other factors. The most often used fluorescents, such as those used in an office building or a supermarket, are the so-called "cool white" lights. They usually photograph with a greenish hue. If no other lights are used, this green hue can be printed out at the lab and the color brought very close to acceptable levels. "Warm white" fluorescent lights are a bit warmer and closer to incandescent and motion picture light in color temperature. Fluorescents balanced to 3200K are also available for motion picture photography. No color-correction gels are needed if these lights are used in conjunction with tungsten motion picture lights. If other lights, such as HMIs, are used in conjunction with cool white fluorescents, an appropriate filter on the tubes, called minus green, will help the color balance. Today's negative stocks are so forgiving, that in almost all instances fluorescent lights can be ignored.

. . . and now, onto the next level of creating the image, *Streets of Fire*.

4

STREETS OF FIRE

From the late sixties on through the seventies and early and mid-eighties, there was a huge change in the look of films, in the art and techniques of cinematography. A new company with a new outlook, the Panavision Company, under the leadership of Bob Gottchalk, was beginning to supply new camera equipment to accommodate the demands, requests, and suggestions of cinematographers who used the equipment. The Mitchell Camera Corporation, the industry leader until this time, like many other American manufacturers, turned a deaf ear to what their customers wanted. The Mitchell Standard, Mitchell NC, and BNC cameras—mainstays of worldwide filmmaking—were fifty years old, so firmly ensconced in the industry that no other cameras were used by the studios. They were fine cameras, but round this time period, other changes were also happening in film production.

Filmed television was born and spreading rapidly into many areas away from Hollywood. The mainstream film industry saw this as an annoyance rather than a threat, and looked down on it and generally tried to ignore it. The major studios stayed away from television—the "enemy"—as more and more new companies sprung up to produce filmed programming for television. This era also saw the birth of an entirely new area of filmmaking—television commercials. As the Majors would have little or nothing to do with these new areas of film production, a new crop of filmmakers emerged, from the top on down. At first, these new filmmakers adapted the best methods of filmmaking as were then practiced by the studios. But they did not buy into all the traditions and unbending hierarchy of the industry, one that in a couple of years would be fighting to keep its head above water.

In spite of booming television film production, the Mitchell Camera Corporation stubbornly refused to listen to the young, new group of filmmakers. I was a member of this group. Within a few years I was working on episodic television, which, incidentally, offered long-term employment as opposed to the sporadic nature of feature film work. I saw an opportunity and purchased my own camera, a Mitchell BNC, which I rented to the production company I worked for. The BNC was a wonderful camera. It was almost a perfect design then for studio sync-sound photography. It had evolved from the Mitchell Standard and Mitchell NC, both of which were still widely used, but mostly in animation or on location where camera noise was not a problem. In spite of its designation—the Mitchell NC, for Noiseless Camera—it was anything but that. It was noisy and could not be used in a studio environment, or where the recording of sound had to accompany the photography. After many stop-gap measures to overcome this problem, the Mitchell BNC (Blimped Noiseless Camera) was born in the early thirties. Since then, its design saw only minimal changes. By the time I bought my first BNC, one could get better lenses, but the camera itself didn't change. Since I was very mechanical, having worked with tools most of my life, I religiously maintained and serviced my camera. As I did, I came to the conclusion that its features could be improved and adapted to the type of filmmaking the new generation filmmakers would welcome. I had an idea that what we needed, certainly in fast-paced television film production, were lighter and smaller cameras, as well as other equipment to accommodate quick and efficient production.

I contacted the Mitchell Corporation and offered to send them my ideas on how the BNC could be reengineered into a smaller, lighter, and much more versatile piece of equipment. After a few weeks of silence, I phoned them and talked with one of the executives of the company who explained their situation. From the early thirties on, the Mitchell Company had had castings of the BNC sitting on its shelves, and each year, on average, they machined, assembled, and sold ten or eleven cameras. The company's government contracts were considerable compared to the film industry orders, and, I figured, they weren't about to make radical changes for the wants of upstarts, such as myself.

By this time, the mid-sixties, I owned two BNCs, #332 and #342. Television production demanded newer equipment. Such items as the crab dolly was born, emerging from the garage workshop of a grip. Likewise, new, smaller, more versatile lighting equipment was built in the home workshops of gaffers. Sound recording equipment and techniques had changed too, and slowly the entire film industry was taking on a new look. The Eastman Kodak Company, unlike other companies, heard and listened to its customers. Acknowledging the pressures from overseas competition, Kodak started bringing out new negative, as well as positive, emulsions. Such a negative emulsion, designated as Kodak 5293, emerged in 1982–83, just preceding the production of *Streets of Fire*.

By this time, I was a member of a select group of cinematographers to whom Kodak sent new, experimental film stock for testing and evaluation. When I received the first couple of 400-foot cans of this new emulsion, identified by handwritten labels, I was eager to test it. I had no idea at the time that I'd be doing a film, *Streets of Fire*, within a very short time. As part of this Kodak test, following up on my photography of the match lighting Rambo, I took shots of my daughter studying by the light of one candle with additional candles in the background. I also mixed the light of the candle with standard, incandescent lighting, provided by household lamps and professional equipment, all of which produced outstanding results.

Following these tests, I took my camera into the cavernous main hall of Grand Central Station in New York City. I had shot there many times before on different projects, and the big problem had always been the low light levels, which necessitated the lighting of the scenes. When lighting the foregrounds, the backgrounds were usually underexposed, or they would disappear, but without lighting we could not have shot. I set up my camera for the Kodak test on the balcony at the west entrance to the station, overlooking the immense main hall, and shot many takes with different focal length lenses. The corridors branching off from the main hall were dark, and, as usual, the main hall itself was dingy. At the same time the gigantic windows facing the camera were way overexposed, too bright, and without detail, totally blown-out. I was hoping for a miracle, and a miracle I got. The blown-out windows, though hot, retained much of their detail. The main hall, as in life, was a bit subdued, but most surprisingly there was detail in the dark tunnels leading out to the platforms. The longer focal length lenses, produced equally amazing results. There was detail everywhere: in the faces of passing travelers, in the detail of the station, even in the brightest spots, such as the windows and the incandescent lighting in the building. One very notable and beautiful result was the balance between incandescent lighting and daylight, which filtered down from the high windows.

I couldn't wait for an opportunity to put this wonderful new emulsion to work, and I didn't have long to wait. My good friend Walter Hill called, wanting to know if I would be available to shoot his next film, *Streets of Fire*. I jumped at the opportunity. Aside from everything else, *Streets of Fire* was going to be a high-budget movie, offering all sorts of opportunities—the best of which was to work with Walter again.

Around this time, one of my colleagues grabbed a few headlines in industry publications, for the then-unimaginable feat of shooting 5293 at 1200 ASA, instead of its designated speed of 250. The speed of this film, 250 ASA, was not new, but it was the first really high-speed, fine-grain film manufactured by Kodak. I had shot a movie on a 250 ASA film stock by an overseas manufacturer, simply because until Kodak 5293 came out, it was the only choice.

My first order of business in Los Angeles was to put together a minimum crew and a small camera package to start testing Kodak

5293, as well as other negative emulsions for comparison, with the upcoming project in mind. Let me say a few words at this point about testing. Regardless of how much experience one has in photography, or with one particular film stock, testing and more testing of an emulsion to be used for an upcoming movie, in my opinion, is one of the most important elements in preparation for the production. Kodak has an array of many sample films and demos, but most of these are made to point out the abilities and advantages of new film stocks. These tests, I prefer to call them demos, are made under controlled, optimum conditions. The tests I prefer are made under the worst conditions. I want to know the limits of a new emulsion, how far I can take it under less than optimum conditions. Most importantly, I want to know if the stock has anything new to offer me, beyond or above Kodak specs, even if the results may not be perfect according to the standards set by Kodak.

By this time in my career, the nonstandard approaches and results had taken priority over the norm in my cinematography. Not that I ignored the norm, for very large portions of each of my films were still photographed according to the best practices of the art, but I had learned to rely heavily on—or at least not reject—anything that could have been at odds with what was considered the norm, as long as it gave me something that in my opinion was right, or a plus, for my movie.

One evening, I assembled my skeleton crew, put the minimal camera package in a panel truck, and, accompanied by a union-specified driver, grip, and electrician, my assistant and I set out to find a suitable location to test the new 5293 negative stock. As *Streets of Fire* was to have large blocks of night photography on location, I wanted to start learning about the film's characteristics in photographing low-key, underlit scenes. I found a street in one of the seedier sections of downtown Los Angeles, which I thought was perfect for my test. It was a curved street in the old industrial section, with one- and two-story buildings lining the street, a pair of railroad tracks in the middle, and one mercury vapor light on top of one of the buildings at about the middle of the block. This one light, with its purple-orange hues, provided the only illumination.

I was struck by how beautiful this real setting was. I was not equipped to change or add to the lighting as I had no lighting equipment or crew with me, but even if I had, I don't think I would have wanted to change anything.

We set up the camera in the middle of the road, looking into the block, and more out of curiosity than any requirements for my test, I took light readings abreast of the mercury vapor light, at pavement level and at eye height in the middle of the street. At pavement level the reading was 4 foot-candles. At eye height, in the middle of the street, I had about 6 foot-candles; and on the wall, just under the light source and as high as I could reach, I had about 12 foot-candles. Even after having heard so much about this new film stock, and after having personally tested it in New York, I didn't think I would have enough light for proper, solid exposure. But I proceeded with the test, rolling about 45 feet of film, a half a minute's worth, using one of my wide-angle lenses with the T-stop wide open. The majority of my lenses by this time were in the T:2.3, T:2.2, and even in the T:2 range. I then shot another 45 feet of film with the lens set at T:2.8, 45 more feet at T:4, and so on, going through the full range of stops to T:16. Obviously, I expected no acceptable results at the extreme settings, but seeing just exactly what one can get at that sort of setting is what I mean by testing a new emulsion under the worst of conditions. Later on, as you will see, this testing not only paid off, but the results of photography in the extreme became a huge part of the photographic success of this film.

I repeated the test with other lenses, going from the wide-angle to medium and long focal lengths and shooting various sections of the street, to see how these lenses would perform under conditions of shooting by a single light source and at below or above the required amount of light for exposure. I was also interested in the color of the shots, as so many of our locations, I knew, would have similar lighting. The dailies the following day blew me away. Not only did I have enough light for exposure, but the results—the richness of the black areas in the image, the detail in shadow, and the ability of this new negative stock to faithfully reproduce color and hold detail in the underexposed areas as well as in the highlights, such as the wall the light was mounted on—were until this point in my career simply not possible. But here it was, everything just as I had seen it the night before. I looked at the tests over and over again. By about the fifth viewing, an idea started to germinate, getting me a huge step closer to the "look," and the style of photography that *Streets of Fire* was to have.

It seemed to me that some underexposed shots looked better than the fully exposed ones. This called for additional testing, under controlled conditions, with set light levels, and with exposures determined by the use of grey cards, grey scales, color charts, and careful measurement of the lights. One more step remained, perhaps the most important portion of the testing process, and that was the reprinting of the tests, taking the original negative all the way through to "release print." This meant the making of an interpositive from the original negative, followed by an internegative made from the interpositive, and a final "release print" made from the internegative. In the course of completing a movie, there are sometimes many more steps that will affect the final release print, but for now I wanted to take the negative through these additional steps to see how the final result, the release print, would look compared to the dailies printed from the original negative. In the past, each such intermediate step would deteriorate the quality of the final print. But now, there was hardly any major deterioration in the "release print" of this test. I concluded that Kodak had once again adhered to its well-known conservative practice and rated this emulsion below its real potential. The conservative rating of this new stock was what Kodak, I'm sure, considered the best for its new film stock. But for me, once again, the industry's or Kodak's definition of the "best" was not to be my interpretation of the "best."

Having gone over the script for *Streets of Fire* many times, I knew that the lessons of the past, particularly the ones I learned while doing the films I have discussed in this book, would come in very handy. Much of this film was to be shot on location, day and night, and a very large portion of the film was to be photographed on the back lot and in the studio. All of these settings will have unique elements, which I will talk about in this chapter. For now, let me introduce the project, tell you how it had come about, and how I proceeded from here on.

The story of *Streets of Fire*, another Walter Hill film, was once again borrowed from Greek mythology. Though it takes many liberties, it is an updated version of Helen of Troy. The heroine, here a rock singer, is kidnapped by a motorcycle gang, and her ex-boyfriend is called on to rescue her. That is the nutshell version of the story. Within that story the action never stops. The script offered many exciting photographic opportunities, which the new film stock was going to make possible for me.

In the case of *First Blood*, it was exciting to shoot a close-up of the star with the light of a match, and a full sequence in a large, elaborate set by the flame of a torch. Here, I was looking forward to the opportunity to shoot an entire movie with unheard of and almost frighteningly low light levels. I still wasn't completely comfortable with 5293, as I still didn't know its full potential. I didn't know how some theories would work in practice, nor was I completely set on the style, the "look," of the movie. This was a pressing issue, as we were already in Chicago where the photography was to start within days, and I still didn't have a clear-cut understanding of what the film was going to look like. The testing continued.

One afternoon, around five o'clock or so, I once again took a small crew and a camera to do some more tests. This time I went to one of our future locations, the platform of an elevated station. I set up the camera and shot film of trains coming in and out, of people getting on and off. I had no supplementary lighting over what existed at the station. It is amazing to me how we look at the world in front of our eyes without really seeing what we are looking at. We take things for granted as we become accustomed to our environs, to familiar places, and move around as though we were not part of those surroundings. We don't bother to look for beauty, or even ignore it when it's right before our eyes. Ugliness stands out more readily, but beauty is taken for granted, or not noticed, as part of an everyday event, place, or situation. Like most of us, I've been on elevated stations many times, but not until I looked through the camera lens that afternoon did I realize how beautiful an elevated station can look on a dreary, wet, winter afternoon. The gently curved platforms and the rails glistened in the drizzle, their texture and highlights accentuated by the string of lamps over the platforms.

I was no longer concerned with exposure. I knew the new film stock was capable of registering whatever I might have in front of the camera, plus some. In fact, by this time, I had made a firm decision to expose this negative at an index of 640ASA, instead of the conservative 250ASA Kodak assigned to it. This by itself is not an extraordinary accomplishment, as the film's rating only increased by about a stop and a quarter, but that exposure allowed me to get the rich look that I knew I wanted *Streets of Fire* to have. The test that afternoon firmly established what that "look" should be. Watching dailies the following afternoon, I became very excited over what I saw. The station looked real, and the image was rich beyond my expectations. I called Walter right away to come to the lab to look at the film. I knew I was on the right track, and he agreed that we had the "look" for the film. It was "reality," which I could now manipulate and improve upon. I called it "enhanced reality." Reality was there for the asking without me trying to imitate it, and I knew that I could enhance it any way I wanted to.

And now, the first "war story" of *Streets of Fire,* which was very helpful in further honing the film's photographic style.

Very few of the Los Angeles crew, myself included, were properly prepared for the severe winter of the Windy City. Because of that, almost the entire crew, as if by a common plan, congregated at the Eddie Bauer store in Chicago, buying every kind of foul weather gear in sight. We got big discounts, but for me the biggest plus was the discovery of a new light source. As I was paying my bill at the cash register, I noticed a small basket full of keychain lights. Everybody has seen these little lights at one time or another—they were little plastic lights that, when squeezed, would turn on a tiny built-in lightbulb (the keys are attached by a small chain). I picked up one of these lights, and as I squeezed it I directed its light into the palm of my hand. It was surprising to see the even and soft light this little gadget produced. Unlike other flashlights, large and small, this light did not have the dark rings and bright spots usually emitted by flashlights. I am fascinated with light, and it immediately occurred to me that this little light could play a big part in the photography of *Streets of Fire*. Joel Silver, one of the film's producers, was standing next to me, and I aimed the light at his face, to see what it would look like in the eyes and on the skin tones. Joel might have thought that I was trying to be funny, or lost my marbles, but when I explained to him what a great find this light was, he, the producer of the movie, immediately offered to buy all the key-chain lights in the store. We bought hundreds of them. I still have some, all dead of course, but one, a fond memento of *Streets of Fire*, still sits on a shelf in my den. My gaffer and his crew, seeing me use the light in a manner I'll describe later, fixed up one of these little lights with miniature barn doors and a blue gel to correct its color temperature.

This was the moment when I realized something very important about the industry. For years, the motion picture industry has strived to develop bigger, more powerful and efficient lights, mainly to help exposure. Suddenly here I was in an Eddie Bauer store in Chicago, realizing that the new film stocks, together with more efficient lenses and processing, were going to demand *less* light and *smaller* sized equipment, which we, the industry, didn't have. Eye lights, for example, the kind that are usually attached to the camera, evolved for years, with increasing light output. For me, as of this moment, they were on the endangered list. This incident suddenly brought into focus that I was going to have to work with lighting units on this film that were going to be too big and too powerful. I realized that in the studio or on the back lot I would have complete control of the environment, and that I would not be strapped for exposure as in the case of *The Warriors*. But I still needed light to mold and create the image—with equipment that was suddenly no longer state-of-the-art. I also realized that it was time to unlearn most of what I knew, most of the experience I had gained over the years. What I didn't know was that at every step of the way, exciting new revelations and opportunities were waiting for me. Old techniques and standards were about to fall, and old tricks of the trade would have to accommodate new applications.

When we see our hero, Tom Cody, played by Michael Paré, for the first time in the movie, I was shooting once again with only the lights built into a subway car. Though these were incandescent and a great deal dimmer than the fluorescent lights of the New York subway cars, I was delighted not to need any other lights to supplement the actual lighting of the car, other than my little key-chain light. I'm sure that most of our crew, some hardened veterans of many years of filmmaking, thought I was nuts as I held this little light next to the lens as the camera moved in for a close-up, or when I moved it back as the camera pulled away. But the results were truly amazing. The low light level allowed me to see every detail in the car, as well as of the city seen through the windows. Even without lighting, wherever I looked I had plenty of light for exposure—in fact, in a few cases, I had too much, which is the subject of the next war story.

The shot was on the platform of the elevated station as a train comes in, stops, opens its doors, and Tom Cody gets off. He walks into his close-up and looks at the torn posters of the concert, during which Ellen Aim, his former girlfriend, was kidnapped. Based on my tests on the same El platform, I was going to do very little lighting for this shot. The most I was hoping to use in addition to the existing lights of the station was the key-chain light, as Cody stops in front of the camera in a big head close-up. But as we rehearsed the scene, the spot where the train stopped every time put his door directly opposite from one of the platform lights, which lit him up (as we say in the business) like a Christmas tree. Let me remind you of what I have already said in previous chapters about the secret of successful location photography: the secret is to be ready to shoot when the conditions are right. In this case, I was ready, but the condition—the bright light right where I didn't want it—was wrong. I wanted Cody to get off the train in a silhouette and gradually become visible as he walks into his lit close-up. The regular train traffic was running, and we only had a limited time before our train had to pull away from the platform. I had to move fast. Turning off the light was out of the question. All the lights of the station, I reasoned, were probably on the same circuit, and turning one off would have turned all of them off. Besides, the lights were most likely operated by a computer somewhere in a central location. Bringing ladders, black wrap, or black fabric from the street below to do away with this light would have taken too long; our train, I knew, would have had to clear the station by then. There was one other solution. My grip, as most grips do, usually keeps a hammer on the dolly. I grabbed this hammer and smashed the five bulbs in the overhead fixture. Some of the production people were aghast, but we got the shot exactly as I wanted to photograph it, before our train had to move. Since then, I have called this method "lighting with a hammer," but I recommend it only under the most extreme conditions. Fortunately, the Chicago Transit Authority did not revoke our permit, and, of course, Universal Pictures paid for replacing the bulbs. Since this incident, I have used the "lighting with a hammer" technique only once (see Figure 4.1).

The rest of the shooting in Chicago was relatively uneventful, though I did have a problem that was a 180-degree turn from my experience on *The Warriors*. With the new fast film stock, all of Chicago's night locations photographed well, with lots of detail even in the darkest, most underlit areas, but shooting overlit sections within a dark shot became a problem. Photographing with the lens openings set for the dark portions of shots would overexpose brightly lit sections; conversely, exposing for the bright sections would lose the detail in the dark portions of the shots. I was back to square one, wishing for the type of control one has in a studio. In spite of my love of real locations, I was beginning to look forward to working on the back lot at Universal without these problems. I had come full circle. In the past, on other films, while creating outdoor shots in the studio, I had wished for real locations. Now, facing the problems afforded me by this wonder-

Figure 4.1 On the crane at the Chicago el station

ful new fast negative film, I was wishing to get back to the studio and the back lot, where I could create lighting without the drastic differences in the light levels of dimly lit Lower Wacker Drive and the brightly lit bridges alongside it over the Chicago River. Of course, one always finds a solution. Whether it is placing a black-fabric-covered truck in front of a Chinese restaurant, or putting a helicopter on a giant lazy Susan made out of a thousand tennis balls, there is always a solution. There has to be! That is what cinematography and being a cinematographer is all about. The lights illuminating the bridges were covered with barber net, a mesh of black netting, several layers of which tamed the lights to my requirements. Adding phony stop signs, street signs, and flags—the type of 3M Scotchlite Hotel and Garage signs I described in Chapter 2, *"The Warriors"*—masked unwanted bright portions of the shots. Facing these frustrating problems and resolving them is part of what makes this work so enjoyable. The solutions usually come from the cinematographer, whose ingenuity and willingness to deviate from the norm, to improvise and use unorthodox remedies, are not described in many books. Nor are there such things as standard solutions, as there are no standard problems.

The major difference in the night photography, as we moved to Los Angeles and Wilmington, California, was that we could finally shed our Eddie Bauer clothes and no longer freeze all night, as we did in Chicago. The new film stock kept opening up new avenues. It offered many new possibilities and taught me whole new approaches, while at the same time it helped me to unlearn over thirty years of experience. Such little tricks as "liquid dimmer" saw more and more applications. The headlamps of motorcycles and police cars, and occasional neon signs on location, were routinely treated with "liquid dimmer." Shooting vast, underlit street scenes without lighting, even for rear projection plates, was no longer a traumatic experience. I learned to realize that if I can see it, I can shoot it. The new film stock had the sensitivity of the human eye, and in some cases, more.

One interesting aspect of location work, particularly at night, is the inconsistencies in atmosphere, such as fog, rain, snow, and brighter or darker nights, which at times can be pretty hard to deal with. I knew this was not going to be the case on the back lot, where we were going to photograph the bulk of the movie, both night and day.

When the company got back to Los Angeles, a big, political problem was waiting for me. Because of the large amount of work, mostly night shooting scheduled for the back lot, we were planning to "tarp in"a large portion of the Universal back lot: the area of New York Street, New York Avenue, and New York Alley, which were to be our main set. By covering this large area with tarpaulin, we were going to be able to shoot the night scenes during the day. This was a welcome prospect, as nobody really likes night work. Universal bought the idea of tarping in the set because of the big advantage of not paying night premiums for a long time period, and because of the longer work hours available during the day. They also thought that such a new facility would allow otherwise expensive night photography even for low-budget, episodic TV series to be done during the day. Universal Studios also hoped to lease out this unique new facility to other production companies. The structure of the tarp was being completed when I visited the back lot as soon as we got back to Los Angeles. It was enormously impressive. Tarping in sets to allow night photography during the day was not new in filmmaking. It was by this time a long-accepted practice, one I had used many times before, but never on this scale. Huge poles surrounded the set with massive "I" beams supporting the tarp. I've heard that eight acres of tarp were used to enclose the set, which was so big that we shot a high-speed automobile chase on it (see Figure 4.2).

As the tarping construction was still going on, the Universal production office sent me a memo inquiring if I could use about $30,000 worth of tarp, which Universal had on hand. I can never figure how or why some inane ideas originate within a large company, but once the ball starts rolling, one has to go through the motions until the ball is stopped. I was flabbergasted to find out that the tarps the Universal production office wanted me to use were relatively small, blue, construction tarps. Somebody in the production office certainly was not understanding the situation, or was out to gather brownie points—even if it cost me my job for refusing to use these blue tarps.

Instead of flatly refusing to use the tarps, even though I knew it would be impossible to do so, I set up a large-scale and expensive demonstration. The initiator of the idea of asking whether I could use these tarps had to approve the cost of this demonstration, particularly as I had invited a number of studio executives. I had one of the blue tarps set up in an empty sound stage, backed

Figure 4.2 The tarp tent over a corner of the Universal backlot set

up by a bank of 10,000-watt lights aimed at the backside of the tarp. At the appointed time as we all gathered at the stage, I made a show of taking a light reading of sunlight outside the stage and noted its level. We then went inside and I had the lights turned on. I pointed out that, although the light level of the powerful lamps was less than half that of sunlight, the bright, blue light coming through the tarp rendered them unusable. This was immediately obvious even to those who weren't well-versed in photographic techniques. Everybody agreed. The issue was put to bed and some long faces indicated a concern over how to justify the expense of this foolhardy, though from my perspective very successful, demonstration.

The night photography on this large set (which I believe was the world's largest enclosed set ever) turned out to be a very interesting and enjoyable experience for me. John Vallone, our production designer who also did *Southern Comfort*, did a sensational job, turning this set into what the opening credits of the movie refer to as "another time, another place." He built an elevated train structure down the middle of the long avenue, complete with a station, and the diner, an important part of the set, underneath the el. As in the case of building the police station on actual location in *First Blood*, this set also allowed me to tie in the exteriors as seen through the windows of the diner. It was a pleasure to create the street lighting, to have the ability to control the light output of street lamps, and to put these lamps to wherever I needed them.

The marquee of the theater, a major point of interest in the street, was another story. Though by now everyone who worked on this movie had heard of my low-light-level photography, only a few were fully aware of just how low the light levels I was working with were. Even though everybody had been notified, the art department and set decorators in their professional zeal (an admirable quality) and because of their extensive experience, did a fine job of decorating the marquee with neon lights, which looked great—except for the fact that they emitted so much light that I couldn't photograph it. Standard incandescent lights can always be dimmed by reducing the electricity, which powers the lights. The light output of gas vapor lights, on the other hand, where there is no glowing, metal filament, is much more difficult to adjust up or down. Fluorescent lights, for example, will flicker if the electricity is lower than the necessary level and go out as the electricity is lowered beyond that point. Neon lights can be dimmed by reducing the voltage to the lights, but only to a point, beyond which neons will also go out. I just about cleaned out all the dimmers from the Universal lighting department and very carefully reduced the light of these neons to a safe, manageable level. But even at this level the lights were still too bright, so far above the lighting of the rest of the street that I knew they would blow out and lose their color. Once again, "liquid dimmer" came to the rescue. Actually, instead of hairspray, which is what I have used for this trick in the past, here the neons were sprayed with a neutral-density lacquer that did not affect the colors. Like all neutral-density filters, however, it reduced the intensity of these lights to the desired levels. (See Color Plate VIII.)

It is interesting to mention that the pre-lighting crew, on orders from the studio's lighting department, was going to place 250 10K units on the rooftops in preparation for the shooting. This was standard studio practice, the rationale being to have more than one needs, so the company won't have to wait and stand down while the director of photography gets one or more lights he might be short of. But I didn't want 250 10,000 watt lights bathing this set, washing every bit of character, artistry, and reality out of it. It was very difficult to convince the electric department to install only 10 of these, and only in places where I wanted them. Even these veterans, who out of politeness would not disagree with me, found it hard to accept my reasoning that if this set were a real street, it would not have 250 10K units on rooftops.

Other techniques that I had acquired over the years, such as wetting down the streets, paid off again. The very first shot of the movie is a reflection of the colorful theater marquee in the wet pavement. It was the idea of my camera operator and good friend of many years, Bob Marta (see Figure 4.3). Because of the lower exposure levels, the puddles of water became bright, black mirrors replaying reflections—with much less contrast than was the case in *The Warriors*. "Reality" in the look of this film, as in most of my previous films, is quite obvious. Light coming from visible or obvious sources renders the scenes believable. When Tom Cody and his sister pull up to the curb and proceed to go into her building, the feel of the image is as though it were photographed on a real location with real lighting as it might exist at that location. In addition, we even put extras, passengers waiting for a train on the elevated station, in the background of the shot to round out the reality of the situation.

Photographing the interior of the bar where Cody meets the character McCoy, played by Amy Madigan, is another example of a new and different approach to photography. It was another opportunity I twisted out of the script. I shot in a real bar, but lit it

Figure 4.3 New York Street with crew on crane

exclusively with neon lights. This is another example of using an unusual light source, in this case neon, for motion picture photography. Well, that is not entirely accurate. There were two other non-neon lights used in the photography of the bar scene. One was a 40-watt, regular household bulb in the ceiling at the entrance to the bar, and the other was my little key-chain light, which provided the eye lights and fill lights in the close-ups. All other illumination came from neon lights I had made and brought to location to light this set with. If you look at and analyze this image, you will notice the nondescript neon shapes on the ceiling, directly over the actors. You will also note the many colorful neon lights all around the bar—generic beer signs, the usual cocktail glasses, and so on—which I moved at will as I needed more or less light in any individual shot.

Like the nondescript or visible but unidentifiable lights in the background of some shots in *The Warriors*, these neon lights also helped create interesting backgrounds, and added light as well as depth to the shots. I was no longer concerned with proper qualities of color. Though color can be scientifically defined, for my purposes, there are so many variables that affect color, not just in photography but in processing and reproduction, that I no longer concern myself with the "reality" of color. In this instance, as applied to this "rock-and-roll fable," the definition of color would not have made any difference anyhow. The true color of neon lights, like the true color of the grass or the sky, is not of major concern to audiences, unless it is blatantly bad or purposely altered from reality to achieve an effect. Contrary to my practices of the past, in *Streets of Fire* I no longer had to be guided by reality or by imitating nature. I could, and did, bend the images to my liking to produce unusual photography that is not often noted by audiences, but nevertheless has a subliminal influence that does help manipulate the audience's feelings and reactions to scenes.

Most of this film was photographed in an unusual manner. Shooting the day scenes, for example, was in some ways more unusual than the night photography and will have its own section later in this chapter.

The concert scenes represented a very interesting portion of the *Streets of Fire* photography. All five musical numbers were filmed at the Wiltern Theater in Los Angeles. This beautiful, old Art Deco theater at the intersection of Wilshire Boulevard and Western Avenue was about to undergo renovation, but Universal was able to get it for the shooting of the concert scenes before the renovation started. The numbers were staged and the concert lighting was done by Marc Brickman, a highly acclaimed and well-known lighting designer of top concerts. He did a wonderful job lighting the concert, to which I added the touches I needed for the photography. My immediate problem was the tremendous fluctuation of light, ranging from levels of no measurable intensity to 15,000 foot-candles, which almost equals sunlight. The cues for light changes were sudden and drastic, allowing no time for exposure adjustment. Though this concert was not a one-time event, I still had a monumental problem figuring out how I could ensure coming up with good images, as there was no single lens setting that could have successfully photographed the never-ending lighting variations of every section of the musical numbers. Even with the new fast film, I knew that good photography of sections where the light level did not register on the meter could only be hoped for, even when those sections were photographed with the widest lens openings possible. At the opposite end of this spectrum, when the lights were burning at their highest intensity, called for the smallest lens openings. I realized that photographing the concert could only be done properly if I shot every number twice, just to cover the low and high light level instances. But my concern for photographing the rest of the portions dictated that I photograph every number at least four, in some cases five, times.

The first time around the lens setting would be wide open, T:2.2 or T:2 where that setting was available, to accommodate the darkest portions of the lighting. The next time the same musical number was photographed, the T-stop was set at 4. I purposely ignored the T:2.8 stop, since even if this stop were called for as the proper exposure, I knew that being off one stop, one way or the other, would make very little difference. The third repetition of the song was at the lens setting of T:8, once again ignoring the intermediate stop of T:5.6. Likewise the fourth go around was at T:16, to photograph the very high light level portions, and once again ignoring the intermediate stop of T:11. In this manner, I hoped to have well-exposed, good photography of all segments of each musical number, though with lots of badly exposed footage in between the usable portions. The badly exposed parts were to be write-offs, discarded in editing. The problem of exposure was thus taken care of.

Because we photographed each number from beginning to end every time, the only way to accomplish full coverage was to use multiple cameras to ensure matching coverage, which was a very important consideration. I decided to use five cameras, one of which was a remotely controlled, overhead camera on a boom. The cuts of close-ups, group shots, special effects, and so on were carefully listed and grouped, with some shots left over to be individually rephotographed after the multiple camera coverage was completed.

Using these techniques, there were a couple of days during the photography of the musical numbers when I exposed 57,000 feet of film each day, of which roughly 55,000 feet were printed. I'm not mentioning this as some kind of a record to be proud of, or apologetic about, but as an interesting aspect of filmmaking, dictated by the circumstances and a solution to a problem. Incidentally, not including the very long TV mini-series *Shogun*, this was the movie I shot the most amount of film on.

The dailies, because of the large amount of film shot, could not be viewed in the usual manner. I would still be sitting in a screening room at Universal if I had to look at all that footage, camera after camera, with normal projection speed. Instead, two flatbed-editing tables were set up in a relatively small room, one with three, the other with two projection screens. I agonized about going to these dailies. I knew that most of the footage was going to be badly exposed write-off, as the lighting went from one extreme to the other. The idea of seeing all that badly exposed footage repeated five times was almost too much to come to terms with. Everyone who was to attend these dailies was forewarned to be prepared for miles of under- and overexposed bad footage, which was to be ignored.

But the dailies were a big surprise. At the first take of the five cameras, as a very overexposed, high light level shot came on and the screens went almost completely white, blown out, more than a few excited voices gasped: "Look at that," "Fantastic," "Incredible," and so on. And when the opposites appeared on the five screens, the badly underexposed shots at low light levels, particularly the takes with T-stops of 11 and 16, the reaction was the same. From the musicians to the studio executives, everyone in the small room loved these very unusual, strange shots, as the well exposed, ordinary shots of the musical numbers seemed to be largely ignored. Here was an extreme illustration of the "bad/good" photography theory. Not that the shots, which were over- or underexposed by six, perhaps as much as ten stops, were "good" photography by any standards, but that within the context of this film, they became the desirable choice. They were different, unusual, interesting, and they made the musical numbers and the visual aspects of the concert exciting. These shots would have been very difficult to design and deliberately plan, but they turned out to be the shots that dominate the musical numbers.

The rest of the photography of the movie fell in step with this new "look," which I referred to in Chapter 2 in connection with the sketchy, quick cuts of the Warrior gang members. I recognized the style then, used it more and more often following *The Warriors*, and in the case of *Streets of Fire* it became the dominating factor in the photography of the entire movie.

I no longer thought it was necessary to make the audience see every aspect of the image. What was important was to let the audience see the most important aspects of the image and let them put together the rest. Bright, color-key lights, or backlit steam, lots of silhouettes, and sketchy, low-key lighting became prevalent and the norm. Though not entirely new by this time, the photography of *Streets of Fire* has caused the film to be quoted often as one of the films that ushered in a new era, a look which is still much used today.

The photographic style of this film allowed me to redo shots I had done in other films in a new way. One such shot presented itself during the final concert sequence. Ellen Aim and Tom Cody are about to part for the last time, presumably forever. They embrace and kiss passionately in a dark corner of the wings. This kiss, as far as I was concerned, was not to be "just another kiss." I needed to enhance it, to point up its finality, its importance in the drama—I needed something to blast it off the screen. In *The Warriors,* the bright, stainless steel sides of the subway train reflecting the brilliant flashes of lights in the dark tunnel provided the visual, while the roar of the train completed the effect that enhanced the drama of the kiss in that film. Here, in *Streets of Fire,* I used bright, quick bursts of vividly colored lights to backlight or shatter the silhouettes of our two performers as the music in the background rises to a high pitch, underlining the drama.

I mentioned earlier that when the look of a film is imitated in television commercials, it is possibly the greatest testimonial a cinematographer can get. This was the case after *Streets of Fire* came out. In fact, I was called to do a series of Chevrolet commercials and was asked to shoot one that was specifically designed not only to have the look of *Streets of Fire,* but even to contain shots resembling footage from *Streets of Fire.* It was interesting that the agency that produced this commercial did not realize that I had, in fact, photographed *Streets of Fire.*

Now another war story, which might be of interest even though it has little to do with photography. What follows is second-hand information, which I picked up as it circulated on the set, but which I never bothered to verify since, beyond its value to amuse, I had no great interest in the story.

In the course of filming the musical numbers, we photographed a song titled "Streets of Fire." It is a well-known Bruce Springsteen number, which was also the name of one of his albums. Not until some time after we finished filming at the Wiltern Theater and the renovation crews had moved in, did we start hearing rumors that our movie, which had the right to use the title *Streets of Fire,* did not have rights to the song. Whoever made the deal with Springsteen might have neglected to clear the rights to the song, perhaps assuming that by buying the name "Streets of Fire," the rights to the song had also been acquired. Apparently this was not the case, and the song "Streets of Fire" could no longer be used in the movie. Having lost the finale song for the movie, a new song had to be composed. But creating the location for shooting the new song turned out to be a big problem. The Wiltern Theater was no longer available, and recreating its interior, according to the rumors, was going to cost $3 million. But we did end up building the interior of the Wiltern Theater.

According to the stories that filtered down, a deal was engineered between Universal and MTV. As I understand it, MTV was to pay for the set, and in return they were going to get a number of music videos assembled from footage of the film. This was interesting and probably true. The set was built at Universal, we did shoot the new song, "Tonight's the Night to Be Young," and the music videos turned out great.

There was a small bonus that grew out of this potential disaster. As long as we were shooting the new song, we used the opportunity to shoot a few additional cuts as well, which Walter thought were needed to round out some of the already edited sequences. One such shot was of Willem Dafoe, playing Raven, the feared leader of the motorcycle gang, entering the theater just before kidnapping Ellen Aim. We had an entrance door constructed (it didn't have to match anything) and backed it up with a nondescript piece of wall, and had the gang, surrounding its leader, push into the crowd in the auditorium. We didn't want to see the faces, until a certain point when the face of the gang leader slowly fades up into full exposure. The backlighting paid off in the heavy atmosphere we introduced in the concert shots, the face faded up, and the shot was in the can. It was a simple shot to make. I shot it in less than fifteen minutes, but I bring it up here because I've been asked many times about how the fade-up was accomplished.

When I discuss this with film students, many theories are advanced, some of which might have some validity. But the way I accomplished this effect was with the use of a device made for this purpose that was put in front of the front key light. This device has a series of horizontal metal slats in a frame, which, when closed, cut off all the light of the lamp, but as it's opened, allow the light of the unit to reach the subject. By placing diffusion between the light and the subject, the shadows of the slats become invisible. This is a technique I used many times for dimming lights up and down for color photography. Ordinary electric dimmers should not be used for color photography, because the color temperature of light changes as the voltage is raised or lowered. Whether one has this commercially made piece of equipment for these kinds of shots or not, the shot can be easily made by using an ordinary venetian blind in front of the light. It is important that the blind be completely opaque and not transmit any light when it's closed. Translucent, plastic blinds will not work for this purpose. Opening the venetian blind will produce the same effect as the one found in Willem Dafoe's shot in *Streets of Fire*.

One more war story, which might be of interest to some, again has to do with low light level photography. When we finally got into the studio to photograph one of our biggest sets, the interior of the motorcycle gang's clubhouse, *Entertainment Tonight* visited the shoot to do their usual coverage of an important film in progress. The problem was that their video cameras did not have the sensitivity of our new film stock, and they could not record anything until I had huge lights brought in, which, of course, totally washed out the modeling of my image.

It struck me then, that not too long before *Streets of Fire,* when I was working on such television series as *The Nurses,* I had shot at light levels of 400 foot-candles. On *Streets of Fire,* the average light level was ranging between 4 to 12 foot-candles. This was a huge difference that necessitated the use of new equipment, without which the photography would not have been possible. I have used the example of needing smaller lighting units, and now I have to mention an equally important item—an extremely sensitive light meter. In the past I would have five mechanical light meters calibrated before starting a shoot or going on location, fearing that one might be dropped or somehow jarred out of calibration. Nor could I rely on light meters that could not accurately measure the very small amounts of light I used shooting *Streets of Fire.* When I was shooting with the illumination of 400 foot-candles, taking a false reading of 200 foot-candles instead of 400 (the loss or addition of an immense amount of light) I would only have been off by one stop, a more or less forgivable mistake at such high light levels. But when one shoots with very low light levels, a mistake of 10 or 20 foot-candles can be disastrous. Today, electronic light meters are sensitive to tenths, even hundredths, of foot-candles. Of course, that degree of accuracy is not required for ordinary photography, nor could it really be applied. Yet the sensitivity of these new meters is a tremendous and very necessary part of today's low light level photography. At this point, let me pass on a thought that I have always considered important.

I never subscribed to the popular notion that a light meter was an "exposure" meter. I know, that is the name these instruments are known by, but I think it is a misnomer as far as the true functions of these instruments are concerned. The basic instrument, in one form or another, will convert light into electricity and express the value as a T-stop or f-stop, or as a unit of footcandles. But the exposure should really come from the person taking the reading. I'm sure you recall me saying how I opted for a certain exposure in connection with Rambo's close-up as he lit the match. Had I decided the lens stop by the read-out of the light meter, the correct exposure would have been the highest reading. In that case, I decided to set the lens below the highest reading, creating a slight overexposure at the brightest portion of the flare. In all cases, whether to accommodate a condition or to achieve a desired effect, the setting of the exposure must be determined by the photographer. Today's modern still cameras automatically set the exposure, an average, which in most instances will be to the liking of the majority of amateur picture takers. With these "smart cameras," everybody becomes an expert photographer, producing sharp pictures focused by the camera, and good color well exposed by the camera: "good" photography. It brings an incident to mind, which has nothing to do with *Streets of Fire*, but one which well illustrates my philosophy.

During the photography of *Shogun* in Japan, we all rushed out to buy the latest Canon camera, the A-1. At that time I was shooting the jail sequences in the mini-series, which were low-key, sketchily lit day and night scenes. I took a bunch of stills with my new camera on the set, exposed the same as the film's footage that was being photographed for the show. When the pictures came back, some of my friends, the producer, the writer of the show—all of whom bought the same camera and also took still shots of the jail sequence—were surprised to see that their pictures had come out much lighter than mine, completely losing the lighting schemes and the mood of the scene. As we all know, the answer lay in the exposure. In their case, the exposure was set by the camera; and in my case, it was set by the photographer, yours truly.

Back to *Streets of Fire*. The one thing even John Vallone's magic couldn't do was to put a real train running on the elevated structure over New York Street at the Universal back lot. I did the next best thing. I had a large drum constructed, not like the flimsy paper drum of *First Blood*, but a well put together metal contraption fabricated at the Universal metal shop. It was about twelve feet in diameter, about four feet high, and its side had a series of slots, eight inches wide each. It was equipped with a motor to turn it and had a very powerful light unit installed in its center. This drum was placed out of view of the cameras, on top of the elevated structure, and as it rotated, it projected a series of moving light spots on the walls, simulating the effect of light coming from the lit windows of a running train. It could be slowed down to a full stop, then started up again, simulating the arrival and departure of a train. An appropriate sound effect rounded out this illusion, which worked exceedingly well, though very little of it ended up in the finished film. That is why production people, who watch the money at studios, always question anything out of the ordinary, and always want to know if it is absolutely necessary, or if the effect could possibly be accomplished by another, less expensive way. They do have a point. And that brings me to another, very expensive proposition, which I had to fight out with some of the studio's production people: the photography of the daytime sequences in *Streets of Fire* on the Universal back lot.

But before I leave our large tent, which allowed us to photograph consistent night photography during the day, I must tell you about one more interesting aspect of working under the tarp.

The Universal back lot has an enormous wildlife population. Not the human kind we read about in pulp magazines, but real animals, such as raccoons, deer, foxes, coyotes, and birds of many species. When the tent went up and we turned on the lamps over New York Street, the raccoons, nocturnal animals that they are, I imagine, couldn't quite figure out why the night wouldn't end. Their homes were now shrouded in two nights, natural and manmade, that followed one another without any daylight in between. Deer, though not nocturnal, were also confused. And so were the birds. They found small openings in the tarp, flew out of night into instant daylight, caught a fly possibly, and flew back into instant night. Due to this confusion, perhaps, at times they all started to chirp excitedly, so loudly that we could not record sound.

Even us humans became confused. My days started at five in the morning, just as daylight was dawning. By the time I got to the lab at six, it would be light, though on most days the light would be diffused by the Los Angeles smog. When I finished at the lab and it was time to report to the set, it would be substantially daylight, which instantly changed to night as I walked into the black tarp-covered set. It was a weird feeling. It became worse when lunchtime arrived, and we walked out of the night of the tent into full daylight to sit down to a big catered lunch outside the tent, only to walk back into night forty-two minutes later. The rest of the day was spent in the night environment, and when the workday ended around seven-thirty or eight o'clock, we left the darkness of night for the last fading rays of daylight, outside the tarped-in area. Soon it was nighttime again. It was confusing.

But the work under the tarp continued, in spite of the mounting complaints from other companies shooting on the lot, as they found the enormous black block of the tent hard to frame out of their shots. Even Universal was beginning to lose faith in the value of the tent. On hot days, as the sun heated up the brass grommets at the tarp's edges, the plasticized tarp became soft and pliable, the grommets would tear out, and the tarp itself began to deteriorate. More and more repairs had to be made, all during the night, so as not to interfere with the shooting. Then the Santa Ana winds came. Gusts of these high winds would lift the top layer of the tent and slam it down with the force of a hurricane. Recording of sound was impossible, and photography came to a halt as sunlight poured through the rips in the tarp. It wasn't long before the winds loosened up portions of the overhead construction.

On one occasion, an "I" beam tore away from the huge wooden poles and hung precariously above the set. The shooting was halted, the set was evacuated, and executives from the black tower, as the executive offices of Universal Pictures are called at times, came to assess the damage. I remember them, clustered in a group, looking up at the loose "I" beam with baleful expressions, but not one of them would call the shoot, or give an order to roll back the tent and try to save it. Of course, if the process of rolling back the tent had started, it would have taken about two days to complete, with an additional two days needed to roll it out again. Four days of shooting would have been lost, or replaced by shooting in cover sets. The order to save the tent was not given. The rationale behind this, I suppose, was that if an order to halt production was given, the resulting loss would have had to be absorbed by Universal. If the winds wrecked the tent and we had to stand down, it would have become an insurance issue—or a lawsuit—and at least some of the company's losses would have been recovered. In the end the tent did become the subject of a lawsuit. But while the photography was going on, the tent was maintained, continually repaired by a crew, and that brings me to talk a bit about the day photography under the tarp. You read it correctly: the day scenes were also photographed under the tarp. Here is why, and how.

Throughout the shoot, up to this point, Walter and I agonized about the look of the day scenes. I recalled all the tests and the time it took to arrive at the determination of the night "look" of the film going almost down to the wire in Chicago. Now, the day schedule was drawing near and I still had no idea how I was going to handle it. What I did know was that neither Walter nor I wanted bright shots with sunlight and hard, deep, contrasty shadows. We reshot a number of scenes in *Southern Comfort* because the look of contrasty shots in the swamp looked bad and didn't fit in with the diffused photography, which was dictated by that film's story. Towards the end of that shoot, as spring brought more and more sunny days, we covered a large portion of the swamp with silk to be able to maintain the diffused look of *Southern Comfort*.

Besides the problem of contrast, I also had a major concern over trying to match the "musical fantasy" look of the night footage and somehow continue the style of the film into the day photography. New York Street, the main portion of our set with the elevated structure overhead, was an east-to-west street. At seven in the morning, just as the work would start, the sun would be shooting directly and almost horizontally into the street from the eastern end. By about eleven, it would be more or less overhead, moving steadily in a westerly direction. After the lunch break, the sun would come from the west, from the opposite direction of the morning light. I knew that by four in the afternoon, direct sunlight would be cut off by the hills at the western end of the street, forcing me to shoot with diffused ambient light for the rest of the day. This is exactly what happened on another film, *Newsies* (1991), which I shot on the same street some years later. On that film I faced these problems everyday and had to juggle the shooting order, breaking away from scenes in the middle of the shoot and going to half-finished scenes that had been started the day before and could be shot only under certain light conditions. Fortunately, this was not the case on *Streets of Fire*.

One morning I left the lab earlier than usual, arriving at New York Street about a half hour early. What greeted me was a miracle. It was a very smoggy, overcast morning and the tarp crew was still working. Here and there the tarp was rolled back, allowing the soft, overhead light of the morning to enter the tent and illuminate large sections of the street with a most beautiful, soft "north light," the favorite of great master painters for centuries. Portions of the street were bright, beautifully modeled in this unmistakable daylight, while other parts of the buildings and the El structure molded into semidarkness under the closed portions of the tarp. Here and there, the dark elevated structure was silhouetted against the buildings that were bathed in daylight, and where the elevated structure was lit, under one of the openings in the tarp, it was backed with darker, unlit buildings behind it. I couldn't believe my eyes. This was magic, a revelation that instantly erased all my concerns about what the day scenes of the film should look like. I immediately told the foreman of the tarp crew to stop working, leave everything as it was with the tarp rolled back, as I wanted Walter to see the street in this light. I called his office and within minutes, he rolled into the set on his bike, toothpick and all. He nodded his agreement.

Now that I had a solution, the problem was how to make the solution work. Waiting for smoggy mornings to shoot in was as far out of the question as discontinuing the photography if or when the smog lifted and allowed direct sunlight into the set. But I knew that one way or another, I was going to have to create this environment for the photography of the day scenes. The solution, at least in theory, wasn't difficult. All I had to do was open the tarp here and there, wherever I knew our action was going to take place, and install silk panels to fill the openings. The silk panels, as in the case of *Southern Comfort*, were going to diffuse the light, smoggy or sunny, and give me a uniform, soft daylight, though of different intensities, depending on the brightness of daylight above the tent. What remained was to get this plan implemented, which turned out to be harder than I thought.

First, as I understand it, the executive producer of the film, Larry Gordon, came up against some stiff opposition from the studio, and the task fell on Joel Silver, Larry's partner, to get to the right people in the tower for approval. The studio did a preliminary cost-analysis and came up with the figure of $13,000 for the silk, not including the fabrication or the installation of the panels. In spite of his enthusiasm and confidence, I believe Joel thought he was going to be turned down, and he dumped the silk problem in my lap. When I went to see the head of production at Universal, he bluntly pointed out what a marvelous thing the tent was. The way he put it, more or less, was that when I finished the night photography, I should have the tarp rolled back and continue working in the natural daylight. This was logical, and no different from the way day photography had been practiced on the lot ever since the first camera was planted on California soil. It was a fact that when the tarp was rolled back, I would have daylight. That is what studio executives expected for the photography of day scenes on the tarpless New York Street. Incidentally, this was the same executive who originated the idea of saving thousands of dollars if I would use the blue tarp. He was also one of the executives who wouldn't order the tarp to be rolled back as it was being torn to shreds by the wind. Now he was telling me to roll the tarp back and I would have plenty of daylight, end of story!

He was right, at least in the respect that I would have daylight, but I knew I would also have hard, contrasty shadows of the elevated structure and the changing direction of the light—or no sunlight at all on smoggy days. I tried to explain that while the main reason behind the silk panels was stylistic, it would also ensure continuity and uniformity between cuts. My reasoning had about as much effect as water on a duck's back. He was adamant, and as a desperate measure I decided to take one more shot. I told him that I'd be shortly sending out a memo to all concerned about the possibility of reshoots, due to weather. I must admit that this was a bit ridiculous in an industry that frowned upon standing down for any reason—particularly for good weather—in sunny California. Of course I didn't say I would be standing down; what I did say was that we might be spending time on reshoots to even up light conditions. Even I was surprised at the absurdity of this statement. Standing down for weather is a possibility, particularly when bad weather is a must when the story calls for bad or any specific weather, and the opposite is true.

This was definitely not the case with me, but memos in the film industry almost always spell trouble. A middle-level executive, such as the production manager I was talking with, in a permanent, relatively secure position at the studio, does not like memos circulating, pointing at him as the possible cause of a problem. At best, his higher-ups, all of whom might have to explain the contents of the memo to their superiors, would ask for explanations. Taking a stand in the film industry is not an everyday event. More often than not, taking a firm position is avoided, under the "let sleeping dogs lie" principle. I've had similar experiences, and most of the time I would have agreed that taking a strong position was not always the most reasonable course of action. But for me, at least, taking a stand worked in most cases. And it did in this case. I never sent the memo, nor do I know if I ever would have, but about a day later I received a memo from the production department stating that the silk panels were approved and would be installed, per my instructions, by the scheduled date of day photography. Now *I* was on the spot if the panels did not work as I had predicted, or for some reason caused loss of production time.

But they did work. If anything, they speeded up production and, in my opinion, resulted in a very interesting look, exactly as I had hoped. There is a short sequence in the film, a torrential downpour with lightning and thunder. It is the background for Ellen Aim and Tom Cody breaking up once again, then hugging and kissing as they make up in the rain to the accompaniment of lightning and thunder. Had I not had the tarp and the silk panels overhead, the rain in the brilliant California sunlight would have looked ridiculous, and the lightning would not have registered strongly enough in the bright daylight. The consistency of the day shots, taken under the silk from morning till noon to late afternoon, day after day after day, became the glue joining the shots and sequences uniformly together.

Streets of Fire is still often referred to as one of the films of that era that started a new look for feature films. This look is still very much in vogue and still evolving. New, improved emulsions covering all contingencies, newer lenses, new techniques, and now electronics, will continue the trend that *Streets of Fire*, among other films started.

And now, a Requiem for a Tarp. The big tent is no longer covering New York Street on the Universal back lot. We barely made it as the winds were ripping it to shreds, and by the time we moved into the studio to finish *Streets of Fire*, the tent was a patched up mess, silk panels and all. I've heard $3 million mentioned as the cost of putting up the tent, not including the silk panels. I suppose, wanting to recover some of this cost, Universal either instituted a suit against the manufacturer of the tarp, or refused to pay claiming that the tarp did not stand up. As I was interviewed by lawyers for both sides, I know that Universal claimed the tarp was of inferior quality, while the manufacturer of the tarp accused Universal of engineering and constructing the supporting structure badly, causing the tarp's failure. Universal's refusal to roll the tarp back in the high winds might also have been a claim by the manufacturers.

I have no idea how the suit was settled. I stayed away from it. But I do know that shortly after finishing the photography of *Streets of Fire*, and some lesser projects, the structure was taken down. A wonderful facility, which could have been a great boon to filmmaking, was gone.

In the late eighties, New York Street and its surrounding area on the Universal back lot burnt to the ground. When it was rebuilt, I once again found myself there shooting another film, called *Newsies*, and it was the first film shot on the new New York Street—minus the tent, but with all the headaches of constantly changing weather conditions for weeks and weeks.

The *Streets of Fire* experience would not have been complete without the traditional still photograph of the camera crew with Walter and me. It shows the neon-lit set behind a happy bunch of people, and it attests to a great experience (see Figure 4.4).

Figure 4.4 The traditional crew still with Walter and me

Q&A *Streets of Fire*

ANDREW QUICKE: At the beginning of the chapter you stated that the Mitchell Camera company only sold ten or eleven cameras per year. That hardly seems enough to make a living. Are you sure about that?

ANDREW LASZLO: As I understand it, the Mitchell company at that time had very large government contracts. They made missile tracking cameras or such and other military hardware in the photographic line. They also marketed two other models in the professional motion picture lines, the Mitchell NC and the Mitchell Standard cameras. They sold only ten or eleven BNCs per year. My first BNC was number 332, and my next camera, which I bought a year later, was number 342.

AQ: What kind of tarp blocks out all light? How high do the tarps have to be?

AL: The tarp has to be completely opaque. No light must pass through it. The height of the tarp is determined by the height of the set. In our case on the Universal back lot, the buildings were four- and five-story New York brownstone-type buildings. The tarp had to be sufficiently above these to allow photography up to and above the height of the buildings. In order to keep all daylight out a complete tent must be constructed over the entire set.

AQ: Should film students learn lighting rules, or come up with their own rules?

AL: I always suggest learning all the rules in order to be able to break them. There are lots of basic rules and techniques to learn, and, of course, it is important that one learns about equipment, what to use when and where, the limitations, electricity, filtration, supporting equipment, attachments, accessories, etc. Beyond that, knowledge of lighting, for example, will be acquired on the basis of practice, analyzing and imitating the work of others, and, of course, experimentation. At a certain point in this process, art will take over from technique, but one never gets to the end of the process of learning. I don't think there were too many days in my career when I didn't learn something.

AQ: You refer to the lights the studio lighting department wanted to install on the rooftops at the Universal back lot as 10K units. How strong are these units and what does the "K" mean?

AL: "K" means thousand. Ten K means that the light is rated at ten thousand watts. In the industry we just call them 10Ks or 5Ks, 2Ks, etc.

AQ: Why were you not concerned with the reality of color?

AL: As I mentioned, color can be defined, but for my purposes, in connection with the photography of *Streets of Fire*, the accuracy of color was not important. As with other elements of any film, accuracy is only important if inaccuracy is due to an obvious error or in a case when a particular effect is desired.

AQ: Define this a little further.

AL: Let's say, for an extreme example, that the color of grass in an ordinary shot is an unrealistic yellowish-green. This discoloration might be due to processing, film stock, the use of wrong filters, or some irregularity in the photographic process, but for lack of a replacement shot, the shot ends up in the movie. As the story dictates no obvious reason to have the grass this unusual color, the audience will consider it a mistake. Now let's say that the grass is a strong purple color, completely unrealistic, but because the nature of the story demands it, the unusual color will be accepted as an interesting effect.

AQ: You keep referring to "liquid dimmer," and sometimes you mention that it is hairspray. Is "liquid dimmer" a trade name?

AL: "Liquid dimmer" is an industry-coined, somewhat humorous name describing the function of reducing the light output of a source, or dimming it, but with liquid (often a hairspray) instead of the usual electric dimmer.

AQ: Can you explain why imitation of the photographic style of a film by television commercials is a great compliment?

AL: The making of television commercials is supposed to be a very creative field. All sorts of creative people are involved. Some of these creative people won't stop short of appropriating the successful work of someone else. In fact, in certain instances, when a proposed TV spot is presented to an advertising client of the agency, the agency puts together a sample commercial from footage of a film, the style of which they intend to imitate. In ad agency jargon, this sample commercial is referred to as a "Stealamatic," meaning that the footage was stolen from somebody else's work.

AQ: How long should someone apprentice to learn the craft of cinema? How long will it take, from grip to DP (director of photography)—5 years, 10 years?

AL: The length of apprenticing in today's world is entirely up to the individual. At one point, one must break from apprenticing and start doing. From there on it is up to the individual and, of course, the breaks. There is no set timeframe for this process. In a specific field, such as cinematography, the transition is very different today than the long-established union-specified time periods. According to union rules, you must qualify first for union membership. This can be simple, or very complicated. Once accepted, you have to work as a "loader, slate person" until someone is willing to hire you as a second assistant. Moving up from second to first assistant can take years. Once you are established in the category of first assistant, the union requires five years in that category before you can move up to operator. Another five years is required to move up to director of photography, provided that there is an offer of bona fide employment.

These were, and to some extent still are, the union-regulated time periods for advancement. In the nonunion world the rules are not as stringent; in fact, in most cases there are no rules at all. If someone is willing to hire you as a director of photography, perhaps a day after graduating from film school, that can happen. If such a person is talented enough and the work is good, he or she might be a director of photography from then on. In a way, I resent this practice and consider it to be very detrimental to the entire industry. As the world of film developed, practices, procedures, techniques, and hierarchies developed and evolved over a long period of time, all of which benefited the industry. Moving up the ladder too fast precludes the acquisition of experience, the opportunities for working with and learning from others, not only regarding one's own craft, but also peripheral issues such as set procedures, decorum, etc.

Incidentally, traditionally one does not advance from grip to DP. These are two different areas that in most aspects are unrelated to one another. I know several people who started out as electricians, became gaffers, and who are now DPs, but there is a strong connection between gaffing and photography.

AQ: How far is too far when trying to fool the audience?

AL: Though I make repeated references to "deception," meaning that some of the images are designed to make the audience believe that what they are looking at is the way things really are, one really never tries to "fool" the audience. Even "deception" is not a good way of putting it. In the instances where the situation is supposed to be real, deceiving or "fooling" the audience might center on creating a believable situation. When the objective is to sell fantasy or impossible situations, well, the deception goes a bit further. It's the same as magic. You know that what you are seeing is not possible, yet you can't dispute what's before your eyes. If it's well done, if the results entertain you, or give you food for thought, or are believable and don't call attention to themselves, the deception works. So, to answer your question, there is no limit as to "how far is too far." Let the story carry the deception, and let the deception help tell the story.

AQ: Talking about deception and fakery—fooling the audience, if you will—was Rambo's close-up while driving the Army truck at night real or was it faked, as the day close-ups were?

AL: You are very observant and I am extremely pleased that you could not tell. The night close-up was also fake, shot in the studio at the same time the day close-ups were shot. This shot might be a good example of good fakery; if the fakery is not detected, most people will accept it without analyzing it.

AQ: When you told the studio executive that you would be sending out a memo, were you trying to put pressure on him? Were you really intending to send out a memo, or were you lying?

AL: Looking back so far it is hard to say what exactly I had in mind. But I probably would have tried anything in my power to get the silk panels, so I don't think I was lying.

AQ: The shot in the film as Tom Cody's train is stopped by the fire set by the motorcycle gang, seems to ring a bell with a similar scene in *The Warriors*.

AL: You are very observant, indeed! The scene is very similar. Somehow an effective scene, which worked well in one of a director's films, can, and at times does find its way into another of the same director's films. In this case, there was an almost identical scene in *The Warriors*. In fact the engineer in the *Streets of Fire* scene was imported from the cast of *The Warriors*. She played the DJ in *The Warriors*.

AQ: What is a normal ratio for shooting a feature? 10:1, or 20:1? Is the expense of raw film as big an issue in commercial filmmaking as it is in student filmmaking?

AL: Any expense in film production is closely scrutinized to fit within the budget of a film. But there is also a saying, "Film is the cheapest part of production." This simply means that if you don't shoot it, you won't have it. Nobody encourages a flagrant disregard of costs, or a squandering of resources, but as in the case of shooting up

57,000 feet of film during several days of concert photography, everyone understood that it was the only way the coverage of the musical numbers could have been assured. In this respect, the two situations, feature and student productions, cannot be compared.

AQ: When the other guys bought the Canons, were they using the auto exposure while you were using manual exposure?

AL: Right on! That was exactly the case.

. . . and now, onto the next level of creating the image, *Innerspace.*

5

INNERSPACE

Innerspace is a science fiction comedy. Though science fiction may be photographed as a very low- or high-key presentation, the consensus in the industry seems to lean towards high-key presentation for comedy. This doesn't mean that every frame must be lit up like a Christmas tree, but most industry professionals, myself included, shy away from extremely dark photography for light comedy. These were some of my thoughts as *Innerspace* was offered to me in 1986.

As it would happen, three films were offered to me at the same time: *Lethal Weapon, The Witches of Eastwick,* and *Innerspace*. All of these films had their own attractions. *The Witches of Eastwick* was a very interesting script, had an all-star cast, and was produced by a friend, Neil Canton, whom I first met on *The Warriors. Lethal Weapon* was produced by Joel Silver, whom I worked with both on *The Warriors* and on *Streets of Fire.* But in the end it was going to be *Innerspace,* directed by Joe Dante of *Gremlins* fame. He and his producer, Mike Finnell, are two hard-working and talented filmmakers. The script by Jeffrey Boam was funny and very well written, with all sorts of opportunities for the cinematographer, which was one of the reasons behind my decision to go with *Innerspace.*

Basically, *Innerspace* was a story about miniaturization. From a military and scientific point of view, miniaturization is a most important new breakthrough (don't ask me why). According to the story, two separate groups are trying to perfect the process: the good guys, operating with little capital in a lab put together from NASA rejects, and the bad guys, working with unlimited money in a state-of-the-art-lab. But it is the good guys, naturally, who come up with the process. The final experiment—to miniaturize a human in a capsule and inject him into the bloodstream of a rabbit—goes off track as the lab is raided by the bad guys. In the ensuing confusion the miniaturized human ends up being injected into the behind of a nerdy hypochondriac supermarket clerk, Potter, played by Martin Short. The script I read was full of special effects, but Steven Spielberg, the executive producer of *Innerspace*, persuaded the studio, Warner Brothers, to add even more special effects to the film.

All the films I have described thus far have had some special effects, but not to the extent that *Innerspace* does, which is why I held off discussing this important aspect of filmmaking—special effects—until now.

There are a number of different types of special effects. When bullets rake the side of a building, it is achieved by special effects. The blowing up of the gas station in *First Blood* was a special effect, as were the fire, the shooting out of the transformers, the carnage at the police station, and the flimsy, rotating paper drum that helped to simulate the motion of a truck. The photography of the helicopter sitting on the giant lazy Susan was a special effect. When special items, such as what we called the "one-man submersible" in *Innerspace*, or the miniaturizer, are needed for a film, a lot of very talented people go to work to create them. In the case of *Innerspace*, ILM took up the bulk of the special effects requirements, and some of the special props and devices were constructed by one of the most talented mechanical special effects experts, Michael Wood. When *Innerspace* received its Oscar for special effects, Mike was somehow overlooked, perhaps because of the popular belief that all special effects were accomplished by Industrial Light & Magic (ILM), George Lucas' fantastic special effects establishment. But the truth is that lots of the film's special effects involved Mike's work, or were accomplished during the photography, in the camera. Creating special effects in the camera goes back to the earliest movies, such as *A Trip to the Moon* (1902), *The Great Train Robbery* (1903), and many others. At the time those films were made, and for some time to follow, there were no other processes available to filmmakers to create special effects. Rear projection, for instance, did not arrive on the scene till many years later. This is why Lillian Gish, as she once described it to me, floated on a real slab of ice on the Niagara river, not too far above the falls in the film *The Adventures of Dolly*.

Though *Innerspace* has very large blocks of ILM-created special effects, using blue screen, green screen, stop motion, miniatures, and so on, some of even those effects were combined with in-camera effects. The special effects that did not require ILM's magic and were to be done in the camera, were for me one of the main attractions to this project. All my life I've been a gadgeteer. I love tools, like to invent and make things, and have several U.S. Patents issued to my name. But most of all I like to repair things and figure out how to make broken-down machinery work. Figuring out how to make things work, or creating or inventing something that will do a special task (like the rotating drum for simulating an elevated train in *Streets of Fire*) is a very satisfying experience. Filmmaking is a constant process of making things work—or at least making them appear to work. When I first visited Mike Wood's shop, the one-man submersible was a most convincing object—a full-size, futuristic, one-man submarine, or space craft (see Color Plate IX). With Lieutenant Pendelton, played by Dennis Quaid, at the helm, it was going to be miniaturized to microscopic proportions. The miniaturization of the one-man submersible was going to be accomplished in an appropriate, very large device in the good guys' lab, the "miniaturizer," also created by Mike Wood and his crew. Filming the miniaturization process fell on me.

According to the story, the "scientific principles of miniaturization" dictated, as part of the process, that the capsule, with its pilot inside it, must be spun at a very high rate. At a certain RPM it disintegrates into its atoms, which are reassembled at microscopic size. Not being a scientist, I can't verify the accuracy of this process, but as a cinematographer and a mechanically inclined person, I knew that we would not be able to spin the submersible even at moderately low revolutions. It was on a turntable and was going to be spun by a powerful electric drive, but to make it appear to spin exceeding the speed of the fastest turbine and become almost transparent in the process—that was my job. In the end, this bit of in-camera special effect was accomplished in a much simpler manner than the description of the scene in the script would have suggested.

Making something appear to move slower, or faster, than normal is not a particularly difficult task in filmmaking. It is, in fact, one of the simplest in-camera special effects to accomplish. When the speed with which the film runs through the camera is increased, the motion of the image slows down in projection. Conversely, when the film travel in the camera is slowed down, the projected image speeds up. I have photographed with camera speeds of 3500 frames per second as a glass vase is shattered by sound waves, and with one frame every five seconds to simulate jet travel before there was any. Most standard cameras used in everyday filmmaking today will allow the cinematographer to increase the camera speed at least three times normal, or reduce it about the same amount. Every time either of these processes is required, an appropriate exposure adjustment must be made to compensate for the resulting faster or slower shutter speed. Once these adjustments are made, the camera is ready to roll and the shot is photographed. When more than three times faster or slower photography is required, special equipment is called for. For extreme slow motion, very-high-speed cameras are used; and in the case of extreme slow camera speeds, an intervalometer triggers the single-frame exposure rate of a standard camera.

I had an added complication in the case of photographing the miniaturization of the one-man submersible. To start with, the capsule stood still on its pad, then started to turn, and finally speeded up to the high revolutions I described above. I started my camera, showing the one-man submersible at a standstill, photographed with normal camera speed as the capsule started to turn and increase its speed to the limit of its mechanical capability. From here on it was my magic that speeded up the spinning of the capsule. Before the capsule reached its top mechanical RPM, I gradually reduced the film's travel speed in the camera to one frame per second. A device called aperture frame control made appropriate adjustments to the T-stops, and therefore to the exposure. In the final result, one sees the capsule speeding up without any noticeable change in picture quality, density, or color. The effect was similar to long time exposures with a still camera. When a time exposure is made, objects that move within the exposure will appear to be blurred and to some extent transparent, or even disappear completely. This property of still photography can be applied to film, and such results as showing a large section of street devoid of traffic or pedestrians, for example, are possible to produce with very slow film travel speed in the camera. I used this technique in other parts of *Innerspace*, and, of course, during the filming of other projects as well.

There are a number of different aperture frame control devices available today, one for just about any camera currently in use. In fact many of the new cameras have this capability built in. There are two very important factors that are necessary to create and accomplish this and most other in-camera special effects. First and foremost, the need for the effect must be established. When a solution for executing the desired effect is found, additional normally photographed shots will be needed to round out the illusion. I photographed the capsule from many angles prior to the actual effect. The sequence also contains shots of surrounding activity—anything that is part of the script-described action, plus some. Many shots show the capsule turning slowly, including shots photographed from inside the capsule, then cutting to the special effects shots as we see the capsule speed up and spin with extreme speed. Supporting shots for such a sequence are very important. I made mention of this fact in connection with the *Rambo* close-ups, when I talked about the shots photographed on actual location that gave us the flavor and reality of the situation.

All "poor man's process" shots should be generously interspersed with actual location shots, or whatever shots will round out and underline the reality of the sequence.

Certain techniques, which I have discussed in the preceding chapters, crop up time and again in this and in most films. In this movie, for example, look for a shot of Lidia, played by Meg Ryan, sitting on a bed as she talks on the telephone from her hotel room. It was photographed by the light of the night table lamp, treated with "liquid dimmer."

In another portion of the script, one of the shots called for the bad guys bringing Meg and Marty up to their laboratory in a freight elevator. The description of this shot in the script simply called for the actors to get out of the elevator, logically assuming that the elevator has just arrived at this floor. In reality, this shot could not have shown the elevator coming up and stopping as the mock-up elevator was built onto the studio floor, and the only parts of it that could move were the horizontal metal-grate doors. But I thought it would be a nice touch if we could add a bit of motion to this elevator, suggesting that in fact it did come up from below. Once again, the floor of the elevator was that of the studio. There was no way I, or anyone else, could have actually made this elevator move. But as you watch the movie, you might swear that the elevator is coming up and comes to a stop. Here is how this little, but very effective, deception was accomplished. I talked to the actors and asked them to do exactly as I was about to do, mimicking my actions in unison with me. I stood next to the camera with bent knees, my back straight and erect, appearing to be about a foot shorter than my normal height. As all the actors assumed the same position in the elevator, I slowly straightened my knees and grew about a foot. So did the actors, but that wasn't all. When my knees were perfectly straight, I continued my upward motion by getting on my toes for an extra couple of inches. As soon as I was on my toes, I dropped back on my heels. After rehearsing this several times, I rolled film and the shot was accomplished. But the effect was still not quite finished. In editing, an appropriate motor whine was added to the sound track, followed by a clang and cling as the motor whine stops—and the actors drop to their heels and the elevator appears to stop. This was an inexpensive bit of deception, which worked well. Complicated, expensive, and effective special effects are a great joy to work on, but nothing, as far as I'm concerned, is more gratifying than pulling a little rabbit, such as this elevator shot, out of nowhere.

For equally effective quick cuts of the capsule traveling throughout the body, we had some devices built, similar to those used in *The Great Train Robbery*. In that film the audience sees the western countryside speed by through the open doors of the Mail Car. It was a primitive, early example of an in-camera special effect. Though the film is not a polished movie by today's standard, the audiences loved it, crude special effects and all. In our case, a very similar, though well executed, effect shows parts of anatomy gliding by the capsule's windows, seen from inside and alongside the capsule. Large portions of the human body were created by ILM and were slowly cranked past the capsule, using the same primitive hand-cranked method of *The Great Train Robbery*. Pat Kehoe, the movie's first assistant director, who had a larger than average sense of humor, labeled these pieces "The Slab of Blab" and "The River of Liver" (see Figure 5.1).

There was another interesting special effect in *Innerspace* created by a light effect. At a specific moment in the miniaturization process, as the capsule and its pilot disintegrate and, near the end of the movie, as they are reenlarged to original proportions, there is a flash of light, similar to an atomic "whiteout." One way I could have achieved this would have been by slowly opening and closing the T-stop of the lens during the shot. Of course, to achieve the degree of the whiteout I envisioned, I would have had to start with photographing this sequence at a very high light level, perhaps T:16, and gradually opening the lens to its full opening. Using this method, the most I could have achieved would have been a six-stop overexposure, perhaps adding one extra stop by starting the shot with the shutter half closed and opening it simultaneously with the T-settings. Closing the shutter and resetting the lens to T:16 would have completed the effect by bringing the

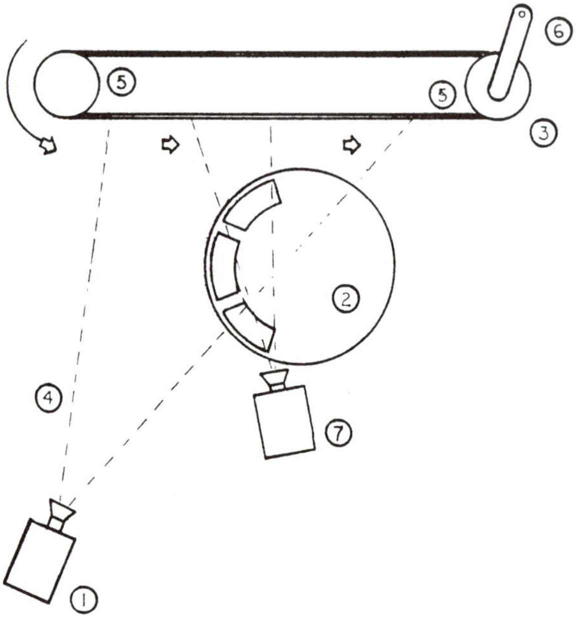

Figure 5.1 Overhead view of the "River of Liver": (1) Camera showing exterior of capsule with River of Liver; (2) capsule; (3) River of Liver; (4) #1 camera view; (5) vertical rollers for River of Liver; (6) River of Liver hand crank; (7) #2 camera showing capsule interior and view of the River of Liver through the capsule's window.

exposure back to normal after the whiteout. The resulting six-stop overexposure probably would have been enough to produce a near whiteout, but by accomplishing this with the shutter and the T-stop, all portions of the picture would have been uniformly affected. I wanted the foreground of the shot—the objects closest to the source of this whiteout—to be more burnt out than objects in the background.

Some time before *Innerspace*, I had an opportunity to work with a little-known item called a long-duration flashbulb. These flashbulbs are made, I believe, by Westinghouse, and have a two-and-a-half second high-intensity, consistently white burn. They are made for extreme high-speed photography, where for a couple of seconds extreme illumination is required, beyond the capability of standard motion picture lighting. I had seventy-five of these bulbs built into the set, out of camera view so only their effect was visible. Seeing the actual bulbs would have given away how the effect was accomplished. It was important to attribute the effect to one segment in the miniaturization or reenlargement process. To achieve the highest degree of whiteout, and to exaggerate the effect, the scene was purposely underlit, allowing me to shoot this shot with a wide-open lens setting.

I had one of the cinematography classes from the American Film Institute visit the set as I was making this shot, and one of the instructors, by then a retired Hollywood cinematographer, was amazed at the very low light level I used to shoot this scene. When the bulbs are set off, the image is blown out to an almost completely white screen. Two and a half seconds later, as the bulbs burn out, the shot becomes visible again, slowly returning to normal densities and exposure. We see this effect three times in the film: first at the good guys' lab as Lieutenant Pendelton and his one-man submersible is miniaturized; next at a much tamer, highly sophisticated miniaturization at the bad guys' lab; and finally, at the end of the movie, as the capsule and its pilot are reenlarged by the good guys.

Such in-camera special effects grew out of the necessity of showing unreal, nonexistent, and at times outlandish aspects of a story. For a very long time in the history of film production, in-camera special effects were the only kind of special effects available. Most cinematographers, myself included, as aficionados of film magic have been fascinated with being able to create illusions of almost anything that a story might call for.

As a young fellow, like so many of my contemporaries who were involved in photography, I experimented with trick photography, such as taking a picture of myself, or of a friend, playing chess with ourselves, appearing as both players in one photograph. These effects then—or later on as I experimented with trick photography in films long before *Innerspace*—could at times be dangerously self-serving. Even when they were interesting, they failed in some instances because audiences did not accept them without question or saw through the deception. An effect can only work if the audience does not see it, is not aware of it, or accepts it as a part of fantasy. Even today, after years of publicity, very few people spot the second story structure of Tara, the plantation house in *Gone with the Wind*, which is a painting. By the time *Gone with the Wind* was made, special effects had developed to a very high level, but nowhere near where they are today.

Very interesting new processes grew out of the increasing demands for better and more interesting filmmaking, in turn spawning even more in-camera special effects, most of which found their way into films such as *Innerspace*. One of the early in-camera special effects techniques was the Shuftan process. Eugene Shuftan, whom I had the privilege to meet in the early fifties, invented a process while he was a collaborator with the director Fritz Lang by which two images could be combined onto one strip of film during one exposure in the camera. It was a rather complicated and tedious process involving a mirror. A certain portion of the mirror's backing was scraped off the glass in the shape of an object, which was to be part of the composite image. This object, photographed through the clear glass portion of the mirror, became part of the shot, which was seen in the mirror. On one occasion, though not while I was shooting *Innerspace*, I combined a modified version of the Shuftan process with my use of Scotchlite. Let me deviate a bit from *Innerspace* to tell you about how I used this combined technique to photograph sinus pain.

As you read this, I'm sure your reaction must be similar or identical to mine when I was asked by an advertising executive if I could photograph sinus pain. Questions such as this, at times bordering on the inane, are not unusual in the advertising business. The idea came into focus as it was further explained that the major portion of the commercial would be a tight shot of a glass head that would be completely transparent with nothing inside. At a specific point in the commercial, the until-then invisible sinus cavities in the clear glass head materialize and start to glow and

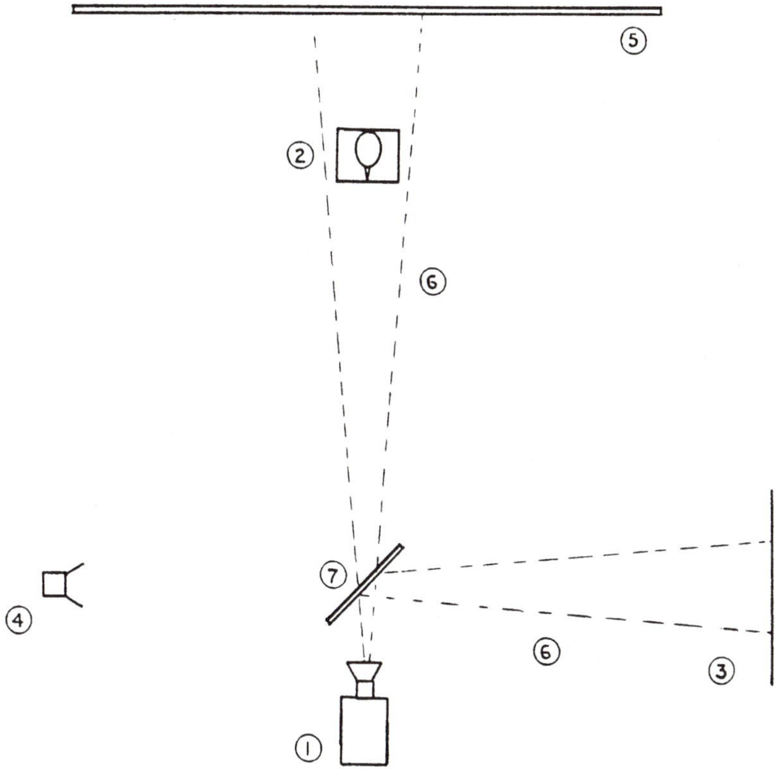

Figure 5.2 "Sinus Pain": (1) Camera; (2) glass head on stand; (3) board with Scotchlite sinus cavity shapes; (4) light for Scotchlite sinus cavity shapes; (5) black backing; (6) camera view; (7) one-way glass.

pulsate with an intense, vibrant red color. The commercial then cuts to the medication, and, as we cut back to the glass head, the glowing sinus cavities lose intensity and disappear. This effect could have been created with animation, but when I came up with the solution of how to photograph sinus pain, the commercial was made. Here is how I did it (see Figure 5.2).

The glass head was set up on a black-fabric-covered pedestal in front of a black backing, about six feet behind the head. The camera, equipped with a relatively long focal length lens, framed a shot of the head, almost filling the frame. When the head was appropriately and attractively lit, I placed a clear sheet of one-way glass in front of and very close to the front element of the lens, at a 45-degree angle to the optical axis of the lens. The glass head was visible through this pane of glass, while the glass panel itself, shaded from all lights, was not visible in the shot. Roughly ten feet from this glass panel—exactly the distance of the glass head from the lens—but at right angles to the optical axis, I placed a black card with shapes of the sinus areas cut out of 3M Scotchlite pasted on it at precise locations. When viewed through the camera, the Scotchlite shapes appeared to be in what would have been the proper locations of the sinus areas in the glass head. A small, very low wattage light unit was placed, perpendicular to the lens' optical axis, on the opposite side from the black card. This light, shooting through the glass was focused on the Scotchlite shapes on the black card and controlled with a standard electric dimmer, which could bring the light up to its full intensity or turn it off. The light had a bright red gel. When the dimmer was slowly turned up, the light came on with increased intensity, illuminating the Scotchlite shapes through the one-way glass. As these shapes became visible and brighter, their reflections were bounced back to the one-way glass panel, which directed their image into the lens. The red, glowing, pulsating sinus shapes appeared at exactly the right locations, floating inside the glass head. That is how the photography of sinus pain was accomplished.

There is no end to the unusual, even weird or impossible request that a cinematographer comes up against, particularly in TV commercial production. It would be impossible to describe the hundreds of requests and hundreds of commercials I have shot with in-camera special effects, which on first hearing seemed impossible. Shooting a hundred-foot-high razor blade with a pitchman on a levitating platform pointing out the blade's virtues was not as difficult as one request that was dumped into my lap during a meeting at one of New York's top advertising agencies. They wanted to shoot a sixty-second commercial advertising a new version of the original Volkswagen Bug. The entire commercial was to be one continuous shot of the car, finished off with the customary logos. The shot was to be a beautiful side view of the car, photographed preferably in dawn light, sitting in open country without a driver. At a specific point in the spot, the car starts to move, picking up speed till the background blurs and simultaneously the rear portion of the car starts to trail out like a comet. The agency wanted to know how this could be accomplished, if indeed it could be accomplished at all. I didn't know, but said I'd think about it.

I never could bypass a challenge, though in some instances I should have. Having been so challenged, by the time I arrived home I had an idea and couldn't wait to get to work in my basement workshop. I cut several seven-by-four-inch pieces of clear Plexiglas. The thickness of these pieces was $\frac{5}{16}$th of an inch. I milled a gentle curve on one of the side edges of all these pieces, but each with a different radius or arc. When the curved edges were buffed to crystal clearness, I modified a device called the Mitchell Variable Diffuser. This device, when installed in front of a camera lens, moved two graduated diffusion filters in opposite directions to increase the effect of the diffusion. I removed the diffusers and installed one of the curved prisms I had made, so that by turning the adjusting knob of the device, my curved prism could be smoothly slid in front of the lens. This was all I needed to begin experimentation to determine the usability of this device.

My house is situated with a long arc of the street in front of the house. I set up my camera near the center of this arc, so a car driving on the street would be more or less the same distance from the camera, going around this curve. My wife was going to drive our car and my son was poised to move the curved prism in front of the lens on my command. As the car drove on and the curved edge of the prism came into the frame, the rear portion of the car became elongated and, to my considerable surprise and amazement, just as the agency had visualized this effect, trailed out like the tail of a comet. I showed the film a few days later at the agency.

Though it was a crude demonstration, it proved the feasibility of shooting the spot. When the project was ready to go, I made several, much more carefully executed Plexiglas prisms, and we went to Seabring, Florida, to shoot the commercial at the old Seabring military airport which had a large, smoothly paved area for the car to drive on. I set up the camera and the car was positioned in a spot that gave us the most attractive background and light on the car. Operated by a hidden driver, the car was to drive in a perfect circle around the camera, maintaining the same distance. At a certain portion of the circle, the plastic prism was cranked in front of the lens, producing a comet-like trail on the car. To further enhance the effect, an aperture frame control device (similar to but not as sophisticated as the one I used in the miniaturization shots of the one-man submersible) speeded up the car, until the car itself became mostly transparent, horizontal lines.

Shooting this was not without problems. Following the car with a long focal length lens, so its relative position in the frame remained steady, was impossible for the entire sixty-second duration of the shot. This was particularly crucial for the sections that introduced and maintained the comet tail effect. If the car moved forward in the frame as this effect came on, the effect slid off the car and would come back as the camera caught up with the car. Because of this, the commercial ended up being presented in edited sections and, though it worked very well, the impact of the special effect was not as impressive as it would have been if the shot could have been made in one, continuous take.

Today, the sinus pain, the hundred-foot razor blade, the comet tail, the atomic whiteout, and so many other effects, can all be easily achieved with state-of-the-art electronic effects and computer-generated, computer-manipulated and composited imaging in postproduction. But my purpose in talking about in-camera special effects is that they are still around and work as well as ever, when money is a consideration or in any instance where in-camera special effects can produce the desired results. Since these considerations are usually the case with most student, beginner, or low-budget film productions, in-camera special effects can offer exciting solutions even to some very complicated problems. And that is the purpose of this discussion. The examples I cited—making an elevator, which was immovable, appear to come up and stop in the shot; seeing the insides of the human body float by the capsule; spinning the capsule to the point of disintegration—are but a few examples of in-camera special effects. Achieving these and other effects was among the most gratifying experiences in my many years of filmmaking.

But the main thrust of this chapter is to demonstrate a very special in-camera special effect—forced perspective photography. I will describe several examples of forced perspective photography, examining and explaining it in detail. But before I proceed, I'd like to comment on the ordinary photography comprising the bulk of *Innerspace.*

Let me start by saying that, as far as I am concerned, whatever the genre of any film, there really isn't such a thing as "ordinary" photography. A comedy may not have very dark, dramatic photography, but that does not mean that the photography should be "ordinary" nor be interesting or expressive. Photography, regardless of the genre, is a major element of the storytelling aspect of film, and as such it should never let up in its goal of affecting, influencing, and impressing audiences. There are many photographic techniques that can add elements of drama, tragedy, and humor, and, in all cases of film presentation, underline and emphasize the points of the story. Let me use the portrayal of the interior of the one-man submersible as an example.

I learned a long time before doing *Innerspace* that a set or location that keeps coming up in connection with a presentation can quickly become boring. The nurse's station, the emergency room, or a standard hospital room in the television series *The Nurses,* or the police station and the Lieutenant's office in the series *Naked City,* would quickly become deadly if nothing is done photographically to make them ever so slightly different from the last time we saw it. The interior of the tiny one-man submersible is an extreme example. I knew from my first reading of the script that as we would keep cutting back to Lieutenant Pendelton in the submersible, the audience would become familiar with every detail of capsule, which, cut after cut after cut, would become uninteresting and boring. That is why I decided to make every shot a little—or in some cases drastically—different. In some shots, Lieutenant Pendelton is fully lit, his facial features clearly visible; in others he is totally underlit or in-between. In short, he and the capsule interior are presented in never-ending variations of lighting schemes. In most cases, the bulk of the lighting is provided by the little goose-neck lamps, designed and built into the capsule as part of its high-tech equipment. Because of these continuous variations, the capsule interior does not become boring and extends a little suspense and interest to each of the shots.

In one shot, Lieutenant Pendelton's face is lit exclusively by the light of a computer monitor in the capsule. The image on the monitor is that of his ex-girlfriend as seen through Potter's eyes. After the miniaturized submersible is injected into the supermarket clerk's bloodstream, Lieutenant Pendelton hooks onto Potter's optic nerve and is able to see whatever Potter looks at, as well as hear everything Potter hears through Potter's ears. In order to photograph the images that Lieutenant Pendelton sees, we attached a small video camera to a motorcycle helmet. The helmet was worn by my camera operator and son, Jeff Laszlo, who watched Marty Short's performance, and, wearing the camera, repeated Marty's actions as the black and white image of the video camera was recorded and later played back on the video monitor in the capsule as the image that Lieutenant Pendelton sees (see Figure 5.3).

The capsule interior is an example of how the "ordinary" photography of a movie, even a comedy, should not be overlooked or dismissed regardless of the genre, for without good images on the screen the story could not be told effectively. With expressive, interesting imagery, the story is enhanced and the enjoyment of the audience can be increased.

Many aspects of this film had a certain, not terribly obvious, stylistic stamp. For instance, every time the color of the image has a bluish overtone, the audience receives a subliminal message that we are in the bad guys' domain, particularly in their lab. The rest of the film, depending on the nature and demands of a particular scene, was treated with varying photographic techniques

Figure 5.3 Operating cameraman Jeff Laszlo with helmet-mounted video camera

that I thought were most appropriate and helped to underscore the situation.

Certain aspects of film production do not change because of the genre. Such an aspect, as I have pointed out in previous chapters, is testing. Constant testing of possible solutions to achieve an effect, a "look," is an important aspect of preparation in all cases. As for *Streets of Fire*, I placed a big emphasis on testing a new emulsion. As I was about to start preproduction on *Innerspace*, yet another new negative stock was being tested by Kodak. It was 5297, the first high-speed daylight negative stock, which also promised fine grain and good color reproduction. It was rated at ASA 250, the same as my all-time favorite emulsion: the 5293 I used for the photography of *Streets of Fire*. Though I didn't think I would need anything for *Innerspace* beyond what was already available for day photography, I was still anxious to test the new film stock as a matter of curiosity. Kodak's Hollywood representative at the time, Bob Rowe, by then a friend for many years, gave me a couple of rolls of this new emulsion to experiment with. I received the cans with the usual handwritten labels, just as the camera gear for the production was about to be tested. It was a new camera, an Arriflex that my son and camera operator Jeff and I owned jointly. We had used it on one other film, which I had shot and my son had operated, in New York and Mexico. I knew the camera was in fine shape, but as I pointed out in previous chapters, there is never such a thing as too much testing and preparation.

As part of these tests, I decided to shoot some shots with the new 5297 emulsion in the lobby of the Clairmont Camera Company. It was a fair-sized lobby with a floor-to-ceiling clear glass entrance door showing a very large portion of the hot sunny California exterior, which, I recall, had a light value of T:22 plus. The interior was relatively dark. Most of it was covered with dark brown and burgundy ceramic tile, and there were several areas of tropical plant arrangements. The lobby had a large chandelier with regular, low-wattage incandescent bulbs with a color temperature in the red end of the spectrum. The camera was at the far end of this hallway, shooting towards the entrance. Once again, as the exposure in various sections of the shot ranged from the very underexposed to the extremely overexposed, I decided to run a full bracket of tests through every setting on some of the lenses. Normally, when shooting for a film under similar conditions, the entrance doors would have been treated by adding neutral gels or netting outside the door to tame the drastic difference between exterior and interior light levels. The interior, depending on the action called for, might also have been supplemented with additional lighting to raise the level of illumination and further balance the difference between the exterior and the interior.

The test results on the new emulsion were surprising, to say the least. The dramatic and extreme difference between exterior and interior light levels was brought into acceptable range without supplementary lighting or any treatment to reduce the high light level outside the building. For the first time, I shot with a new daylight balanced negative stock that allowed me to get away with a condition that in the past would have been difficult, even prohibitive.

The photography of *Innerspace* was scheduled to start within days, and the first portion of the schedule called for the photography of scenes that the new emulsion would have been ideal for. But the new emulsion wasn't commercially available yet. It was scheduled to become available about a month and a half later, but by that time I would have finished the photography of the scenes for which I would have liked to use this new emulsion. Bob Rowe from Kodak came to the rescue. He contacted every cinematographer he gave test rolls to and borrowed them back. He would come to my office on the Warner Brothers lot in Burbank almost daily, carrying an armful of hand-labeled cans. By the first day of shooting, I had enough of this wonderful new emulsion to make do with until the new stock became available. The new emulsion worked well for *Innerspace* and became a part of my arsenal in the photography of a number of other films.

And now, as I promised, let me start tackling the main interest of this chapter—forced perspective photography. Forced perspective relates to the relative size of something as it is compared to the known size of something else. Films such as *Darby O'Gill and the Little People* (1959) photographed actors against oversized backgrounds in huge sets where enormous beds, chairs, and other props made the actors seem very small. Likewise, *Fantastic Voyage* (1966) (which, incidentally, was photographed by my namesake, the well-known, Academy Award-winning cinematographer Ernest Laszlo) "miniaturized" a group of scientists and "injected" them into the bloodstream of a human. The special effects of *The Incredible Shrinking Man* (1957) also made the cast of the film appear very small as compared to large sets and props, such as a pair of gigantic scissors and a telephone-pole-sized pencil.

Innerspace was to follow the same techniques. That is how two of the film's bad guys, Kevin McCarthy and Fiona Lewis, after they are reduced to 50 percent of their normal size, appear to be half size in the film. There are three major examples of forced perspective photography in the film. First, two half-sized people in the backseat of a car fight with two normal-sized people in the front seat; this was by far the most complicated and difficult sequence to accomplish. Second, the half-sized people make a telephone call from a phone booth by San Francisco Bay, which was moderately complicated. The third, least complicated effect was to see these two cast members, reduced to half their size, in a suitcase. I'll start with that one.

How and why these two heavies were reduced to half their normal size for the purpose of this illustration is not important. Those who have seen the movie will know, and those who haven't probably will after reading this. At this point in the story, the two actors are half their normal size. They are in a suitcase, which is placed into the trunk of a limo. Once the description and the purpose of the shot, as defined in the script, was understood, this was a relatively simple effect to accomplish. The elements of such a shot are listed, the components are fabricated, and when everything that is needed is in place, the shot is photographed. Here is how the sequence proceeds. The Cowboy, played by Robert Picardo, one of the bad guys now dressed as the limousine driver, is approaching the limo just after the wedding scene. He is carrying a normal-sized suitcase. He opens the limo's trunk, lifts the suitcase in, and opens it. In the suitcase, somewhat obscured by double-sized feminine items of clothing, are the two half-shrunk bad guys. After the exchange of a few lines of dialogue, the Cowboy closes the suitcase and the trunk. We cut to the original exterior wide shot of the real car and the Cowboy.

First and foremost, we had to have a suitcase, twice normal size, identical in every detail to the real normal-sized suitcase the Cowboy places in the trunk and large enough for two full-sized people to curl into. (See Color Plate X.) The rest of the suitcase was filled with twice-normal-sized articles of clothing. This suitcase was then placed into a twice-normal-sized car trunk with the lid open. All of the details inside the trunk were recreated at twice the normal size, including two additional suitcases, a fire extinguisher, and other items that belong in the trunk. A very important element was the twice-normal-sized replica of the two hands and arms of the Cowboy, which was attached to the suitcase lid. So, as the lid closes, it appears as if the Cowboy's arms and hands have closed it. Additional peripheral shots rounded out the sequence and provided the detail, which made the scene believable within the context of the story.

The telephone scene was accomplished following the same technique. We needed the elements that established the relative size of the actors. The cement balustrade at the edge of the San Francisco Bay was replaced by one of twice normal size. The telephone booth adjoining this balustrade was also twice the normal size, about twenty-two feet high, with all its features and appointments—the phone, phone book, door—identical to real objects, but all twice the normal size (see Figures 5.4 and 5.5). The benches (see Figure 5.6) facing out to the bay were also twice normal size and were visible in the left portion of the shot. The bucket, fishing rod, and tackle box next to the phone booth were all twice normal size. Alcatraz Island in the distance was of course full size, but because of the distance its size was not relevant and did not affect the shot. Neither did the size of boats out in the bay. But we had to keep seagulls away from the set, as any of them would have looked the size of sparrows in the vicinity of the gigantic phone booth.

The cameras were placed on a platform, with the lenses roughly eleven feet high (that's twice the normal average eye height) roughly level with Kevin McCarthy's eye height as he is standing on Fiona's shoulders and talks on the oversized phone. The relative size of actors was thus established, but to round out the deception we needed additional references. One of these was a fisherman standing at the balustrade (camera right of the phone booth) looking into and reacting to the half-sized man standing on the shoulders of a half-size woman and making a telephone call. As the shot is made, this man could not have been standing next to the phone booth; he would have appeared to be half normal size, like the people in the booth. In order to have him appear normal in size, we had to move the normal-sized cement balustrade in front of him, and move it, as well as the fisherman, back towards the

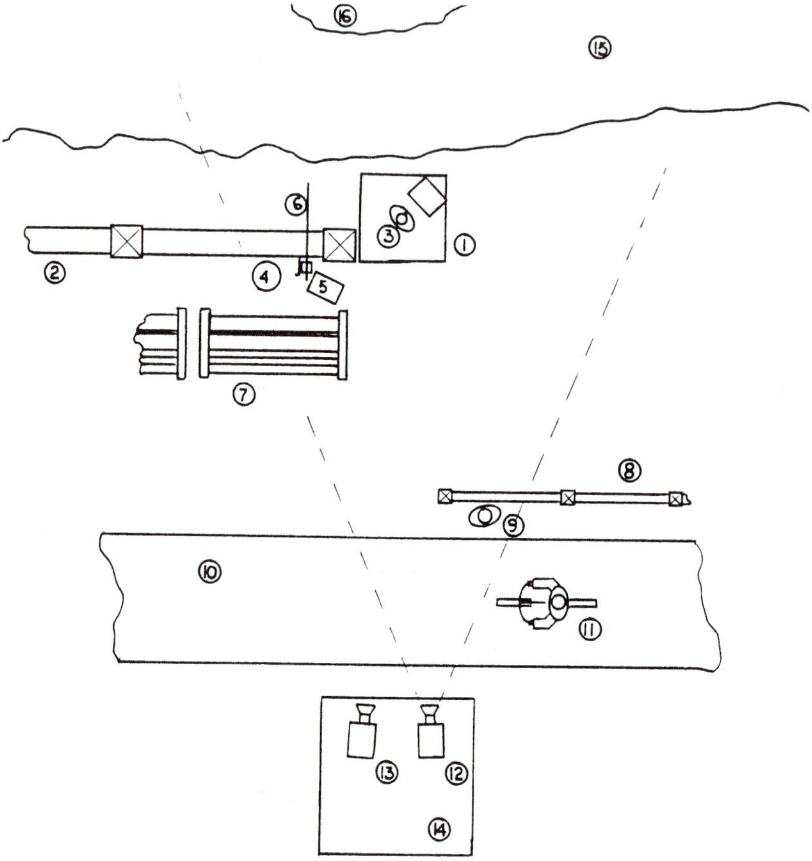

Figure 5.4 Phone booth floor plan: (1) oversized phone booth, (2) oversized balustrade, (3) actors in phone booth, (4) oversized bucket, (5) oversized tackle box, (6) oversized fishing rod, (7) oversized benches, (8) normal-sized balustrade, (9) fisherman, (10) elevated roadway, (11) bicyclist on elevated roadway, (12) tied off #1 camera, (13) close-up camera, (14) camera platform, (15) San Francisco Bay, (16) Alcatraz Island.

Figure 5.5 The phone booth being readied for the shot. Author at left of group.

camera to a point where he and the balustrade in front appeared to be normal size compared to everything else in the shot. Looking sharply to his left, the fisherman in the shot appears to be looking into the phone booth (see Color Plate XI). Because the camera was elevated, he and the balustrade in front of him had to be elevated proportionately.

One additional element, a bicyclist crossing close in front of the camera, was added to this deception. A roadway had to be built for him to make his height appear correct in the camera. The camera had to be locked off, as any camera movement, even the slightest left or right, would have replaced the position of the lens to which all elements of the shot were positioned. A right-to-left pan would have immediately given away that the telephone booth was not attached to the balustrade to the right of it. In fact, though it is hardly visible, we painted a shadow of this balustrade

Figure 5.6 The author taking a few seconds rest on a giant bench

where the shadow would have been if it were in fact next to the phone booth. The deception works well in the film.

Unlike the primitive, oversized, possibly out-of-scale props of *The Incredible Shrinking Man*, careful sizing of all props in the case of the phone booth sequence, or in the trunk scene, made these scenes completely realistic within the context of the story. But whatever effects are in films, audiences will never fully believe them outside the story line. No deception seen on the screen is completely believable if the audience knows that such an effect in reality would not be possible. Of course, in the case of a science fiction film or a good comedy, audiences will make allowances or get so involved in the story and the action that at times even the most outlandish deception will work. That was the case in the next example of forced perspective: the fight between half-sized and full-sized people in the car.

The script clearly described the sequence and the action within the story. This particular bit of action involved the two bad guys, having been shrunk to half their normal size, having a fight with two normal-sized good guys. The two bad guys, played by Kevin McCarthy and Fiona Lewis, are in the backseat of a car as Martin Short drives with Meg Ryan in the front passenger seat. Forced perspective was clearly the technique to accomplish this very funny and, I might add, effective bit of special effects deception. All the elements of the sequence, the props and the surroundings, once again had to be constructed, in some cases double and in some cases half their normal size. A large number of people went to work—Mike Wood and his crew; the ILM people; Jim Spencer, the production designer of *Innerspace*; and many others—and so did I. The combined talents resulted in one of the most hilarious sequences of the movie.

The first item this deception needed was the black Volvo sedan, which was cut in half. The front section was retained for the normal-size actors, but the backseat and the entire rear portion of the car had to be reconstructed to twice normal-size. Every aspect of the original was recreated to the minutest detail. The normal-size front section and the twice-normal rear section of the Volvo were mounted on a platform, which was roughly forty feet long and ten feet wide. The rear section sat on the floor of this huge platform, while the front half had to be elevated to a height that when seen from the camera's vantage point appeared to join the rear section of the car (see Figure 5.7). The camera's vantage point for the master shot of this sequence was from the front, looking through the windshield at the two good guys in the front, with the back seat and the half-size bad guys some twelve feet behind the front seat in the back portion of the car. From this

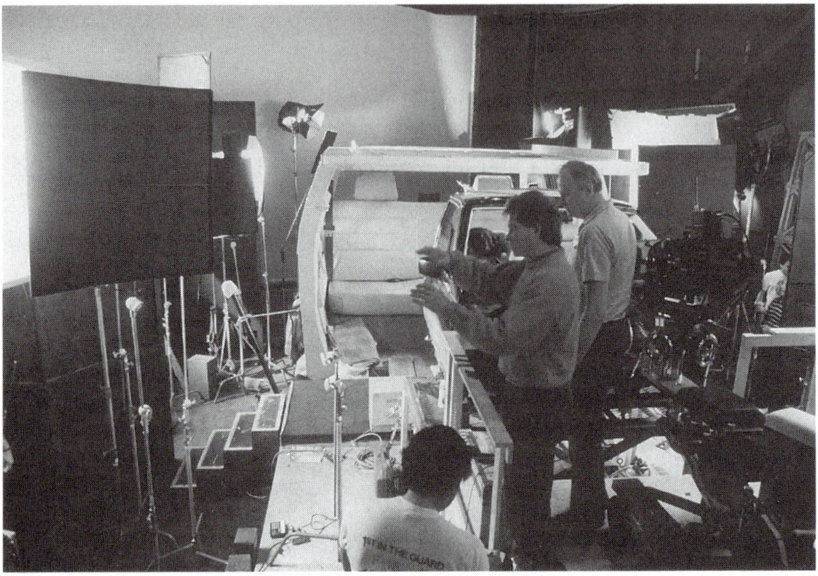

Figure 5.7 Volvo components on platform with operating cameraman Jeff Laszlo and Dennis Muren, ILM special effects supervisor.

vantage point, the two halves appeared to be one normal size car, except for the two bad guys in the backseat who now appeared to be half their normal size. The two car halves were bolted to the platform, which held the sections firmly in place and also anchored the camera solidly in its proper position. The platform was supported by a series of hydraulic controls that could move and rock it in a manner simulating the motions of a car driving at high speeds and making the dangerous hairpin turns, just as we see our real stunt car driving through the steep, picturesque San Francisco streets. This set-up was to be the most important basic element of this bit of deception (see Figure 5.8).

It was at this early stage that the first danger flag went up. It became obvious to me that it was going to be the execution, not the preparation, of this in-camera special effect that was going to cause problems. I had no idea just how difficult some of the new problems, caused by the solutions of the old problems, were going

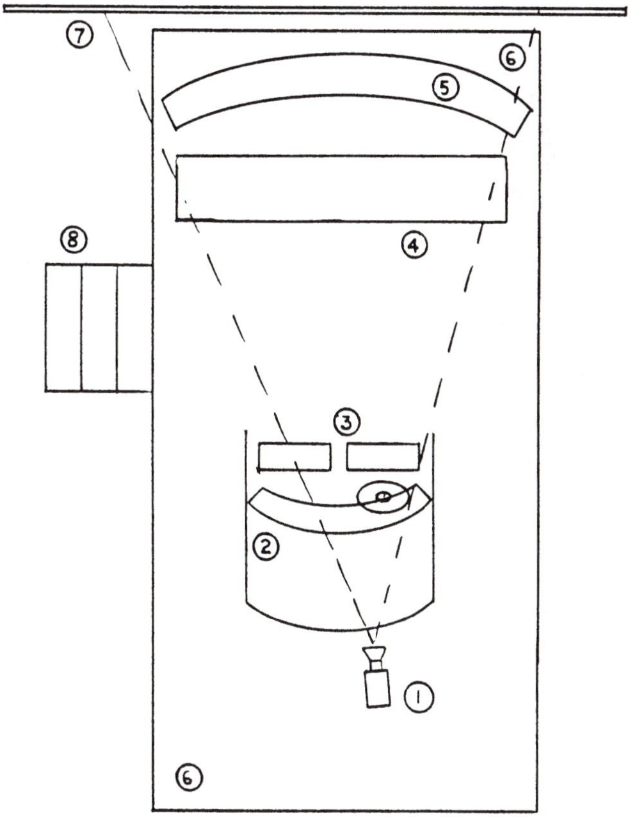

Figure 5.8 Volvo floor plan: (1) camera, (2) normal-size front half of Volvo, (3) normal-size front seats, (4) oversized backseat, (5) oversized rear window, (6) hydraulically operated platform, (7) rear-projection screen, (8) steps.

to be. For example, in order to keep both the front seat and back-seat passengers in acceptable focus, I would have to work with higher than normal light levels to achieve the necessary depth of field. If this action were taking place in a real car, the four- or five-foot distance between the front and rear sections could easily have been photographed with relatively low light levels. In this case, the distance of some twelve feet between the seats required a high

Figure 5.9 The author and camera operator Jeff Laszlo, demonstrating the lack of depth of field in the mock-up Volvo with oversized back seat.

light level to effectively carry this unusual depth of field (see Figure 5.9). As this set-up was erected in a soundstage, increasing the light to a level needed to produce this depth of field was not particularly difficult. All I had to do was use bigger, more powerful lighting units, raising the exposure to just about any level I wanted to.

But I had a limit, which was dictated by the fact that the image of the San Francisco streets visible through the car's rear window was going to be provided by rear projection. The projector could not produce images bright enough to surpass the light level I needed for the car's interior in order to carry the depth. Normally, if one was to photograph this sort of action on actual location, in this case the San Francisco streets, the interior light level of the car would be at least a stop, a stop and a half, and in some cases more, below the light levels of the street. I knew that I could live with a light level of T:5.6, which meant that the projected image on the rear projection screen was to be at least T:8, preferably T:11. No rear projection equipment at that time was capable of providing that high a light level. So now, as the technique for accomplishing this effect had been solved, its execution had become a major stumbling block.

To help you better understand the problem, let me just mention a few of the factors that for years regulated the technique of "process," or rear projection, photography. The number one limiting factor was always the amount of light the projector could generate. The next factor was the light-transmission ability of the projector's lens, followed by the size of the image to be projected, which at least partially determined the distance between the screen and the projector. A larger image required a longer distance, and the longer distance resulted in a darker image. In our case, because of the extra-large size of the rear portion of the car, the projection screen also had to be unusually large. To fill this oversized screen with the projected image, the projector had to be moved further than usual from the screen. In fact, this distance was so long that a portion of the studio wall had to be opened up and an addition, housing the projector at the proper distance from the screen, had to be built onto the studio. In turn, this extra-long distance diminished the light output of the projector to the point where it was hopelessly below the level needed for acceptable results. The projector's light apparatus had to be completely rebuilt to use much heavier carbons to be burnt at greatly increased amperage. The "plates," as the projected film is referred to, were also printed lighter, so as to help me get a brighter, higher light level background.

Let me take a couple of minutes and talk a bit about these background "plates." They are called "plates" because when this technique was first introduced, glass slides (or plates) were used, projecting a still image as a background to a scene. The name "plate" carried over to motion picture film that provided a moving background. When process, rear projection photography is prepared, appropriate images must be photographed that when projected behind the action, will provide the proper backgrounds. It is important that these background plates be photographed at the location where the action and the location portions of the sequence are photographed. In other words, the studio photography must match the scenery and the quality of the conditions of the location photography. If it was raining during the portions photographed on location, the plates must also be photographed in the rain. In most cases, particularly at locations where seasonal changes are a possibility, it is very important to photograph the plates as soon after the location portions are photographed as possible. Even a slightly cloudy day during the plate photography can present big problems if the original location photography was done under bright, sunny conditions. Additionally, making all the plates, or as many as possible, at the same time is very important. If, for example, a car travels twenty blocks, the plates needed to provide backgrounds for all the angles of that travel should be photographed at the same time. These plates must be longer than needed for the exact distance of travel, allowing for a run-up and a run-out, so a performance should not have to be cut before the scene is played out because the plate was too short and ran out of the projector. The plates should be made in one pass so the conditions will match between plates.

The technique of making plates is relatively simple. A specially designed and outfitted "camera car," also called an "insert car," is used because of its special suspension and smooth travel. One camera is mounted on the back of the insert car, looking straight backwards at a height matching the height of the studio camera as it will be used during the process photography. All cameras should be mounted at this height onto the insert car. The rear-looking camera is generally designated as the "twelve o'clock" camera, producing the "twelve o'clock" plate. A second camera mounted on the front of the insert car, looking straight forward, is designated as the "six o'clock" camera. Two additional cameras mounted on the sides of the insert car, looking out at right angles to the sides, are designated the "three o'clock" and the "nine o'clock" cameras. These are the most necessary, basic angles, producing the most often used backgrounds for rear projection photography of a moving car.

When the plate cameras are set, a pass is filmed, driving the same route the subject car drove during location photography, under the same conditions, with the same speed, at the same time of the day, and with, it is hoped, the same traffic patterns of the original photography. Care should be taken that no unusual conditions are photographed that did not exist during the original photography. For example, a brightly colored car that might follow the insert car during the photography of the plates would ruin the footage, if it had not been seen in the shots of the subject car on location. This would constitute an easily spotted, serious mismatch in the rear projected portions of the sequence. To avoid this, the car should be surrounded by picture vehicles whenever possible during the photography of the subject car. The same picture vehicles will maintain their positions around the insert car, as they did during the location shooting of the subject car, and create a matching background during the plate photography. In certain cases, additional angles are needed and extra cameras are mounted on the insert car, or the basic cameras are repositioned and the insert car makes a second pass over the same route. After these plates are photographed, they are generally printed with at least three different densities to produce lighter or darkened values for the process photography.

Now that the technical requirements of how to accomplish the photography of the scene had been solved, a tremendous amount of additional details had to be attended to. The fight between the half-size and full-size people in the car required close contact between the participants, and we had to come up with solutions as to how this was to be accomplished. One thing we knew from the start was that the people in the back of the car, appearing to be half size as they sat on the oversized backseat, could not move forward at all. If they did, they would rapidly grow to normal size, equaling the scale of the two actors on the front seat. Consequently, the action of the real actors in the backseat was to be restricted to being recognized as the real participants, appearing half normal-size on the twice normal-size backseat. From here on the rest of the scene was to be photographed with half-size puppets fighting with full-size people, or full-size people fighting with twice normal-size puppets. These puppets were outstanding life-like reproductions of the actors, wearing the same clothes and identical in every detail to their human counterparts, including jewelry, such as Meg Ryan's earrings or Kevin McCarthy's large ruby ring. This little detail, the large ring, was a calculated portion of the deception. We knew that in addition to the puppets, we were going to need two articulated arms and hands, half-size replicas of Kevin's real arms and hands, which were going to grab and tug at Martin Short's face and lips in some of the shots. The ring was to be a very important part of the deception, an easily recognizable object that was a reminder that the hands belonged to the bad guy. Other props were just as carefully created. Meg Ryan's twice normal-size seat belt, worn by the twice normal-size puppet, appears twice normal-size in the real Fiona Lewis' tiny hands as it extends into the back portion of the car. When Fiona is seen tugging on Meg's earring, the earring, Meg's ear, and Meg's head are twice normal-size, as is the portion of the seat that is visible in the picture. (See Color Plate XII and Figure 5.10.)

As Marty drags the half-size Kevin puppet over his shoulder during the fight, the upside down, kicking puppet slides down Marty's leg below the steering wheel. In the next cut, the white-suited bad guy who bites Marty's leg is the real actor, biting a twice normal-size leg in the twice normal-size front section of the car. The white-clad figure of the bad guy climbs back up on Marty, punches Marty in the face, and gets punched in the nose by Marty. But neither the real bad guy, Kevin, or his puppet were actually in the shot. As we look over Marty's shoulder, we see Marty frantically trying to avoid collisions with buses and other cars, as he is fighting the half-size bad guy who isn't there. What was before Marty was the rear projected image of Kevin, composited onto the "six o'clock" plate. As we look forward, Marty is turning the steering wheel reacting to the traffic in front of him on

Figure 5.10 Fiona Lewis fights a double-size Meg Ryan puppet. Note oversized earring

the rear projection screen and snapping his head as the projected image of Kevin bites his nose. Likewise, timing his action perfectly, he throws a punch at Kevin at the precise moment, just a split second before Kevin's rear-projected image snaps his head as he is hit. It is easy to see how important it is for the actors to be able to interact with puppets and projected images in order to ensure the success of such a large-scale deception.

It is also very important that the audience is prepared to expect, accept, and be so engaged in the action that the obvious unreality of the situation is no longer an important consideration. It would become important if any blatantly flawed facets of this effect were easily noticeable. And almost any of these facets would become unreal if the camera were allowed to dwell on any of the shots long enough for the audience to critically examine and analyze them. The cuts must not be allowed to linger on the screen; the action must be furious, presented in very quick cuts one after the other, and generously interspersed with the supporting shots taken at location to add realism to the situation.

As this sequence was presented in *Innerspace*, it was an almost perfect deception within the context of the story. It had no other purpose than to amuse the audience with a highly impossible, fantastic, outrageous sequence.

The film has many more similarly brazen aspects, one of which is the transformation of Jack Potter, the nerdy, hypochondriac supermarket clerk played by Martin Short, into the image of the Cowboy, played by Robert Picardo. This sequence starts after Marty and Meg tie up the Cowboy and put him in the tub in the hotel bathroom. Lieutenant Pendelton, in his submersible inside Marty, tells Marty to go to the mirror for he is about to change Marty's face. The opening shot of this sequence, a close shot of Marty from the mirror's point of view, shows Marty's lips balloon out as his face contorts in pain. This was a simple shot to make. Just below the camera's lens, a compressed air nozzle was aimed at Marty's lips. As he opens his mouth, a shot of compressed air blows up his cheeks and lips. The pressure of the compressed air was very carefully adjusted, so as not to be dangerous.

Additional shots show Marty's head rapidly moving from side to side, lips extended. The side-to-side motion was photographed with slower than normal camera speeds to speed up the action. There are no other shots showing Marty actually going through the transformation. When we see him emerge from the bathroom, his hair is changed slightly, but the face definitely belongs to the Cowboy. In fact, from this point on in the story, Marty's part is played by Robert Picardo. With some appropriate dialogue and a bit of action, the sequence convinces Meg Ryan, and the audience, that the Cowboy we now see is in fact Potter, the supermarket clerk, with Lieutenant Tuck Pendelton and the miniaturized submersible inside him. Changing the Cowboy back to Potter was a bit more complicated, and this is where extensive special effects were needed.

Three life-size, completely lifelike, heads were constructed. One was of Potter, another was of the Cowboy, and the third was half-Cowboy and half-Potter. All three of these heads were mounted on a device, which was able to shake and twist the heads, and all had inflatable bladders under the skin in various parts of the heads. As the heads shook, these bladders were alternately inflated and deflated to add grotesque expressions to the faces during the transformation process. Further outrageousness was accomplished for this piece of action with the technique of aperture frame control. As the Cowboy becomes Potter again, the camera speed was adjusted to gradually lower film travel speed to about six frames per second, adding to the speed and violence of the shaking heads. The shots of the three heads are intercut at such frequency that it is impossible to identify which head we are looking at. The half-Potter, half-Cowboy head alternately flashes as one or the other of the actors, but they change so rapidly that the two images and the individual features of the actors meld into one just before the Cowboy is changed back to Potter. To further divert attention from the mechanics of this bit of special effect, the camera moves continuously on a circular track around the shaking head. This camera motion, and the moving background it produces, adds to the element of confusion while focusing attention on the heads in the center of the shot. This confusion is just another element that helps round out the overall effect. This special effect of the head transformation, as the other effects in the film, helped make *Innerspace* a popular and successful film (see Figures 5.11–5.14).

Since *Innerspace*, produced in 1986–87, rapidly developing new techniques are changing the way special effects are accomplished today. Never before in the history of motion pictures have changes developed at such a pace and intensity. If *Innerspace* were made today, very few of the techniques described above would be used. Though the use of blue and green screen was considerable in creating some of the special effects for *Innerspace*, today there would be little or no application for the "Slab of Blab" or the "River of Liver." Nor would today's filmmakers have to construct

Figure 5.11 Filming the face transformation scene

Figure 5.12 Another expression in the face transformation process

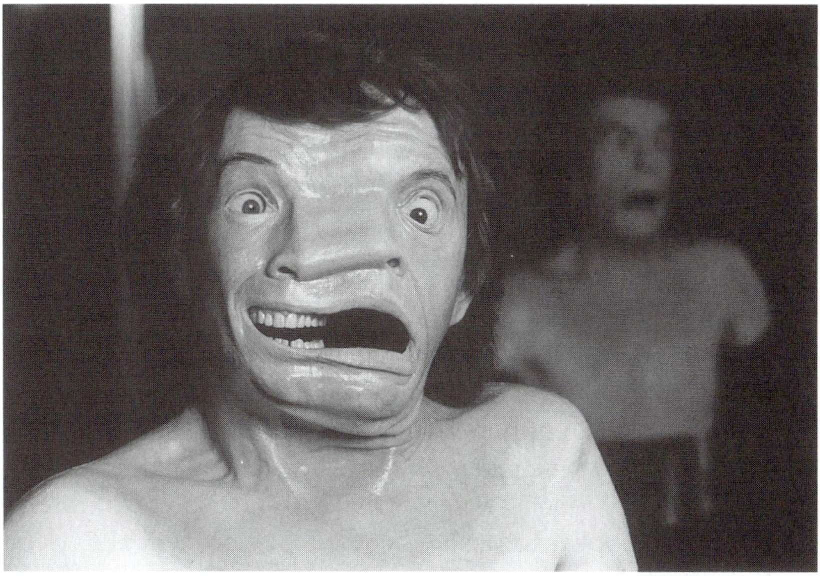

Figure 5.13 Double-faced head in action

Figure 5.14 Filming face transformation on a circular dolly track

huge suitcases in equally oversized trunks, or cut cars in half with double-size rear portions. All of these could be accomplished with computer-generated, or computer-composited and manipulated, imaging. The atomic whiteout effect could easily be accomplished by punching a few buttons on a keyboard at a workstation, without any need for long-duration flashbulbs. Almost all special effects and filmmaking techniques and practices are changing daily, with new techniques creating until now unheard of possibilities and results. But let me emphasize one more time how important it is to be aware of in-camera special effects, particularly for up-and-coming young filmmakers operating with limited budgets.

At this plateau of filmmaking even the sky is no longer the limit; the limit is where today's filmmakers' imagination ends. But little on-the-spot touches, such as making an absolutely immovable elevator appear to rise and come to a stop, will always be welcome additions, however films might be made.

The rapid development of new techniques threw the industry into a bit of a tailspin. As is the case with all new techniques and equipment, filmmaking has the tendency to go overboard in the use of new capabilities. Case in point, the extreme overuse of zoom shots following the introduction of the zoom lens. But the zoom lens did not do away with dolly shots, as was advertised, nor did the steadicam replace the crane. When the novelty wore off, both of these new devices found their proper niche in filmmaking and became valuable new weapons in the arsenal of filmmakers. I suspect this will be the case with electronic imaging and electronic post-production, and when the dust settles, at least a portion of filmmaking (or whatever the medium will be) will return to that magical and wonderful world of storytelling that motion pictures can be. Effects that are nonexistent in the real world will always be interesting to see on the screen. Large explosions and natural, unnatural, and supernatural events and disasters will hold the interest of audiences, but more and more, I hope, they will become less gratuitous, less self-serving and self-indulgent, and be presented only as demanded by the story. Already there are indications of such trends, and the list of small films with solid stories about people, places, and things is again on the upswing, providing the values of classical entertainment to enlighten, amuse, or sadden us. Regardless of the techniques, the inner strength of filmmaking will continue to come from the imagination and creativity of filmmakers dedicated to the art.

Q&A *Innerspace*

ANDREW QUICKE: What is to stop us from using in-camera special effects today?

ANDREW LASZLO: Nothing. Absolutely nothing. In fact, as I pointed out, in-camera special effects remain a wonderful resource for independent and low-budget filmmakers and for student productions where budget is usually a tight consideration.

AQ: What can we do if our camera has a fixed-speed motor?

AL: I take it you are referring to making high-speed or low-speed shots. Most modern cameras have variable speed drives, offering a limited range of high- and low-speed photography. Older or less expensive cameras can usually be fitted with variable-speed motors that are available from camera rental houses. If no such motors are available or where extreme low and high speeds are required, it is generally best to rent a camera offering the required speeds.

AQ: If the correct exposure at 24 frames per second were F:5.6, is there a rule of thumb calculation for "slow-motion" exposures at 32fps, 48fps, 72fps?

AL: The general rule of thumb is that every time the film speed doubles, or gets cut in half (i.e., the camera runs at 48fps or 12fps), the exposure is decreased, or increased, by one stop. In between film travel can be calculated on that basis. Incidentally, a Kodak (or other make) calculator gives precise exposure adjustment for all film speeds.

AQ: What happens if the lens is not fast enough to offer proper adjustment for exposure?

AL: There are three possible solutions, all within limits, of course: (1) The light must be increased; (2) a more sensitive film stock must be used; and (3) the film must be pushed in developing. The increased lighting or the more sensitive film stock would be preferable to forced developing.

AQ: If the correct exposure at 24 frames per second were F:5.6, is there a rule of thumb calculation for "fast motion?"

AL: The above formula of an additional stop of exposure required every time the film speed is doubled should apply. For shots of extremely slow film speed, such as stop motion of a flower blooming, the exposure is usually dictated by the use of an intervalometer. This is a bit more complicated, for here we are no longer talking about motion pictures. Instead, every frame is a still photograph, and the exposures must be calculated on the basis of the camera's shutter angle, the duration of a single revolution of the shutter, or the level of the illumination, which in these instances is usually provided by electronic flash, which sets its own exposure. All of these factors must be taken into consideration. In even more extreme cases (catching a balloon burst, a bullet striking a light bulb, etc.), highly special equipment is used, demanding special exposure calculations.

AQ: For the complex exposure adjustments required for *Innerspace*, an aperture frame control device was essential. Can these be rented from camera rental companies?

AL: Yes, but not all cameras used today may be fitted with these devices.

AQ: In your "whiteout" sequence, how did you trigger off seventy-five long-duration flashbulbs all at the same time?

AL: That was not particularly difficult. All the flashbulbs were wired into the same circuit and triggered by a single switch.

AQ: In your account of simulating sinus pain, how did you get the red sinus shapes to pulsate?

AL: The single light, having a red gel over its lens, provided exposure and color. The pulsation was achieved by alternately increasing and decreasing the intensity of this light by a dimmer that sent high and low voltages of electricity to the light.

AQ: Did you personally supervise shooting the "plates" for your back-projection sequences, or is that sort of work handled by the second unit photographer?

AL: On a large budget film, a unit of specialists usually handle rear-projection sequences. This was the case with *Innerspace*, *Streets of Fire*, *Star Trek V*, and other films of mine. In all cases, the first unit was involved, and as much as possible, I prefer to shoot my own plates.

AQ: Looking back on shooting *Innerspace*, what might you have done differently, without using computer generated images?

AL: That is a very hard question to answer. There isn't a film I've ever done that I have not redone in my mind a dozen times. There are very few films that have more than a single release. Those that are rereleased some time after their initial release, might contain some footage that was not seen in the original, though shot during the film's production. Every film can be made in a zillion different ways, and in my opinion it is usually the first version that is the best. If I were a wise guy, I could answer the question of "What would I have done differently" by saying, "I would ask for more money."

AQ: Wonderful as the in-camera special effects are, would you agree that part of the reason the film works so well is because it had a strong story line and good acting, so that we the viewers want to believe all the wonders you show us?

AL: I would agree totally and without hesitation. You might recall me saying many times throughout this book that the most important element in film is the story. No element of a movie, wonderful as it may be, could survive without a strong story to start with. On the other hand, even a halfway well-executed film may become successful if it has a good, strong, intelligent, and interesting story line. Every other element of a film must be subject to and support the story.

AQ: Sometimes students ask me whether I would recommend the career of the professional advertising cinematographer who spends all his time making commercial spots? Which do you prefer?

AL: I much prefer the world I spent nearly a half a century in, which is entertainment films, both theatrical features and television. Of course, I'm sure you recall me talking about working on television commercials, which I enjoyed as a wonderful proving ground that allowed for experimentation. But one has to be cut out for one or the other of these fields as a full-time occupation. As much as I liked working on TV spots, I don't think I'd like it as a full-time, exclusive commitment.

AQ: I know you have extensive experience of both worlds, but is it not difficult to graduate to feature motion pictures from the advertising side of the industry?

AL: It is very difficult. I know many very talented cinematographers who tried, and failed. The mentalities of these areas are widely different, and they're difficult to adjust to or come to terms with.

AQ: Having seen the thousands of photographs you amassed during fifty years of filmmaking, why have you not included more pictures here, particularly some of the other big stars you worked with?

AL: Because of the nature of this book, I have used photographs only in the places where they figure in the illustration of a technique, or the subject matter I talk about. Besides, because of the special nature of this book, there may be only one or two more stars whose pictures I could have included. But another aspect of the story is this: though the copyrights of the photos belong to me, as a professional courtesy I contacted a number of the stars of the films I talk about in this book, seeking their consent to include their pictures in the book. Most replied immediately and positively, but some did not. The way I look at it is that most of the big stars are usually surrounded by a small army of people who, in one way or another, depend on the stars for their livelihood. In order to earn their keep—and, of course, in order to protect the stars—sometimes they take a negative position regarding the stars' pictures being published. Most often this is justified and necessary. Though in a case such as this book, in my opinion, a star's picture would not help sell the book, deprive him or her of monetary gain, nor would it be detrimental to their image or standing. Yet, possibly based on advice from their people, some stars hesitate, and in those instances I prefer not to force the issue. I've been fortunate to have had wonderful relationships with most of the stars and performers I have worked with. Out of respect for them, in the absence of their consent, I did not include their pictures.

AQ: You promised, at the beginning of the book, to tell us what the secret of photography is.

AL: I was hoping you wouldn't remember. Since that question first came up, I have been searching for and hoping to come up with some sort of definition. But I can't. At least not with a precise, all-encompassing explanation of what the secret of photography is. If there is such a secret, it must be a culmination of talent, desire, dedication, ingenuity, knowledge, experience, a hunger to create, and much, much more. The word *religion* might apply here. A devotion to a concept, to creation, to the extreme joy of seeing the results of one's imagination and efforts. Let me tell you one last war story, which might get us a bit closer to the secret.

Some years ago, during the sixties, I was shooting a film on location when a young fellow, a hippie, came up to me as I was taking light readings. I don't know if you recall what an archetypal "hippie" looked like. This one, answering all descriptions, had long, straight, unwashed blond hair parted in the middle. He wore a white, dirty, embroidered shirt, wrinkled white pajama-style pants, and sandals. "Like man," he asked, "how do you get into this business?" Though I didn't particularly care for him, I like to talk with young people, so I asked what he was interested in, what he wanted to do. He shook his head, shrugged his shoulders, and said, "I don't care, man." I looked at him for a second as his answer sank in and I told him that if he didn't care, he shouldn't get into this business, and walked away.

Perhaps that is where the answer is. One has to care. If one does, if one has the desire, dedication, perseverance, vision, and interest to pursue and practice the art, then the secret might lie in the images of high quality and interest, which one produces without trying to evoke "the secret."

Perhaps, one of these days, you might come across someone who can give a precise definition of the secret of photography. When you do, I hope you'll pass it on to me.

GLOSSARY

ACADEMY APERTURE A frame size and shape, having an aspect ratio of 1.37:1, that allows space for an optical sound track alongside the frame area.

ANAMORPHIC A process that squeezes the image of a wide screen format onto a standard, 35mm negative by an additional element in the camera's lens. The same element on a projector lens unsqueezes the image to a wide screen format.

ANAMORPHIC LENS A camera or a projection lens, which squeezes or unsqueezes the image.

APERTURE A general reference in photography to the "f-" or "T-" stop setting of a lens. At times, aperture is also used to describe the size and shape of the camera's gate.

ARRIFLEX A German camera make.

ASPECT RATIO The height versus width proportions of a motion picture frame.

BLACK DOT FILTERS A set of glass camera filters with dots and translucent blotches of varying size, density, and shape in a random pattern. These filters come in five grades, from 1, the lightest, to 5, the most dense. They are generally used to soften the image and reduce contrast.

BLACKWRAP Black-coated aluminum foil to wrap lights with to eliminate unwanted light leaks.

BLUE SCREEN/GREEN SCREEN A blue- or green-colored screen in front of which a portion of a shot is photographed to be composited into a background.

BOUCHERIE A French word meaning "butcher shop," which is used in the Cajun language to also mean a party where pigs are butchered, cooked on an open pit, and served.

BRACKETING In most cases refers to multiple exposures of the same subject. Under- and overexposing the image, in order to select the most desirable exposure after the film is developed, particularly when accurate exposure determination is not possible.

BUDGET The cost of a motion picture.

CAMERA CAR A specially constructed and outfitted light truck for motion picture photography. It generally has front and rear camera mounts, a small generator, towing capability, and room for crew. Also known as an INSERT CAR.

CAMERA LEFT/RIGHT Positions of objects and/or performers within the frame as related to the image seen by the camera.

CENTURY STAND A stand used by grips to support flags, gobos, and other objects, in a myriad of positions.

CINEMASCOPE Trade name of an early wide screen process used by Twentieth Century Fox, which initiated the use of an "anamorphiciser" element in front of camera and projection lens, to squeeze and unsqueeze an image that is photographed on standard 35mm film stock. The image ratio of this system was 2.35:1.

CINEMATOGRAPHER A person who actually accomplishes the photography of a motion picture. All DIRECTORS OF PHOTOGRAPHY are necessarily cinematographers, but not all cinematographers are Directors of Photography.

CINERAMA The forerunner of all wide screen processes, using three, side-by-side cameras to photograph three segments of one image. This image was projected by three projectors onto a giant, curved screen, creating a sensational, huge image that almost wrapped around the audience. Surroundsound enhanced this image, but the unavoidable seams between the three images, and the development of better wide screen systems, eventually rendered this process obsolete.

CLIP LIGHT Generally a small lighting unit, which can be attached to an object by its spring-loaded grips.

COLOR TEMPERATURE A definition of color as part of the color spectrum in Kelvin degrees. Color motion picture film is generally balanced for 3200 Kelvin to 3400 Kelvin Tungsten Illumination, or 5500 Kelvin to 6000 Kelvin for daylight balanced film. Higher numbers indicate bluer shades, while lower numbers denote red hues.

CONTRAST The ratio between the darkest and brightest portions of the image.

CORRECTED, UNCORRECTED FOOTAGE Corrected footage generally refers to dailies that were printed in the laboratory to correct defects in exposure, color, or certain other abnormalities. Uncorrected footage generally refers to dailies that the laboratory prints at their so-called mid-range, without affecting density and/or color.

COVER See COVER SET.

COVER SET A substitute set, or location to be used, in case the scheduled set becomes unavailable.

CRAB DOLLY A dolly designed to accommodate camera moves on a smooth surface without the need for dolly tracks. In addition to straight forward and backward motion, the dolly is capable of moving in any direction, sideways, and in a circular path.

CRANE A camera mount that can raise and move the camera. Two well-known types are the Atlas and the Titan.

C-STAND See CENTURY STAND.

CUTTER Designed to cut a portion of a lamp's light output when placed in front of a lamp, cutters may be made from thin plywood, black fabric, or any solid object.

DEPTH OF FIELD An area of the image between the sharpest point closest to the lens and the sharpest point furthest from the lens.

DIFFUSION FILTERS Generally a glass filter to be placed in front of the camera lens to soften the image quality.

DIOPTER Refers to the power of a lens. In motion picture jargon the name "diopter" is generally meant to describe a single element lens that, when attached to a regular lens, alters the focal length of the lens. They are generally used in close-up photography. SPLIT DIOPTERS, regular diopter lenses cut in half, will effect the focal length properties of only the half portion of a normal lens, which they are in front of. DIOPTERS or SPLIT DIOPTERS come in strengths of ½, 1, 2, and 3. They may be used in combination with one another to increase their strength. The more these diopters are combined the more negatively they affect their resolution.

DIRECTOR OF PHOTOGRAPHY See CINEMATOGRAPHER.

DISSOLVE An optical effect of one shot changing into another.

DOLLY TRACKS A precision set of tracks, which facilitates the smooth movement of a camera dolly.

DUPE A print of a motion picture negative, or positive image, made to create a new negative or positive DUPE from which prints or additional negatives may be made. The purpose of a DUPE NEGATIVE is to preserve the original negative. Further DUPE positives of negatives may combine additional images which are not found in the original negative.

DUPE NEGATIVE See DUPE.

E-FAN A small but powerful electric fan to produce minor wind effects.

EFFECTS See SPECIAL EFFECTS.

EMULSION A layer of gelatin on a transparent backing, which contains the light-sensitive silver particles, called halides, that, when exposed to light, will form the photographic image. "Emulsion" is sometimes used to describe film stock.

EXPOSURE—UNDER/OVER The amount of light permitted to reach the film in the camera. Too much light reaching the film will produce overexposure, while less than the proper amount will result in underexposure.

EYE LIGHT Usually a small light directed at a performer's eyes to eliminate shadows and to add a reflection, sparkle, to the performer's eyes.

FAST MOTION An effect achieved by running the film in the camera slower than 24 frames per second, which shows objects or people moving faster than normal in projection.

F-STOP See LENS STOP.

FADES An optical effect of an image fading to black, or fading up to full density.

FILL LIGHT Usually a soft light used to brighten up, fill in, shadow areas of an image and reduce contrast.

FILTER A gelatin, or glass, square or rectangle to be placed in front of, or in some cases behind, the camera's lens. Filters come in many colors and densities. Their purpose is to affect the color, or the density, or impose an affect on the image.

FLAG A rectangular, black shape created by stretching opaque material over a wire frame. Flags, at times called "gobos," are used to produce shadows, or restrict light from reaching a portion of the set. Also see CUTTER.

FLARE Light entering the lens, causing optical and color distortions.

FLUORESCENT LIGHT A glass tube containing an inert gas, Argon, that produces a glow on the inside surfaces of the glass tube coated with a chemical, phosphor. For color temperature and color correction refer to manufacturer's spec sheets, or *The American Cinematographer Manual.*

FOCAL LENGTH A designation of one of the characteristics of a lens: a point within the lens where light rays entering the lens converge.

Wide-angle lenses have short focal lengths; telephoto or long lenses have long focal lengths.

FOGGING An optically or chemically induced effect, which results in a veil-like haze over the image, reducing the contrast and giving the picture a softer look.

FOOT-CANDLE A unit of light value. Roughly the amount of light emitted by one candle at a one-foot distance from the flame.

FORCED DEVELOPING Also known as PUSHING. The negative film is overdeveloped to compensate for underexposure or to achieve an effect, such as creating a grainy effect.

FORCED PERSPECTIVE PHOTOGRAPHY Photographing an object or person in an over- or undersized environment, or compared to smaller or larger objects, thereby creating an effect of reducing or enlarging the size of objects or persons.

FPS Frames per second. The number of frames traveling through the camera's gate per second.

FRAMES PER SECOND See FPS.

GAFFER A member of the crew, charged with the supervision of all electrical activity and equipment. He works closely with and executes the lighting design of the Director of Photography.

GATOR CLIP Also referred to as gator grip. See CLIP LIGHT.

GOBO See FLAG.

GOOD PHOTOGRAPHY A term describing photography executed to exact specifications, such as correct exposure of a sharp image with good color.

GOPHER See PA.

GRADUATED FILTERS A filter having varying values of its qualities effecting portions of a frame differently. Also see NEUTRAL-DENSITY FILTERS.

GRAIN Silver halide particles in the light-sensitive emulsion of a film stock.

GREY, OR GRAY, CARD A neutral grey color card, which reflects 18 percent of the light it receives. It is also referred to as a mid-grey card between full black and total white.

GREEN SCREEN See BLUE SCREEN/GREEN SCREEN.

GRIP A crew member concerned with such set operations as the handling of the camera dolly, cranes, light construction work, and assisting the DIRECTOR OF PHOTOGRAPHY with creating certain lighting effects.

HARD LIGHT An item of motion picture lighting equipment which, in addition to having a bulb of various intensity, also has a curved mirror behind the bulb and a lens in front of the bulb. By changing the position of the bulb between the mirror and the lens, the light beam can be adjusted to cover a wider or narrower area to be illuminated, with a brighter or dimmer intensity of light.

"HEAVIES" A motion picture term generally referring to the "bad guys" in a movie.

HIGH HAT A camera mount that enables the camera to be placed low to the ground.

HIGH-SPEED CAMERA A camera designed to allow the film to travel through the gate at high speeds, therefore producing slow motion when the film is projected.

HMI Trademark name by which most metal halide enclosed arc lights have become known. The units range from relatively low to very high light output. Most are in the 5500 Kelvin to 6000 Kelvin color temperature range, well suited for daylight photography. Because the lights have a cyclic rate, care must be taken with HMI lights during high- or low-speed photography to avoid strobing effects.

IN-CAMERA EFFECTS See SPECIAL EFFECTS.

INCANDESCENT A light in which an electrically heated metal element glows and produces light.

INKY A small, 150-watt to 300-watt light.

INSERT CAR See CAMERA CAR.

INTERNEGATIVE A negative image of a scene or an entire movie, made from an INTERPOSITIVE, which is made from the ORIGINAL NEGATIVE. The INTERNEGATIVE, containing optical effects, is necessary to make multiple release prints.

INTERPOSITIVE A positive image made from the ORIGINAL NEGATIVE for the purpose of creating a DUPE, or INTERNEGATIVE. The visual qualities of an Interpositive are different from a regular positive print made from the Original Negative, in order to produce the Internegative from which multiple, or RELEASE PRINTs are made.

INTERVALOMETER A device that can regulate the frame rate of a camera.

JUNIOR A 2000-watt light unit with a lens.

KELVIN See COLOR TEMPERATURE.

LAZY SUSAN A turntable placed on a dining table for condiments, or any turntable. In our case, one large enough to support a helicopter to simulate the motion of the helicopter in flight.

LENS STOP The setting of a lens aperture denoting its light transmission value. Stops are generally designated in "f" or "T" values. The smaller the number, the more light a lens transmits.

LIQUID DIMMER An industry-coined name for reducing the flare of lights within a shot by applying hairspray or other spray paint to the bulb or fixture.

LOCATION A place where an exterior portion of a movie is filmed. Real interior sets, which exist away from the studio, are also referred to as location.

LONG-DURATION FLASHBULB A flashbulb that will produce a high-intensity light of longer duration then an ordinary flashbulb.

LOOK/STYLE Alteration of the image by adding or withholding elements beyond the normal scope of photography used to truthfully record an image. It is the artistic element the cinematographer imposes on the image.

MAGIC HOUR A short time period, generally at the end of the day just before and immediately following sunset. The sunlit portions of the shot turn warm, or reddish, and the sky is an accentuated blue. After sunset, daylight exposures are still possible, though most ambient lit portions of the shot will appear more bluish and colder than normal, and certain other elements, such as streetlights and the head- and taillights of cars, appear more saturated than normal.

MINIATURES Small-scale reproductions of actual objects to be used in special effect photography.

MISMATCH An inconsistency within the image from one cut to the next, or to subsequent cuts. Example: the length of an actor's cigarette from one cut to the next, or wet pavement in a sequence to dry pavement some cuts away, but within the same sequence.

MITCHELL An American camera make.

MIX OR MIXING Refers to the process of combining the various elements of the soundtrack—such as dialogue, narration, musical score, sound effects, and noises—in proper proportions into one soundtrack.

MONOCHROMATIC An image consisting of one color over a background of black or white. Black and white photography is considered monochromatic, although other techniques, such as sepia tone may also be referred to as monochromatic.

MOVIOLA A machine used by film editors to view film usually interlocked with the sound track. Newer machines, such as flatbed editing machines have largely replaced the old-fashioned moviolas.

NEGATIVE EMULSION See EMULSION.

NEON, NEON LIGHTS From the Greek word neos (new), a colorless gas, which in a glass tube, produces a reddish glow in conjunction with an electric charge. With the addition of other chemicals, many colors can be produced in glass tubes bent into any shape.

NETS Wire or fabric netting designed to reduce the overall intensity of a light. Fine silk netting is sometimes used to soften the image, when placed in front of or behind a lens during photography.

NEUTRAL-DENSITY FILTERS A set of glass filters, which reduce the amount of light passing through them. These filters do not affect color. The most popular designations are 30, 60, and 90, referring to the transmission characteristic of the filter. A 30 neutral-density filter will reduce the light reaching the film by one stop; a 60 neutral filter will reduce the exposure by two stops; and so on. These filters may be used in combination with other filters. They are also available in "half" filters (also known as GRADUATED NEUTRAL DENSITY FILTERS), meaning that only a portion of the filter effects the exposure. These filters are generally used to darken light portions of the frame, such as bright sky. Graduated filters are also available in different colors to achieve an artistically pleasing affect.

NUMBER 85 FILTER A gelatin or glass filter placed in front of the camera's lens to correct the Tungsten-balanced characteristics of film to daylight color balance.

OFF-CAMERA A motion picture phrase, generally meaning an object that figures in the creation of a shot but is out of the frame area and therefore not visible in the picture.

ONE-BY-THREE Also referred to as a "one by," a piece of lumber measuring one by three inches.

OPTICALS Certain visual effects, such as fades and dissolves.

ORIGINAL NEGATIVE Developed film stock used for photography.

OVEREXPOSURE See EXPOSURE.

PA Production assistant. An entry-level position in film production, also know as a "gopher"—go for this, go for that.

PARALLELS Portable camera platforms, which can be assembled from components to various heights for high-angle camera shots.

PERFORATION Also referred to as PERF, the rectangular holes along both edges of the film stock, which facilitate the film's travel and stabilization in the camera or projector.

PICTURE VEHICLE Cars or trucks in the background of scenes in a movie, owned and controlled by the production.

PLATE Motion picture film used to project a background. See REAR PROJECTION.

POV Short for Point of View. Generally a shot of what someone sees.

PRODUCTION VALUE Generally refers to all elements in a frame, which are interesting, pleasing, larger than life, and so on. At times, unexpected elements that appear in the frame, a flight of birds in a landscape, for example, may be referred to as additional production value.

PULL DEVELOPING See PULLING.

PULLING A form of negative processing, which allows the negative stock less than normal time in the developing solution, therefore producing an underdeveloped, less contrasty negative.

PUSHING See FORCED DEVELOPING.

REAR PROJECTION An image projected on the back of a translucent screen and viewed or photographed from the front. Used to create a moving background to the action, which is photographed in front of the screen.

RELEASE PRINT The final version of a movie containing all elements, such as picture, sound, titles, and opticals.

ROUGH ASSEMBLY Unedited takes of a scene spliced together in proper chronology.

RPM Revolutions per minute.

RUNNING SERIES A television series of individual episodes running weekly.

SCHEDULE The duration of time allocated for a production.

SCOTCHLITE The trademark name of a light-reflecting product manufactured by the Minnesota Mining Company.

SENIOR A 5000-watt light having a lens.

SET An architectural construction built to provide interior or exterior locations for filming. Real locations, exterior or interior, are sometimes referred to as sets.

SHOW CARD A black on one side, white on the other piece of cardboard, roughly thirty by forty inches. Used for multiple applications, such as cue cards, or blocking or reflecting light, or wherever a small black or white background is desired in a shot.

SILKS OR SILKING A technique of stretching silk panels over the action of a scene, or in front of large light sources, to soften the quality of light. In smaller sizes, stretched on wire frames, silks are used in front of lights to diffuse and soften the quality of the light.

SLOW MOTION An effect, achieved by running the film in the camera faster than 24 frames per second, thus showing objects or people moving slower than normal speed.

SOFT LIGHT An item of motion picture lighting equipment, which has a bulb in a housing, the inside of which is painted with a matte white color. This housing reflects the bulb's light over a wide area. The light output of this sort of light is referred to as "soft" light. The light is used to soften the contrast of the image by filling in the shadow areas of the image and reducing contrast.

SOUNDTRACK OR AUDIO TRACK A portion of the positive release print that contains the film's audio portion, such as dialogue, effects, music, and anything that is heard while watching a movie.

SPECIAL EFFECTS Unusual or unreal effects created to accommodate a particular story line. Difficult sequences, such as storms at sea, are at times photographed in the safety of the special effects stage, creating effects that might appear even more severe than if the sequence were photographed under actual conditions. Some effects require extensive preparations, miniatures, actual-size buildings to be destroyed during the shot, etc. Some special effects can be achieved in the camera.

SPEED RAIL Steel pipes and clamps that can be quickly assembled in many configurations to form structures attaching cameras, lights, and other gear to cars, trucks, or buildings to facilitate motion picture photography.

SPLIT DIOPTERS OR HALF DIOPTERS See DIOPTERS.

SQUIBS A small, electrically detonated explosive charge used to simulate bullet hits.

STOP MOTION Stop-motion photography is used to achieve a special effect. Instead of the standard 24 frames per second film travel in the camera, each frame is exposed at great intervals to create an effect such as a flower rapidly blooming.

SUBJECT CAR An automobile that figures in the film's story.

SUPPLY HOUSE A business concern that sells or rents equipment to motion picture productions. Some of these companies specialize in certain equipment, such as cameras, or lighting and grip equipment.

TARPS OR TARPING Covering windows of a building or covering entire outdoor sets with black tarpaulins to create a night effect. A good technique for creating day-for-night shots.

THIN NEGATIVE Usually refers to an underexposed image.

TODD-AO Trade name of an early, wide screen process. A joint effort between Michael Todd and the American Optical Company, therefore, TODD-AO.

T-STOP See LENS STOP.

UNDERCRANK When the film is traveling through the camera at less then the 24-fps rate. Undercranked footage results in fast motion in projection.

UNDEREXPOSURE See EXPOSURE.

VIDEO TAP A small video camera built into most modern film cameras. It monitors the same image the film camera sees and can record on videotape an identical image being photographed with the film camera.

VISTA-VISION Trade name of an early wide screen process by Paramount Pictures. The negative film in this process ran through the camera horizontally, exposing an eight-perforation area of the negative to produce a wide screen format. This process is still used for special effects photography.

WIDE OPEN The iris of a lens opened to its widest "f" or "T" stop setting, which, oddly enough, is designated by the smallest number. At this setting the lens transmits the most light and is considered "wide open."

WRAP An expression indicating the end of a workday.

FILMOGRAPHY OF ANDREW LASZLO, A.S.C.

American Society of Cinematographers
International Cinematographers Guild
Directors Guild of America
National Academy of Motion Picture Arts and Sciences
National Academy of Television Arts and Sciences

LIST OF CREDITS

Feature Motion Pictures

Newsies (1991)—Walt Disney Pictures
Ghostdad (1989)—Universal Pictures
Star Trek V—The Final Frontier (1988)—Paramount Pictures
Innerspace (1986)—Amblin Entertainment–Warner Bros.
Poltergeist II (1985)—MGM
Remo Williams, The Adventure Begins (1985)—Orion Pictures
Thief of Hearts (1984)—Paramount Pictures
Streets of Fire (1983)—Universal Pictures
Love is Forever (1982)—Twentieth Century Fox
First Blood (1982)—Carolco–Orion pictures
I, The Jury (1981)—American Cinema–Twentieth Century Fox
Southern Comfort (1981)—Twentieth Century Fox
Funhouse (1980)—Universal Pictures

Shogun (1979)—Paramount Pictures (The Feature)
The Warriors (1978)—Paramount Pictures
Somebody Killed Her Husband (1977)—Martin Poll/Columbia Pictures
Angela (1976)—Zev Braun, Carlo Ponti Productions
Thieves (1975)—Paramount Pictures
Countdown at Kussini (1974)—Independent
Class of 44 (1972)—Warner Bros.
To Find A Man (1971)—Rastar–Columbia Pictures
Jennifer On My Mind (1971)—United Artists
The Owl and the Pussycat (1971)—Rastar–Columbia Pictures
Lovers and Other Strangers (1970)—ABC Films/Cinerama
The Out of Towners (1969)—Paramount Pictures
Popi (1968)—United Artists
The Night They Raided Minsky's (1968)—United Artists
You're a Big Boy Now (1966)—Warner Bros./Seven Arts Productions
One Potato, Two Potato (1963)—Independent

Television Mini-Series

Shogun (1979)—Paramount Television
Top of the Hill (1978)—Paramount Television
The Dain Curse (1978)—Martin Poll Productions/CBS
Washington Behind Close Doors (1977)—Paramount TV

Television Features and Pilot Films

Thin Ice (1980)—CBS
Spanner's Key (1978)—Paramount Television
The Unwanted (1974)—John Secondary Productions
The Man Without a Country (1972)—Norman Rosemont Productions
Blue Water Gold (1969)—Metromedia Productions
Teacher, Teacher (1967)—Hallmark Hall of Fame
Daphne (1966)—CBS TV
The Cliffdwellers (1965)—Bing Crosby Productions
The Happeners (1965)—Plautus Productions

Television Specials

Bell Telephone Hour Special, Easter Sunrise Services
A performance of Handel's *Messiah* by the Mormon Tabernacle Choir and the Denver Symphony
Ed Sullivan, Vietnam Veterans Easter Special 1970—CBS TV
Ed Sullivan in Cuba—CBS TV
Ed Sullivan in Ireland—CBS TV
Ed Sullivan in Alaska—CBS TV
Ed Sullivan in Portugal—CBS TV
The Beatles at Shea Stadium—Ed Sullivan Productions/ABC
New York, New York—CBS TV

Television Series

Coronet Blue—Plautus Productions
The Doctors and Nurses—Plautus Productions
The Nurses—Plautus Productions
Naked City—Columbia Pictures/ Screen Gems
Brenner—CBS TV
Mama—CBS TV
Joe and Mabel—CBS TV
The Phil Silvers Show—CBS TV

Television Documentaries

The Twentieth Century—CBS TV
High Adventure with Lowell Thomas—Odyssey Productions/CBS

INDEX

WATKINS COLLEGE OF ART
Every frame a Rembrandt : art
778.5 Las
10504